# Building Energy Management Systems

Other titles from E & FN Spon

Air Conditioning
A practical introduction
D.V. Chadderton

Building Services Engineering
D.V. Chadderton

Combustion Engineering and Gas Utilization
3rd edn
British Gas

Illustrated Encyclopedia of Building Services
D. Kut

International Dictionary of Heating, Ventilating and Air
Conditioning
2nd edn
REHVA

Ventilation of Buildings
H.B. Awbi

For more information about these and other titles please contact:
The Promotion Department, E & FN Spon,
2–6 Boundary Row, London SE1 8HN

# Building Energy Management Systems

## An application to heating and control

## G. J. LEVERMORE

*Department of Building Engineering, UMIST, UK*

**E & FN SPON**
An Imprint of Chapman & Hall

London · Glasgow · Weinheim · New York · Tokyo · Melbourne · Madras

Published by E & FN Spon, an imprint of Chapman & Hall,
2-6 Boundary Row, London SE1 8HN, UK

Chapman & Hall, 2-6 Boundary Row, London SE1 8HN, UK

Blackie Academic & Professional, Wester Cleddens Road, Bishopbriggs,
Glasgow G64 2NZ, UK

Chapman & Hall GmbH, Pappelallee 3, 69469 Weinheim, Germany

Chapman & Hall USA., One Penn Plaza, 41st Floor, New York,
NY10119, USA

Chapman & Hall Japan, ITP-Japan, Kyowa Building, 3F, 2-2-1
Hirakawacho, Chiyoda-ku, Tokyo 102, Japan

Chapman & Hall Australia, Thomas Nelson Australia, 102 Dodds
Street, South Melbourne, Victoria 3205, Australia

Chapman & Hall India, R. Seshadri, 32 Second Main Road, CIT East,
Madras 600 035, India

First edition 1992
Reprinted 1994

© 1992 G. J. Levermore

Typeset in 10/12 pt Times by Pure Tech Corporation, India
Printed in Great Britain St Edmundsbury Press, Bury St Edmunds

ISBN   0 419 15290 3

A Catalogue record for this book is available from the British Library

∞ Printed on permanent acid-free text paper, manufactured in
   accordance with ANSI/NISO Z39.48-1992 and ANSI/NISO Z39.48-
   1984 (Permanence of Paper)

# Contents

# Acknowledgements

Acknowledgements for reproducing the following figures are due to:
Trend Control Systems Ltd – Figs 2.1, 3.2, 3.3, 3.10, 3.12, 4.3, 10.2;
Satchwell Control Systems Ltd – Figs 2.1, 2.3, 2.4, 3.12;
Drayton Controls (Engineering) Ltd – Fig 2.1;
The Chartered Institution of Building Services Engineers – Fig. 8.17;
Honeywell Ltd – Fig. 4.2.

# Foreword

This book is intended as both a student text on the control of a building services plant and a practitioner's guide to the basics of practical control. With the advent of the microprocessor the building energy management system takes a prominent position in the book, hence its title.

As an energy manager I found that there was little understanding of controls, even though they were crucial to energy efficiency and comfort in buildings. Then, as a lecturer, I discovered the difficulty of teaching control, with most of the textbooks relating to electronic or process control where the reaction times are much faster than those of a building. I also found in teaching short courses and in some consultancy work that the potential of BEMSs was not being realised, partly due to a lack of training and understanding but also due to insufficient time and money allowed on the design, installation and commissioning of plant and controls. Indeed I often ask consultants, clients and students to tell me of any building that they know which works properly after commissioning, but the response is rare and little. This book, I hope, will help alleviate these problems.

As control is a large subject it was decided to devote this book to the application of control to heating and energy efficiency to appeal to energy managers and consultants as well as to students. At the heart of the control of heating and energy efficiency are the building and plant responses. These contribute to the difficulties of using standard control texts and theory as the building fabric can take hours, even days, to heat whereas the plant can respond in minutes, perhaps seconds. So Chapter 7, on building heat loss and heating, has been included. In Chapter 9 on optimiser control this response is treated in a simplified manner as a first order differential equation in order to give an appreciation of the physical processes occurring. To treat the response in more detail with numerical solutions would have overly complicated the treatment.

The book starts by detailing the development of BEMSs, the advantages and disadvantages from case studies and the future prospects. Some of these case studies are ETSU Demonstration Schemes, which are now a little dated but they illustrate cardinal points which later studies do not cover in such depth.

Chapter 2 is devoted to the outstation, its structure, operation and configuration. Of necessity there is some electronics here, such as the operational amplifier, but no previous knowledge of electronics is assumed. Chapter 3 covers the central station, its elements and software, which is the heart of a BEMS.

There is a tendency amongst some traditional engineers that unless they can measure the temperature on a gauge or with a thermometer then somehow any other reading is suspect. Perhaps this has evolved from the extensive use of strap on sensors used in retrofit BEMs installations. Chapter 4 addresses the problem of strap-on sensors and also emphasizes that all measurements contain inaccuracies, but that these can be limited.

Chapters 5 and 6 develop basic control into three term PID control. Although there is more theory here than in earlier chapters, the explanation of the use of BEMSs for analysing temperature curves will be of particular use to practitioners who have to examine their plant and buildings' operation. The control strategies adopted in the book are based as far as possible on those in commercial BEMSs, although there are a number of alterations to simplify the explanation.

Compensator control of heating systems is covered in Chapter 8, with sufficient explanation for the reader to appreciate the implications of the control settings and the size of the heating plant on the internal temperature attained. Chapter 9 deals with the other important heating control, the optimiser.

A major use of BEMS is for monitoring plant and buildings' energy consumption and the subsequent targeting of the consumptions. This is dealt with in Chapter 10. If this chapter alone is read and acted upon then the book will have produced a reasonable payback.

In producing this book I was helped by a number of people, including many of my students who provided their feedback on my lectures mainly by their exam marks. In the actual production of the book I would particularly like to thank the late Mark Coppens, Mrs Pat Cross and Shashi Patel for translating my rough sketches into good graphics. Also I would like to record my appreciation of conversations and discussions with Chris Chapman and Bill Freshwater of Trend Control Systems Ltd and Malcolm Clapp and Sultan Siddiqui of Satchwell Control Systems Ltd. Colleagues, Professors Ken Letherman, Keith Shepherd and Tony Sung kindly commented on a number of the chapters.

I would finally like to express my thanks to my wife Carolyn for her help and useful advice in the writing of this book, and also to my parents, and Alison and Tom for helping me in many various ways to write this book.

There will undoubtedly be some mistakes that have crept into the book, for which I take responsibility. Feedback on these and any other points in the book will be gratefully appreciated.

Geoff Levermore

# 1
# The development and use of building energy management systems (BEMSs)

**Building energy management systems** (BEMSs) have made a substantial impact on the control of building services plant and on energy efficiency. Their development has been extremely rapid; there were few systems in 1980, whereas most new commercial, industrial and public buildings in the 1990s have some form of a BEMS. Perhaps because of this rapid development, there is still a lot of unused potential in many current BEMSs. In this chapter the development of BEMSs is traced; the benefits and problems are considered and amplified in the examination of case studies, and people's reactions are considered. Finally, future developments are assessed.

In this book the term 'building energy management system' is used, but there are many variations such as building management systems (BMSs), energy management systems (EMSs) and building automation systems (BASs). All of these terms basically refer to the same equipment.

## 1.1 The development of BEMSs

Building energy management systems have developed alongside, and been a result of, the microelectronics and computing revolution of recent years. This is because BEMSs are simply microcomputer systems used for controlling and monitoring building services plant. BEMSs have also benefited from the knowledge and technology in the application of computer control to manufacturing and the process industry.

The earliest ancestor of the BEMS was the hard-wired centralized control system. It first appeared in the 1960s and was employed in large buildings [1]. The system was basically an extension of the conventional control wires to a central console, with dials, indicator lights and a chart recorder, which enabled an operator at the console to monitor distant plant and to see temperatures displayed. No computers or microelectronics were involved, and it relied on the operator to change control settings and times [2].

These hard-wired systems were then improved with the telephone technology of the day to enable individual items of plant to be switched, via **data gathering panels** local to the plant, into a central, multicore trunk cable running around the building from the central console. This switching, or **multiplexing**, saved on cabling by utilizing the same trunk cable for a number of data gathering panels.

Another development was the addition of a back-projected slide screen, linked in to the switching, to show a diagram of the selected plant.

With the rapid advances of microelectronics, and hundreds of transistor devices being integrated on to one **large-scale integrated** (LSI) chip of silicon about 5 mm$^2$, the first computer-based monitoring and control systems emerged. These early BEMS were **centralized energy management systems** and first appeared in the 1970s [3], having been developed in the USA. The **central station** was based on a minicomputer, which contained the only

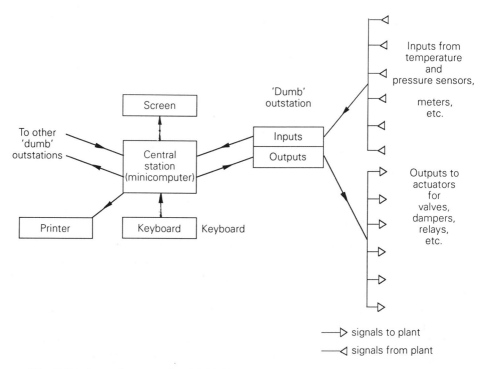

**Fig. 1.1**  An early centralized BEMS.

computing power or 'intelligence' in the system, with 'dumb' or unintelligent **outstations** which were boxes or cabinets for relays and connections to sensors and actuators, similar to the earlier data gathering panels (Fig. 1.1). The term 'intelligent' is used as the central station (the minicomputer) had the ability to calculate and make decisions based on the data it received from the outstations.

The systems were expensive (at approximately £100 000 installed) and so were viable only for large sites. Such sites were often prestige air conditioned headquarters offices of over 12 000 m², or hospitals with over 500 beds, large building complexes (e.g. Heathrow Airport terminals) and industrial sites and factories with over 2000 employees [4]. Although these systems related initially to the control and monitoring of heating, ventilating and air conditioning (HVAC) plant and were therefore energy management systems, they were also capable of controlling the lighting, the lifts, and the monitoring of the security and fire alarms, although the latter two were rarely linked to BEMSs in the UK due to regulatory bodies. In fact the systems were considered as building management systems to help in the management of large and complex sites, without specifically saving energy. These early building energy management systems were in fact in existence before the Energy Crisis of 1973–4.

Although these early BEMSs were capable of monitoring and controlling fire and security systems, they rarely did so, as dedicated systems were used for the potentially life-saving fire detection devices and also security devices. There are still problems in integrating all systems such as fire alarm systems and security systems into BEMSs today, mostly due to the different regulatory bodies and standards – and to the different manufacturing companies involved – rather than the technology.

Since about 1980, with the rapid development of LSI and very large-scale integration (VLSI) to thousands of devices per chip, microcomputers often called **personal computers** (PCs) became as powerful as the previous minicomputer, if not more so. Also the outstations, which are themselves small microcomputers, or more correctly, they have microprocessor chips, have gained considerably in processing power giving them 'intelligence' (Fig. 1.2).

This enables them to operate on their own, or to become 'stand-alone' outstations, being dependent only on the central station for a small proportion of their operating time. These outstations have considerably more control functions than the older, 'dumb' outstations, which tended to have more of a monitoring role. Indeed each intelligent outstation can control a small building on its own, and it is economic to install these intelligent outstations in medium- and small-sized buildings. The cost of such an outstation varies from just over £100 to £4000, although the former cost would apply only to a small outstation with limited control and monitoring capability. It is now considered by many that a BEMS outstation of the appropriate size is competitive with conventional controls, so the tendency is for most new commercial buildings

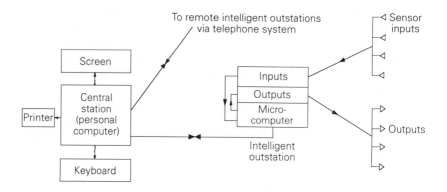

**Fig. 1.2**   A microprocessor-based BEMS with intelligent outstations.

to have BEMS. Figure 1.3 shows the relative cost of a BEMS to an ordinary controller.

The cost per *point* relates to the total cost of an input or an output – e.g. a sensor input or a control signal output. A general rule of thumb is that the cost of a BEMS point (at 1991 prices) with its wiring and programming is £200–£300. With the point cost at £300, the breakdown of this price, normalized to one point, is shown in Table 1.1. The minimum cost of a complete BEMS has also drastically dropped through the 1980s, as is shown in Fig. 1.4.

**Table 1.1**   Breakdown of the cost of outstation

| Element | Cost (£) |
|---|---|
| Outstation | 50 |
| Input/output device | 30 |
| Programming point | 50 |
| Cabling | 100 |
| Fixing | 20 |
| Administration | 50 |
| Total | 300 |

The BEMS costing £1000 in Fig. 1.4 would be a very basic system, and generally a basic BEMS consisting of a central station and an outstation would be approximately £5000–£6000. However, the buyer must beware of the implications of marginal costing [5] and a 'loss leader' pricing policy to gain entry to an organization in the hope that the system will later be expanded, when the vendor will hope to recoup its profit [6].

The distributed intelligence BEMS is particularly appropriate for the UK and Europe with their predominantly smaller, heated-only buildings. Conse-

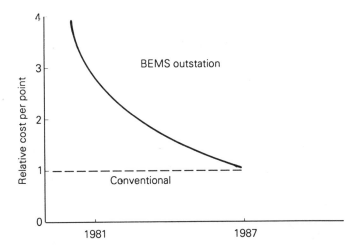

**Fig. 1.3** Comparative cost of a BEMS outstation.

quently the UK has been in the forefront of the development of distributed intelligence BEMS.

Also as a consequence of the computing revolution, the central station is based on standard PCs with sufficient memory and software capabilities. The central station can communicate with many outstations when it needs to, either on a local communications network or to remote outstations over telephone

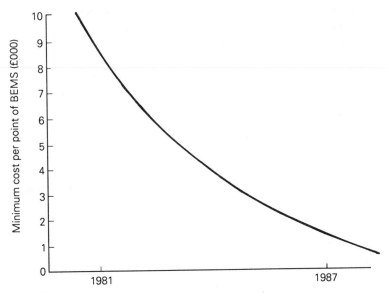

**Fig. 1.4** The cost of BEMS.

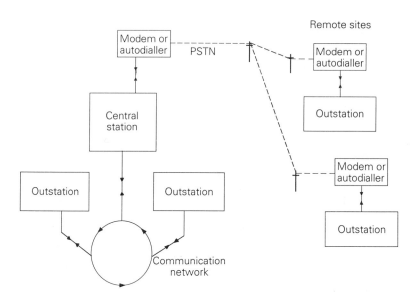

**Fig. 1.5**  BEMS communications.

lines (the Public Switched Telephone Network, PSTN), as is shown in Fig. 1.5, using modems and autodiallers, which are explained in Section 1.2.2 on communication.

Some conventional controls, which are **serially interfaceable** (see Chapter 3), can be connected to computers, to show set points and allow adjustment of them. However, these do not have the full capabilities of most BEMS.

As microprocessors have become more powerful and cheaper, so outstations have become very much smaller and cheaper such that they can control individual items of plant: the plant is becoming intelligent. The manufacturers of BEMSs are supplying these small outstations to other equipment manufacturers (OEMs), so that their plant can be commissioned at the factory and simply connected into the BEMS communication system when delivered to site.

Communications networks are being developed to allow small building services equipment, even down to light switches, with silicon chips added, to communicate; this is dealt with in more detail in Chapter 3.

## 1.2  Some benefits of BEMSs

To highlight the advantage of a BEMS some of the more prominent benefits are briefly discussed before considering some of the disadvantages and problems in Section 1.3.

## 1.2.1 Monitoring

One of the main benefits of BEMSs has been the constant monitoring of the plant, and the ability to recall the monitored data at a later time. This has enabled engineers and technicians to achieve a better understanding of their buildings and plant and has often led to plant improvements and energy saving as a result. Energy efficiency can be checked as a BEMS can monitor and log data from fuel and electricity meters.

## 1.2.2 Communication

An added bonus of the BEMS is that this information can be communicated from remote sites over the telephone system to the central station some distance from the outstation and its host building. This saves the considerable time and effort involved in travelling to and from site to check the plant, unless there is a local plant operator.

An example of the use of the monitoring and communication of a BEMS can be shown by considering a building without a BEMS and the work involved as a result of this deficiency. The building was a local authority swimming-pool, where the ventilation fans had to be run 24 hours a day to stop condensation (there was no pool cover). It was decided by the authority's Energy Unit to install two-speed fan motors, and to run the fans at half-speed at night to save energy when the evaporation of water would be reduced. Also the heating was reduced at night to save energy. However, when this work was done there appeared to be no night-time saving of fuel. A technician visited the site to check the heating control, which seemed to be working satisfactorily. Additionally, a temperature sensor connected to a chart recorder, was placed in the supply air duct as a further check. A few days later, he returned to see that the chart recorder showed no evidence that the heating controller was reducing the heating at night.

Two further site visits were made to meet technicians from the controls company, who asserted that the controller was indeed working satisfactorily when they tested it. Eventually after a copy of the chart recorder temperature trace had been sent to him, a senior technician came from the company. Again, he was sure the controller was satisfactory, but a check of the heater battery valve, in a rather inaccessible place, showed that the valve stem had broken. Although the controller was working, it was not moving the control valve, so there was no control of the heating.

If the swimming-pool had had a BEMS, then the local authority technician could have checked the heating system from his central station in the Civic Centre, realized that it was not working and may even have been able to identify the fault. If the controls company also had a central station, then it could have dialled up the pool and checked it. Many man-hours of visits and checking would have been saved.

### 1.2.3  Manpower savings and maintenance

There are also manpower savings to be made with BEMSs. The local boiler-man, caretaker or plant operator can often be replaced by a communicating BEMS outstation, or one operator can cover more buildings. Primarily because of this remote monitoring facility, and its consequent manpower saving, most London boroughs now have BEMSs installed.

Many maintenance contractors and energy management bureaux offer to run clients' buildings and plant for them using outstations communicating regularly with the central station at the organization's headquarters. Alarms are automatically sent from the outstations if problems arise – e.g. a low temperature or a boiler is off – and the situation restored to normality often before the client is aware of any plant malfunction. Additionally, BEMSs can allow the plant condition to be monitored (condition monitoring), which enables better maintenance.

### 1.2.4  Commissioning

Slowly BEMSs are becoming used in aiding the commissioning of plant in newly constructed buildings. This is especially true in large air conditioned office blocks with many small outstations on the air conditioning units around the building. However, there are still many logistical problems in ensuring that the BEMS is in place and operative before the plant it controls is commissioned. There are also cost implications in making commissioning valves and measuring devices interfaceable to outstations. But to offset this extra cost there is the advantage that the BEMS's outstations can communicate, so that the main contractor, consultant or client can check the commissioning off-site.

Further benefits are mentioned in the case studies in Section 1.4, but it is interesting that the benefits mentioned here are primarily management related as opposed to better control *per se*.

## 1.3  Some problems with BEMSs

Although there are many benefits from a BEMS properly applied and used, it would be naïve to assume that people do not experience problems. BEMSs are simply computers monitoring and controlling plant, and naturally the problems associated with BEMS are often those associated with computers themselves. Like computers, BEMS have large user manuals to explain the many functions and operations that they can perform. Therefore, while the basics can be mastered fairly quickly, some study is required to master the whole system. Also many user manuals are not particularly well written or 'user-friendly' for beginners, so that users have to rely on manufacturers' training courses. This training is not to be decried, as future operators may well cause problems and upset plant operation by experimenting in order to learn. However, training courses are expensive and not all operators are sent on them; experienced operators can also change jobs or leave the organization, so impairing the benefits of the BEMS. The BEMS programs (or 'software') and equipment will often be updated as technology advances and this will often necessitate further study or training.

Another common problem is that inexperienced users can program the BEMS to generate a considerable amount of data, wishing to use as much of the data logging function and alarm reporting facilities as possible. Consequently, the BEMS spews out data and alarms as if it were suffering from 'data diarrhoea', and after the initial enthusiasm of the operator wanes the BEMS becomes a hindrance rather than a help to efficient management. The manipulation of energy data for monitoring and targeting buildings is also a problem with BEMSs. A survey in 1990 [8] of 50 energy managers showed that 82% had BEMSs but only 2% could use them for targeting. Clearly, BEMSs are not being used to their full potential.

Prospective purchasers of BEMS should be aware that different manufacturers' BEMS are not compatible with one another. For instance, one cannot easily link one manufacturer's outstation to another's central station or use another's sensors. This is a problem stemming from the incompatibility of computer systems, programs and communications. In fact the BEMS Centre, initially set up by the Energy Efficiency Office of the Department of Energy, and partly funded by the industry itself, proposed a communication standard to make all BEMS compatible [7] (see Chapter 3 for further details). This should avoid users getting locked into any one manufacturer's system.

## 1.4  Case studies

In-depth case studies have been conducted by the Energy Technology Support Unit (ETSU) of BEMSs installed with grants from the Energy Efficiency Demonstration Scheme, (EEDS). These grants were up to 25% of the capital cost of the scheme, and 100% of the cost of monitoring the scheme. The scheme had to involve the use of new technology which could save energy. Most of the schemes therefore relate to the early to mid-1980s, when BEMSs were new technology. Although some of the schemes are now dated, there are some useful analyses and still some useful lessons to be learnt.

A number of case studies of more modern schemes are also available from the Department of Energy, through ETSU [24]. The reports of these schemes are much shorter and less detailed than the earlier reports, presenting details of selected successful projects which have been undertaken since the initial Energy Efficiency Demonstration Schemes, for BEMSs. The reported performances are based on results from the 'host' organizations (the users), whereas the earlier reports were by independent consultants.

The ETSU booklet, *Energy Management Systems*, gives details of the earlier EEDS projects [4], four of which are considered here:

(i)   Scheme 35, a BEMS for 9 large schools and colleges in the Grampian Regional Council [4], [33].
(ii)  Scheme 62, a BEMS for 50 various sized schools in Hereford and Worcester County Council [9].
(iii) Scheme 64, 3 coal-fired schools controlled by a BEMS [10].
(iv)  Scheme 127, a BEMS central station used for remote energy management as a bureau service to 10 tenanted office buildings [11].

**Table 1.2**   Comparison of costs and payback

| Scheme | Details | Expected | | Actual | |
|---|---|---|---|---|---|
| | | Costs (£) | Payback (yrs) | Costs (£) | Payback (yrs) |
| 35 | 9 large schools and colleges | 257 806 | 3 | — | — |
| 62 | 50 schools | 238 330 | 3 | 376 138 | 3.6[‡] |
| 64 | 3 coal-fired schools [*] | 17 595 | 1.5–2 | 20 591 | 3.8 |
| 127 | 10 tenanted offices | 137 100 | 1.8 | 153 300[†] | 1.7–2.9 |

[*]  A pilot scheme preceding the introduction to 21 schools.
[†]  Operating costs of the bureau not included.
[‡]  This is based on the scheme when it was initially extended from three to 21 schools.

Most of the schemes were completed by 1985. It is revealing to look at the estimated cost of the schemes, as shown in Table 1.2. From the table it can be seen that Scheme 35 was certainly very expensive compared with Scheme 62 which was for more schools and was cheaper. A later Expanded Project Profile on Scheme 35 [33] reported that the BEMS manufacturer, Atlantic Instruments Ltd, was no longer in business, and that a new central station had been installed. New outstations to expand the system were cheaper than the first outstations, costing £16 000 each at 1986 prices. The original BEMS, using a minicomputer as a central station, produced a lot of data. Each school had a weather station connected to the BEMS, and there were problems analysing all the data produced. A separate system was later installed to produce graphs on a flat bed plotter, which helped to alleviate matters.

The other three schemes cost more than expected and produced longer paybacks than predicted. However, it must be remembered that these were pioneering schemes breaking new ground.

## 1.4.1   Scheme 62, Hereford and Worcester

The BEMS used in this scheme was a Transmitton Micropower 2000, with 52 outstations at 50 sites in 44 individual schools. The outstations could operate independently of the central station, the latter communicating with the outstations over telephone lines from the council offices in Worcester. Completion of the scheme was delayed by about a year, to 1983, due to 'immaturity of the software and unfamiliarity of the Council staff in the application of the equip-

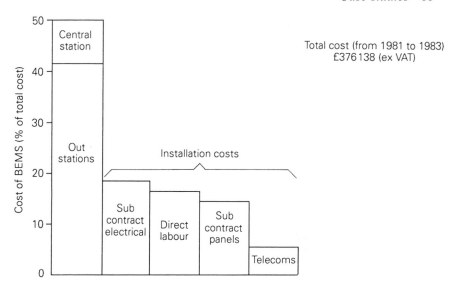

**Fig. 1.6** Breakdown of the cost of a BEMS.

ment' [9]. A breakdown of the costs of the BEMS installation are shown in Fig. 1.6.

The report on the scheme [9] emphasized, in the summary, that continued savings would depend on the effort and skill of the council staff in using the BEMS as an effective management tool. In common with early BEMS, the data presentation was not good. So a separate PC was later purchased to do off-line data processing and graphics.

The local authority took full responsibility for the installation, commissioning and maintenance of the system. The quality of contractors' work was variable and contractors with experience of installing systems showed their worth. Introducing an outstation to each site usually took five man-days. Further work by the council staff in ensuring correct operation and liaising with school staff took about 2 man-days. Unforeseen post-commissioning work required one full-time member of the council's technical staff. Progress in installation was much more rapid as the BEMS matured and as experience of the system was gained. An interim report on this project did indicate that some schools had their heating updated before the BEMS was installed, which would have helped the payback obtained [12].

### 1.4.2 Scheme 64, Staffordshire

Staffordshire County Council also used a Transmitton Micropower 2000 BEMS but the installation was put in later than that of Hereford and Worcester. After a pilot scheme of three schools, the BEMS was extended to 21 schools.

By careful management of specification, installation and commissioning of outstations few problems were encountered at site. The savings made at the coal-fired schools were almost entirely due to reductions in heating times and improved set point control. The performance of the Transmitton BEMS was reported to be 'very satisfactory' [10], although an off-line data analysis facility was later added to aid monitoring and targeting.

Assurances were given that there would be no redundancies because of the installation of the BEMS. Caretakers had to be persuaded to keep high coal-feed rates to the boilers, so that the BEMS could control the heating. The energy conservation staff established a good relationship with the caretaking staff, and problems were contained to manageable proportions. Without this level of cooperation, it is doubtful whether such progress as was actually made would have been made.

The monitoring organization did not measure coal consumption directly, but used local authority data, based on monthly coal deliveries, to determine the good savings that were made by the scheme.

### 1.4.3   Scheme 127, Ten tenanted buildings

In this scheme a Trend Controls System BEMS was used by Energy Technique to monitor and control remotely ten buildings from their own offices in Basingstoke. Seven Trend 550 controllers and four IQ150 systems were used, with two IQ150s in one building. The systems were commissioned between February 1983 and July 1984. Few teething problems were encountered with the BEMS and, in most instances, difficulties were due to peculiarities of the individual building rather than new technology [11].

**Table 1.3**   Costs and savings at ten office buildings

| Building (name or situation) | Cost of BEMS (+ operating cost) (£000s) | Annual savings Fuel (£000s) | Electricity (£000s) |
|---|---|---|---|
| York House | 10 (+2) | 7.8 | 0 |
| Fenchurch Street | 15 (+3.4) | 3.4 | 7 |
| Leicester Square | 19.5 (+3.6) | 4.2 | 8.4 |
| Rothschild House | 27.5 (+4.4) | 8.6 | 8.7 |
| Intercity House | 15 (+3.7) | 4.4 | 5.3 |
| Greyfriars | 17.3 (+3.1) | 5.1 | 4.7 |
| C. P. House | 16 (+3.4) | 6.2 | 0.6 |
| Hagley Road | 25 (+3.1) | 4.7 | 0 |
| Windsor House | 4 (+0.8) | 0 | 0 |
| St James Square | 4 (+0.8 ) | 0 | 0 |

Table 1.3 shows the savings that were made at the ten buildings. Although the overall scheme was successful, two buildings, Windsor House and the

office at St James's Square, made no savings. Seven of the office buildings were air conditioned and Windsor House, St James's Square and York House were heated only. Electricity savings were made at most of the air conditioned buildings, since air conditioning uses large amounts of electricity whereas heating uses little (except electrical heating, which these buildings did not have).

The lack of savings at St James's Square was attributed to a change in tenant and extended working hours [11]. Windsor House saved nothing due to the heating inexplicably coming on during some weekends; one explanation could be that voltage fluctuations could switch the outstation from a weekend schedule to a weekday schedule. Although Hagley Road showed savings, they were rather low. This was attributed to the presence of a resident technician who ran the building very well. He retired when the BEMS was installed, and there was little improvement that the BEMS could make upon his performance.

It is interesting to look at the costs of the ten BEMS outstations, although it should be borne in mind that the costs relate to 1983–4. Since then the costs of BEMSs have reduced as the electronics revolution has progressed, but the labour cost for installation has increased, so the costs actually may not be at variance with current overall costs. Table 1.4 shows the costs, both total and per square metre of floor area. The BEMSs for the air conditioned buildings are shown to be more expensive as there are more points required for air conditioned plant.

**Table 1.4** Costs of BEMSs outstations at ten office buildings

| Building (name or location) | Total cost of BEMS (A) (£000s) | Building floor area (B) (1000 m$^2$) | A/B (£/m$^2$) | Heated (H) or air conditioned (A/C) |
|---|---|---|---|---|
| Windsor House | 4 | 5.0 | 0.8 | H |
| St James's Square | 4 | 5.0 | 0.8 | H |
| York House | 10 | 9.5 | 1.1 | H |
| Intercity House | 15 | 9.5 | 1.6 | A/C |
| Greyfriars | 17.3 | 10.0 | 1.7 | A/C |
| Hagley Road | 25 | 13.2 | 1.9 | A/C |
| Leicester Square | 19.5 | 9.0 | 2.2 | A/C |
| Rothschild House | 27.5 | 9.0 | 3.1 | A/C |
| C. P. House | 16 | 5.0 | 3.2 | A/C |
| Fenchurch Street | 15 | 4.5 | 3.3 | A/C |

This ETSU scheme was particularly successful and good savings were made. The conclusion of the ETSU report noted that when the outstations were installed, it was found that 'much of the plants' equipment (especially compensator controllers) were found to be inoperative due to poor maintenance'. Also the conclusion remarked that during BEMS operation 'inadequacies of the original plant were revealed, e.g. the need for more heating zones'. This implies that the buildings were not in a well-maintained condition prior to the installation of the BEMS, and that the BEMS was useful in highlighting this poor state.

### 1.4.4   Office BEMS survey

A detailed analysis of the improvements and savings that a BEMS can make in a building are contained in a study by Birtles and John [13]. They monitored detailed energy flows, plant efficiencies and environmental conditions in a building on a before-and-after basis to provide an accurate assessment of a BEMS installation. The before period was 130 days of the 1981–82 heating season and the after period was the following heating season, (1982–83), with the BEMS installed.

The office building monitored had a gross floor area of 4,500 m$^2$ on seven storeys. It was a 'medium-weight' building with a reinforced concrete frame with brick cladding and approx. 50% external glazing. Half of the office accommodation was open plan, and the other half cellular offices. Heating of the building was by two oil-fired boilers, both of approx. 300–400 kW; domestic hot-water services were electrically heated. Before the BEMS was installed, the heating controls were an optimizer and a weather compensator (these controls are discussed in detail in later chapters). An average annual energy consumption of 0.85 GJ m$^{-2}$ (236 kWh m$^{-2}$) (for oil and electricity), prior to the installation of the BEMS, showed the building to have a good energy performance in comparison to similar types of offices.

In the latter half of 1982 the BEMS was installed. From that date it can be seen that it was an early BEMS, although it had a stand-alone outstation in the building which communicated over a leased telephone line with a central station at a Property Services Agency (PSA), district works office. Communication with the central station was under the exceptional circumstances of alarm reporting, or when initiated by the operator.

There were seven monitoring functions in the outstation and six control functions. Three of the control functions had been in existence in the previous control system. Those additional controls in the outstation were for stopping the heating system at the optimum time near the end of the occupancy period, sequencing of the two boilers, and holiday scheduling.

As many factors influenced the savings, a model of linear equations was developed, relating the energy consumptions and internal temperatures to meteorological, occupancy and comfort factors. This analysis enabled an estimation of a 27% saving in the annual fuel consumption. Table 1.5 shows how the savings were achieved.

A number of the savings in Table 1.5 were due in part to the 'before' monitoring, and subsequent remedial action. For instance, the heating system efficiency was improved when monitoring revealed that the high/low flame burner

**Table 1.5** Analysis of fuel savings due to BEMS

| Source of saving | Percentage fuel saved |
|---|---|
| Increased heating system efficiency | 6.6 |
| Improved starting of heating at optimum start time in morning | 5.1 |
| Reduced inside temperature | 4.6 |
| Public holiday schedule | 4.1 |
| Stopping of heating at optimum time at end of occupancy | 3.1 |
| Heating pump over-run to use residual boiler heat | 1.6 |
| Use of gains from lighting | 1.0 |
| Heating turned off on warm days in spring | 1.0 |
| Total savings | 27.1 |

nozzles on one boiler were in the wrong position, and they were changed over. Some floors were found to be getting warmer than others, so the heating system was rebalanced. This allowed the overall building temperature to be reduced.

Based on saving 27.1% of the fuel, the simple payback was estimated at 5.8 years. Allowing for a possible saving in maintenance cost, Birtles and John estimated a lower payback of 4.8 years.

## 1.5 User reaction

Although there are a number of useful lessons to be learnt from the case studies, above, many of the technical problems were associated with teething problems of new systems and/or inexperience of contractors and users with new BEMSs. At the end of the 1980s, the industry was more mature and teething problems were reported to be no longer as significant as they had been [15], and that a manufacturer's most up-to-date system could be purchased with confidence, provided that the manufacturer had a good record with previous systems.

A review of 21 BEMSs (three from each of seven manufacturers) was carried out in 1984 (Phase I), and a further 21 BEMSs were reviewed in 1987 (Phase II), covering eleven manufacturers' systems [15]. The reviews assessed the users' reactions to their systems' performances. The BEMSs had been installed for between one and three years. Phase III, completed in 1989, examined the long-term performance of five early BEMSs [16].

There was a large increase in user satisfaction in BEMSs between Phases I and II. Figure 1.7 [16] shows the user responses when users were asked if their expectations had been fulfilled.

Two-thirds of the reasons given for purchasing BEMSs, deduced in Phases I and II, were to save energy, although 30% of users had appeared to make no attempt to quantify the savings! Where savings had been assessed, they were

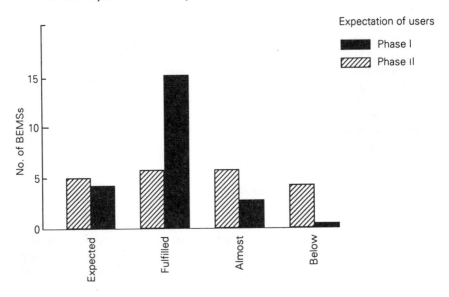

**Fig. 1.7**   User satisfaction with BEMSs.

typically between 10% and 20%, rising to between 10% and 30% where major refurbishment work, such as re-zoning and re-boilering, had been carried out.

In Phase II 45% of users perceived improvements in comfort, irrespective of whether refurbishment had been done. Manpower savings were also reported by a number of users.

Phase III, a survey of five BEMSs that had been operational for five to eight years, showed that both the long-term performance of the BEMSs and their reliability was good. However, Phase I and II revealed that a significant number of users had problems with temperature sensors. Many of these related to **strap-on sensors,** which are clamped on to the outside of pipes and cylinders and give only approximate readings (this is dealt with in more detail in Chapter 4 on sensors). The problems related to failure rate, drift and location. It was concluded that a tighter and improved specification of sensors would have alleviated many of these problems.

During the interviews of the BEMSs users, it became apparent to the interviewer that the ability and enthusiasm of the operator was a critical factor in the success of a system. This means, then, that when a BEMS is installed, there must be personnel within the organization willing and capable of competent operation: either training is required, for which the BEMS manufacturer will probably charge, or 'new blood' will have to be recruited. Also implicit here is the ease with which the BEMS can be operated, or how good is the **man–machine interface.** Most BEMS users in the survey felt that this was the area where BEMSs could be improved, as is shown in Fig. 1.8.

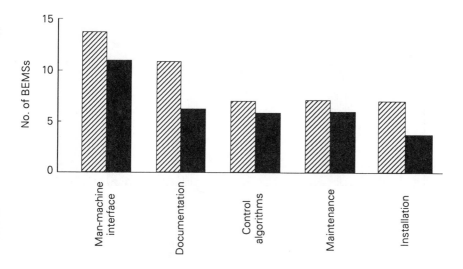

**Fig. 1.8**   Areas users consider could be improved.

## 1.6  Staff reaction

When new technology is introduced into the workplace, naturally it changes the jobs of those people who operate it, if it does not actually make some redundant. There is an additional factor that BEMSs may also affect the environment in which people work. So the reaction of staff, both those directly involved with operating the plant and those working in the controlled environment, is important to the success of a BEMS installation [14].

   In the Hereford and Worcester project it was noted that 'continued savings would depend on the effort and skill of the Council staff in using the BEMS as an effective management tool'. In the Staffordshire project 'assurances were given that there would be no redundancies because of the installation of the BEMS'. Unfortunately, in the study of a BEMS in an office [13], discussed above, when the monitoring team left the BEMS in the hands of the local operators at the district works office, the operators had neither the time nor expertise effectively to use the BEMS. In fact the BEMS (being an early model) was rather user-unfriendly. Consequently, the savings were not maintained.

   Building occupants can also react against managements who install BEMSs. In one case, an occupant phoned the maintenance operative to complain of the low temperature in his office. The operative checked the temperature on the BEMS central station and found that it was rather low. He opened up the

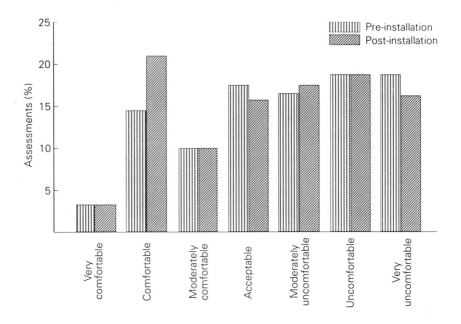

**Fig. 1.9**   Teachers' assessments of comfort on Monday mornings.

heating valve on the appropriate zone by communicating with the relevant outstation and saw the zone temperature, displayed at the central station, gradually rise. However, the operative was later confronted by the occupant, who was now quite angry and demanded to know why the operative had not come to his office to check the temperature. The occupant had no knowledge of the new BEMS or how it operated.

Such staff reactions are well known to industrial psychologists whose work makes useful reading for managements about to install BEMSs. J.A.C. Brown in his excellent book, *The Social Psychology of Industry* [17], relates the staff dissatisfaction, in the early 1950s, following the replacement of tungsten lighting by fluorescent lighting in a drawing office. Within a short time of the change being made, many of the men in the drawing office were visiting the medical department complaining of eyestrain, sore eyes, headaches and even double vision. A little later the men told management that they could not continue their work because of eyestrain caused by the fluorescent lighting.

In fact the fluorescent lighting was a considerable improvement on the tungsten lights, and expert opinion confirmed this. When a meeting was held with the men, it was found that the lighting was held scapegoat for poor management and the fact that the men had not been consulted on the change of lighting before it first took place. After the meeting, there were no further complaints of eyestrain.

A behavioural study was carried out in the schools of the Hereford and Worcester BEMS scheme [9] to determine changes in relevant behaviour, attitudes and experiences of those working in the schools, due to the introduction of the BEMS. The study was conducted in three phases. The first phase was conducted before the BEMS was installed, followed by the second phase of a survey of the same people after the BEMS had been installed and commissioned; this revealed first impressions. The third phase was conducted some time later and was intended to confirm any permanent effects of the BEMS. Sixteen schools were used for the study, involving a considerable number of members of staff at the schools, although only 71 took part in phase three.

The teachers noted an improvement in comfort levels at the start of the week due to the BEMS, as is shown in Fig. 1.9. There was a noticeable improvement in the comfort level during cold weather; the teachers' responses demonstrate this (Fig. 1.10).

Although the teachers' responses showed a perception of increased comfort levels in cold weather, and to a lesser extent on Mondays, there were significant minorities of teachers (31%), caretakers (37%) and headteachers (22%), who were dissatisfied with the way the scheme had been introduced. The dissatisfaction was frequently ascribed to low levels of consultation and infor-

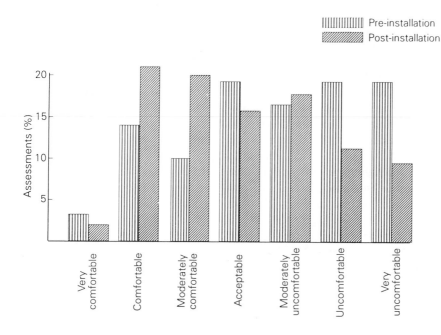

**Fig. 1.10** Teachers' assessments of comfort in cold weather.

mation. Only 68% of teachers knew that the primary purpose of the BEMS was to save energy. The teachers' opinions of their knowledge of the BEMS is shown in Table 1.6, based on data from the ETSU report [9] (which inexplicably has the second percentage column adding up to 98%). There was also a marked increase in the response of teachers after the installation, that the best mode of temperature control in their classrooms was that of opening windows.

**Table 1.6**   Teachers' opinions of their knowledge of the BEMS

| Opinion | Before installation of BEMS (%) | After installation of BEMS (%) |
|---------|---------------------------------|--------------------------------|
| All I want | 2 | 4 |
| Most | 4 | 12 |
| Only some | 41 | 56 |
| Nothing | 53 | 26 |

## 1.6.1  Industrial psychology

To understand people's reactions to BEMSs it is necessary to appreciate industrial psychology, or how people react and interact in the working environment. J.A.C. Brown traces the origin of industrial psychology to the work of Elton Mayo at the Hawthorne Works in Chicago between 1924 and 1927 [17].

Production at the works, which manufactured telephone equipment, was low and there was dissatisfaction among the 30 000 employees. For the time, the employer was considered progressive, with the provision of pension schemes, sickness benefit schemes, recreational and other facilities.

Mayo's work started by assessing the environmental conditions of the workplace, on the assumption that people produce maximum output in perfect environmental conditions and perfected methods of working.

Mayo examined the influence of increasing the lighting levels on production. To do this he took two groups of employees. For one group, the control group, the lighting level was unchanged, while the level for the other group was raised. Production in the latter group increased, but unexpectedly it also increased in the control group. This was puzzling as the lighting had remained constant in the control group.

The lighting level was then reduced, the control group's level remaining constant. Again, the production increased and once more it was for both groups. Clearly, other factors were at work than just the lighting, and it would not make sense to reduce the lighting levels to increase production in the long term. Mayo for many years researched into these factors, and his conclusions are extensive (for a full discussion of them the interested reader is referred to Brown's book [17]). The main conclusions of interest to the installers of BEMS are that the production levels for both groups increased as the employees felt their status had been respected and they did not consider that they had been treated as 'cogs in the works'. Also work is a group activity, and as shown in the Hawthorne experiment, social factors influenced the production.

Hence the moral for installers of BEMSs is that those affected by BEMSs should be informed, even consulted, about their implementation [14], [6]. It is worth remembering that in the Hereford and Worcester scheme 37% of caretakers, 31% of teachers and 22% of headteachers were dissatisfied with the way the scheme had been introduced. The dissatisfaction was frequently ascribed to low levels of consultation and information. It was also written in the ETSU report that 'continued savings would depend on the effort and skill of the Council staff in using the BEMS as an effective management tool'. In the Staffordshire project, 'assurances were given that there would be no redundancies because of the installation of the BEMS'. Also the BEMS scheme studied by Birtles and John, although making initial good savings, was not too successful when left to the resident technicians as they had neither the time nor expertise to use the system fully.

Another useful conclusion from the Hawthorne experiment was that complaints were not necessarily an objective recital of fact; they were commonly symptoms manifesting themselves as a problem regarding an individual's status. Thus a complaint about a BEMS may not in fact be about the BEMS itself, but rather about the organization and people using it.

Mayo's work was conducted many years ago and there has since been extensive discussion and some criticism of it. But more recent work related to energy efficiency supports the importance of the human factor in operating buildings efficiently [18].

One study, on the installation of energy efficiency measures in nine identical children's homes in a local authority [19] showed that measures taken to save fuel worked. Staff in the children's homes had been briefly informed of the work, and its purpose explained, before it was carried out. Although the measures were only to save fuel, it was found that all the homes had also saved a considerable amount of electricity, analogous to production increasing at the Hawthorne Works.

## 1.7 Future developments

As the power of PCs increases and electronic chips become even more powerful, so BEMSs' central stations will become more sophisticated and small outstations for individual items of plant will become cheaper. These small outstations are being supplied to manufacturers of plant (often referred to by BEMS manufacturers as other equipment manufacturers (OEMs), for fitting to their factory commissioned equipment. Installation of the plant on-site is then completed by simply connecting the packaged plant to the **communication bus**, or BEMS **local area network** (LAN) (see Chapter 3). Consequently, the BEMS will have an increasing role in the commissioning of all of the building's services.

It is rapidly becoming economic for small buildings to have microprocessor communicating devices and controls. Even sensors are becoming intelligent, or smart, with the sensor and chips on one piece of silicon [20], [21].

Buildings and plant will then become 'intelligent' [22], and this intelligence will spread to smaller and smaller buildings, down to the home. Intelligent light and power switches have been developed and standard bus systems are available [23] (see Chapter 3).

Communications standards are being developed such that different manufacturers' equipment will be able to 'talk' to each other, so that users will not be tied in to one manufacturer. Central station programs are also being centred on common **operating systems** and **window environment** software (Chapter 3).

### 1.7.1 Expert systems

One interesting area of development is in **artificial intelligence**, and the use of **expert systems**. Artificial intelligence (AI) is the study and process of enabling computers to mimic human learning and decision-making [25]. The AI systems cover **natural language processors** that eliminate the need for computer users to learn a computer language; **robotics** that enables a machine to learn (**machine learning**) and to have **automated vision**; and finally, there is the expert system.

An expert system is a computer program that learns, deduces, diagnoses and advises [25]. A more formal definition is that it is the embodiment in a computer of a knowledge-based component from an expert that offers intelligent advice or takes an intelligent decision and, in addition, is able to justify its own line of reasoning. The style adopted to attain these characteristics is **rule-based** programming [26]. The rules are based on logic and a standard computing statement such as

IF..............THEN

is a common element of expert systems [27], as are

YES/NO

answers to questions. Standard probability theory and Bayes' theorem also contribute to expert systems [28]. If hard 'yes' or 'no' answers, or definite probabilities, are not easy or possible to give, then **fuzzy logic** can be used for approximate reasoning [29]. Three of the best-known proven expert systems are: PROSPECTOR, DENDRAL and MYCIN.

The earliest expert system (work started on it in 1964) and a significant advance was DENDRAL, which identifies molecular compounds from their mass spectrograms. It performs better than the best human experts and has made some worthwhile contributions [27].

PROSPECTOR was developed in 1978; it is designed to help geologists in their search for ore deposits and the mineral potential of large areas of land. Tests against known sites of exploration revealed a 7% agreement [28].

Development on MYCIN started in the USA, in 1974, at Stanford University, California, USA. The program helps doctors to diagnose and treat bacterial infection. Although it is successful, it takes 20–30 min per consultation and is mostly used for teaching [28].

MYCIN, like other expert systems, has two main elements: the **knowledge base** and the **inference engine**. The former contains the expert's knowledge, such as the answers to questions and the consequences of IF...THEN statements, whereas the inference engine uses the facts and rules to answer logically questions posed by the user. Further work on MYCIN stripped out the medical knowledge to leave the inference engine and a system for adding new rules to create EMYCIN (Essential MYCIN), effectively an **expert system shell**. Expert system shells are programs or software that allow users to set up their own expert systems in any area, or 'domain', of expertise. This avoids the need to write the expert system program in LISP or PROLOG, common languages for such programs.

An example of an expert system, or **knowledge-based system** (KBS), applied to a BEMS is BREXBAS, developed as a prototype by the Building Research Establishment (BRE) to demonstrate the use of expert systems in analysing data from a BEMS for fault diagnosis [30]. After some initial tests, BREXBAS was then redesigned to monitor and interpret information from an on-line BEMS at a building in Epsom [31]. The KBS supplies advice on the performance of one of two heating plants and the underfloor heating in the atrium. Various flow temperatures and plant item statuses are monitored, as well as the space temperature of the building. The knowledge of the heating system was obtained and structured for the expert shell by a programmer discussing the heating with the designer. Three main tasks performed by BREXBAS are:

(i) to ascertain the current space temperature;
(ii) to evaluate the current conditions to determine acceptability and, if unacceptable, to diagnose the cause of the problem;
(iii) to provide advice and/or potential remedies to the user.

The general structure of the KBS on its own computer, linked to the BEMS central station, is shown in Fig. 1.11.

Expert systems can be useful for monitoring plant, as BREXBAS, but they will be useful for energy monitoring and targeting, and also setting up the required control strategy for the building. In fact it may soon be possible that when a BEMS is first installed in a building, it will simply declare that the

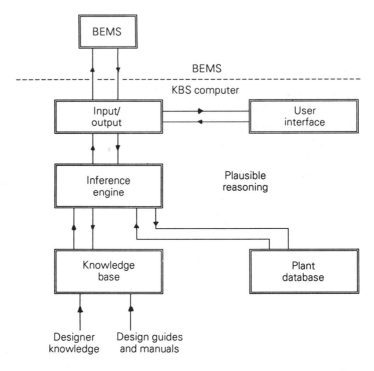

**Fig. 1.11**   General structure of BREXBAS.

building cannot be adequately controlled for comfort as the architect has put in too much glazing and the building services engineer has not put in a large enough heating system and the solar gain in summer will be too much for the air conditioning refrigeration system. Perhaps it will then be necessary to consult a legal expert system!

At the outstation end of the BEMS, rule-based control programs will become more widely used [32]. By using fuzzy logic operators' experience of controlling plant can be incorporated into the program. These programs will be able not only to control individual items of plant, but also look at all plant operation and control it for optimum performance, which is **global optimization**. The era of the BEMS is only just beginning.

## References

[1]  Haines, R. W. (1987) *Control Systems for Heating, Ventilating and Air Conditioning*, 4th edn, Van Nostrand Reinhold, New York.

[2]  Clapp, M. D. and Wortham, R. H. (1989) 'Developments in building-management systems', *GEC Review*, **5**, 1.

[3] Gardner P. R. and Ward, L. (1987) *Energy Management Systems in Buildings*, Energy Publications, Newmarket.

[4] ETSU (1986) Energy Management Systems, Energy Technology series No. 1, Energy Efficiency Office of the Department of Energy, Harwell.

[5] Bull, R. J. (1972) *Accounting in Business*, Butterworths, London.

[6] Levermore, G. J. (1989) *Presenting a Case for a Building Energy Management System*, BEMS Centre, Bracknell.

[7] *The Development of an Application Level Communications Standard for Building Energy Management Systems*, BEMS Centre, Bracknell, 1989.

[8] Hobbs, D. (1990) MSc Thesis, A review of current appraisal methods used for energy efficiency in sectors of the United Kingdom economy. South Bank Polytechnic, London.

[9] ETSU (1987) *Central Monitoring and Control of Heating Schemes. A Demonstration at Hereford and Worcester Council*, ETSU Final Report ED/136/62, Harwell.

[10] ETSU (1987) *Automatic Remote Monitoring and Control of Coal-fired Boiler Plant in Schools. A Demonstration in Staffordshire County Council Schools*, ETSU Final Report ED/111/64, Harwell.

[11] ETSU (1986) *Monitoring of a Microprocessor-based Energy Management System. A Demonstration Project at Various Tenanted Office Buildings*, ETSU Final Report ED/105/127 1986, Harwell.

[12] ETSU (1984) The evaluation of an energy management system for the central control of a number of remote school heating installations in Hereford and Worcester, Interim ETSU Report I/47/84/62 (Harwell).

[13] Birtles, A. B. and John, R. W. (1984) Study of the performance of an energy management system, *Building Services Engineering Research and Technology* (London), 4.

[14] Levermore, G. J. (1989) *Staff Reaction to BEMSs*. BEMS Centre, Bracknell.

[15] John, R. W., Fargus, R. S. and Smith, G. P. (1989) *Building Management Systems: User Experiences*, BRE Information Paper IP 10/89, Building Research Establishment, Watford.

[16] John, R. W. and Smith, G. P. (1990) Building management systems – end-user experiences, CIBSE BMS Selection and Specification Conference, Dublin, April.

[17] Brown, J. A. C. (1977) *The Social Psychology of Industry*, Penguin, Harmondsworth.

[18] Watson, B. M. (1982) *Employee Participation in Energy-saving Programmes*, Energy Publications/Grafton Consultants, Cambridge.

[19] Levermore, G. J. (1985) Monitoring and targeting, Construction Industry Conference on Energy Experience, London, May.

[20] Wilkins, J. and Wills, S. (1990) What are smart sensors? *CIBSE Building Services Journal*, **12**, 12, December.

[21] Europe heads for the smart sensor, *Sensor Review*, **9**, 4, October 1989.

[22] Life saving through intelligence. *CIBSE Building Services Journal*, **11**, 5, May, 1989; based on paper by A. Bentley and R. McNeill, presented at CIBSE Technical Conference, Warwick, 1989.

[23] Communications standards for building and energy management systems. BEMS Centre Colloquium, October, 1990.

[24] Building energy management system in Liverpool tenanted offices, Case Study 20, February 1989, Energy Efficiency Office, Department of Energy; available from ETSU, Building 156, Harwell Laboratory, Didcot, Oxon OX11 ORA.

[25] Colantonio, E. S. (1989) *Microcomputers and Applications*, D.C. Heath, Lexington, Mass.

[26] Naylor, C. (1983) *Build Your Own Expert System*, Sigma Technical Press, Wilmslow.

[27] Hartnell, T. (1985) *Exploring Expert Systems on Your Microcomputer*, Interface Publications, London.

[28] Sell, P. S. (1985) *Expert Systems – a Practical Introduction*. Macmillan, London.

[29] Zimmermann, H. -J. (1984) *Fuzzy Set Theory – and its Applications*, Kluwer Nijhoff Amsterdam.

[30] Shaw, M. (1988) Applying expert systems to environmental management and control problems, Proceedings of the Intelligent Buildings Conference.

[31] Shaw, M. and Willis, S. (1991) Intelligent building services control and management systems, Proceedings of the CIBSE National Conference, April 1991, Canterbury.

[32] John, R. W. and Dexter, A. L. (1989) Intelligent controls for building services. Building Services Engineering Research and Technology, **10**, 4.

[33] *Centralised Energy Management of Schools*, Energy Efficiency Demonstration Scheme, Expanded Project Profile 35. Energy Efficiency Office, Department of Energy, August 1986; available from ETSU, Building 156, Harwell Laboratory, Didcot, Oxon OX11 ORA. August 1986.

# 2
# The outstation

We have already discussed the benefits and problems of BEMSs in Chapter 1, but in this chapter the nature and details of the BEMS will be examined. First, the **outstation** will be considered. This is the BEMS unit closest to the sensors and actuators and is often situated in the plant room. Other terms for the outstation are **field processing unit** (FPU) [1], **data gathering panel** (DGP), **distributed processing unit** (DPU) [1], **field interface device** (FID) and **substation** [2]. The term FPU implies limited local processing power, as opposed to the DPU which is more like a modern outstation, as referred to in this book.

## 2.1 Elements of an outstation

A typical BEMS, with its central station, which is often a personal computer (PC), together with a number of outstations, is shown in Figs 2.1 and 2.2. Here the BEMS outstation is defined as the unit with inputs and outputs that controls the plant; but it does not have the large keyboard and screen of a central station, although it may have a small display, similar to that on a calculator, and keypad, a small keyboard or set of pressure pads often with cursor arrows for limited access.

A representation of the function of a typical outstation is given in Fig. 3.16, p. 83. Inputs basically come in from sensors and switches. The outstation can then use this data either for a **control loop** or a **function**. The output from the control loop goes to the output section of the outstation to control the action of, for instance, a valve, whereas a function relates to time schedules, optimisers and **logic** expressions; and again, it sends signals to the outstation's output unit. (This outstation is only briefly described here, as the rest of this

**Fig. 2.1**   Central stations with outstations of different manufacture.

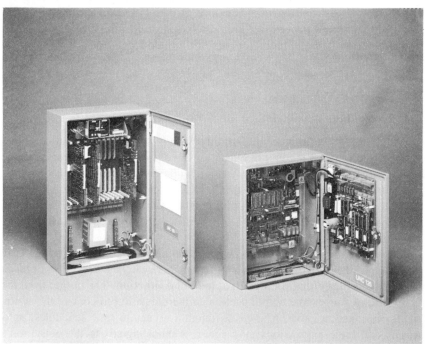

**Fig. 2.2**   As Fig. 2.1.

chapter is devoted to its components and operation functions are dealt with in detail in Chapter 5, and control loops in Chapter 6.)

## 2.2 The intelligent outstation

As we have found in the alternative terms for an outstation in Section 2.1, the DGP and, to a lesser extent, the FPU refer to older outstations that carried out the first stage of processing of the input and output signals for transmission back to the central station. In this book the outstations referred to are more powerful, having their own microprocessor and hence commonly referred to as 'intelligent'. Fig. 3.16 is a representation of an intelligent outstation.

Intelligent outstations range from a single, main circuit-board type (Fig. 2.3) to larger outstations with many printed circuit boards (PCBs) (or cards), plugged in to a **rack** or **backplane** (a metal chassis with electrical connections to the PCBs) (Fig. 2.4).

A third outstation is the **modular** type, which is similar to the rack-mounted PCB outstation except that here the electronics are housed in individual plastic or metal modules mounted next to one another on rails or a baseplate with suitable connections.

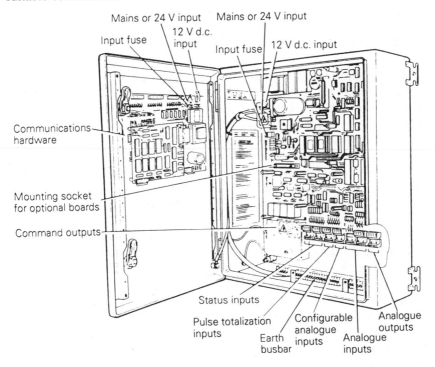

**Fig. 2.3** Single-board outstation.

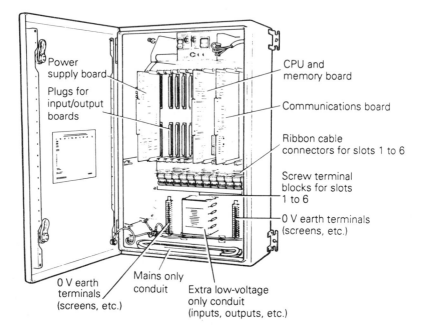

Power supply board

Plugs for input/output boards

CPU and memory board

Communications board

Ribbon cable connectors for slots 1 to 6

Screw terminal blocks for slots 1 to 6

0 V earth terminals (screens, etc.)

0 V earth terminals (screens, etc.)

Mains only conduit

Extra low-voltage only conduit (inputs, outputs, etc.)

**Fig. 2.4**  Multiple-board outstation.

In the multiple-board and modular outstations each PCB or module has a certain function, e.g. for inputs, outputs, communication and for the microprocessor. Thus, with these outstations, users have the advantage of being able to increase the number of PCBs and modules, for example, for adding more inputs and outputs to expand the outstation. Also, if there is a fault, an individual unit can be replaced rather than the whole outstation.

The single-board outstations are limited to the number of inputs and outputs provided; they cannot be expanded. Some of them, however, are very small and cheap, sometimes being dedicated to particular functions and equipment (e.g. boiler control).

The single-board versions are often contained in integral metal boxes, housed in electrical cabinets or control panels with the associated relays and connections, whereas the multiple-board versions are already contained within their own electrical cabinets. But whatever the type, all outstation electronics and circuitry must be protected from dust and damp in plant rooms, to prevent electrical breakdown and tracking of stray electrical currents across the PCBs. To establish how protective the casings and cabinets are there is an **ingress protection** (IP) system, where protection is designated by the letters 'IP' followed by two numerals [3]. The first numeral indicates the degree of protection from dust, 0 being non-protected, up to 6 being dust-tight; and the second numeral indicates protection from water penetration, 0 being non-protected, up to 8 indicating protection against submersion.

Also metal cabinets offer protection against electromagnetic interference and noise, which can impair the performance of microprocessor equipment operating with low voltage signals [4], [5]. This is particularly important when the outstation is located in a plant room where there are discharge lamps and motors for pumps and burners, which can generate significant electromagnetic radiation.

Some outstations have small keyboards or keypads, and small display panels of a few lines, for limited access to the outstation's data by staff in the plant room. Access to the outstation's data and programs can be restricted by use of a **password**, so that the heating temperature set point, for instance, cannot be increased by unauthorized persons; thus it is **password protected**. Differing security levels, or **operator access levels** (often signified by two-digit numbers attached to the password), can be set in the outstation for various passwords, so that low-level information such as the outside air temperature can be easily accessed, whereas only restricted, higher-level passwords allow one into the control parameters such as temperature set points. Numerical passwords, or **personal identification numbers** (PINs) are used on some BEMS.

### 2.2.1 Outstation structure

A simplified diagram of a single-board outstation, with its cover off revealing the basics of the printed circuit board, is shown in Fig. 2.5. The outstation is powered by an internal 24 V d.c. power supply which transforms and rectifies the 240 V a.c. supply. The outstation's microelectronics only operate on low-voltage d.c., and large a.c. voltages would damage them. The 24 V is primarily used for driving sensor circuitry and output controlling circuitry; the internal microprocessor circuitry uses typically up to 5 V.

In case of a mains power cut, or the mains having to be switched off for maintenance, then the outstation memory is powered by the battery back-up. Without this, most of the user's control programs resident in the outstation would be lost. Although the outstation could be set to 'fail safe' (i.e. leave the heating on, or switch off all plant for safety), it is extremely important that the battery back-up is reliable, of adequate life expectancy and of sufficient capacity to retain the outstation memory programs for sufficient time until mains power is restored.

In Fig. 2.5 the input from one temperature sensor is shown, although seven more sensors or input devices could be connected to this outstation. Similarly, seven more outputs could be employed than just the one shown (controlling the valve actuator). The temperature sensor cable is connected via terminals on the outstation to an input section, or **input unit** (a set of electronic chips and circuitry on the PCB, not identifiable as a single, discrete component).

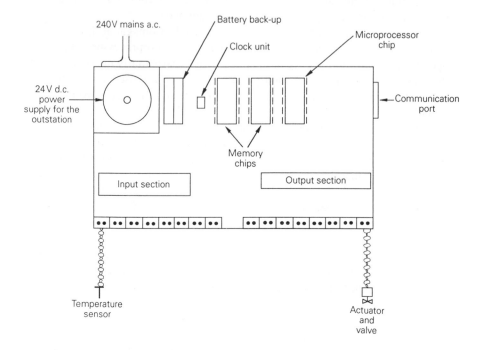

**Fig. 2.5**   Outstation structure.

The cable to the valve comes from terminals connected to the **output unit** of the outstation (again, this is a set of electronic chips and circuitry).

The **communications port** in Fig. 2.5 is the electrical access point for communications, a port being a connection point in an electronic circuit where a signal may be input or output. Inside the outstation would be an additional, small circuit board, not shown in Fig. 2.5, to interface either to a modem or a LAN (both explained in Chapter 3). This board is often referred to as a **communications node controller** (CNC). For communication purposes each outstation would have its individual identification number and name. If the outstation did not have a keypad and display, then there would be an additional communications port for connecting to a portable PC for local programming and re-configuration.

Basically the outstation is a microcomputer controlling the plant, except that it does not have a large keyboard as an input, or a monitor and a printer as outputs. It has merely sensors as inputs and actuators or relays as outputs, but just like a microcomputer, the outstation has a microprocessor chip and memory chips, as shown in Fig. 2.5.

## 2.3 The microprocessor

The microprocessor – or central processing unit (CPU), or even microprocessor unit (MPU) as it is sometimes referred to – is the principal component both of the microcomputer, used as the BEMS central station, and the outstation. It is a microelectronic chip produced by large-scale integrated (LSI) circuit manufacturing techniques on a small chip of silicon (about 5 mm$^2$), and it is the 'brains' of a microcomputer. Later microprocessors are VLSI chips and correspondingly more powerful. The actual microprocessor chip is often contained in a *dual-in-line* (DIL) package with between 16 and 64 pins, like legs holding up the package.

A simplified schematic diagram of the microprocessor, shown in Fig. 2.6, has several of the vital components of the complete microcomputer: the **control unit**, a small store or memory, consisting of **registers**, and the **arithmetic and logic unit** (ALU).

The arithmetic and logic unit is the operational unit. Here, as its name aptly suggests, calculations are performed, such as addition and multiplication, as

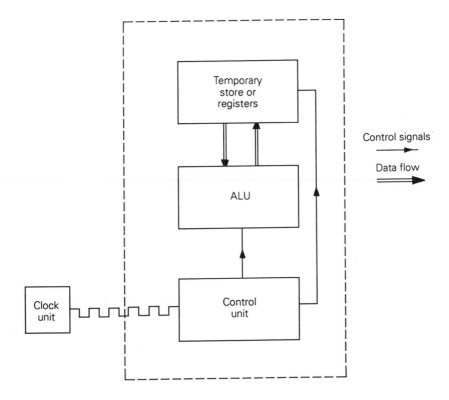

**Fig. 2.6**  The microprocessor or CPU.

well as logical decision-making processes of selecting, sorting and comparing of data (as described later).

Controlling operations of the microprocessor ALU and other associated chips, such as memory chips, is the control unit. This unit co-ordinates all the microcomputer's functions, and interprets the instructions in the program to perform the control functions necessary to run that program. For instance, it will enable the latest temperature reading from a sensor to be accessed, for the ALU to compare with the required temperature, when the program requires this.

The temporary store is a small memory, composed of a number of registers, which will hold both the temperatures and the immediately required program instructions for the ALU and control unit to work on.

Also shown in Fig. 2.6 is the **clock unit**, which sends out timing pulses from a quartz crystal. This enables the control unit to time and synchronize the operations of the microprocessor. Microprocessors operate at high speeds and the Intel 8080 microprocessor, a well-used LSI CPU chip, employs a 20 MHz crystal oscillator in its clock circuit. A frequency of 20 MHz means 20 million cycles or pulses a second! The clock unit speed is a main determinant of the length of the **processor cycle time** (or machine cycle time), which is the basic speed of executing an average program instruction of approx. 250 ns ($250 \times 10^{-9}$ s).

The outstation itself will also contain a clock unit, a chip separate from the microprocessor but driven by it (Fig. 2.5), which is a **real time clock** that keeps time of day and date and enables the outstation to control plant items on a time program, or schedule. This means that the outstation has its own clock for timing the switching of plant, to switch it off at night and during weekends and holidays.

How the microprocessor chip is connected to the memory unit and the input and output units is shown in Fig. 2.7, all units having their own microelectronic chips. Connection between the microprocessor and the other chips is by **buses**, 'bus' being short for busbar, a set of parallel wires. The **data bus**, for example, is for the transfer of data between chips, for transferring the sensor temperature from the input unit to the microprocessor temporary store – ready for the ALU to compare it to the required set point.

The **address bus** is for locating where in the memory or register the required data is, or where a program instruction is located; the address appears like a telephone number or postal address. Every piece of data or program instruction stored in the microprocessor outstation must have an address. There could be many sensors connected to the input unit of the outstation, and each will have its own address and storage area in the memory set aside for sensor readings.

Once the address of a piece of data or an instruction has been located by the microprocessor on the address bus, then the microprocessor control unit sends a signal on the **control bus** to that address for the data or instruction to

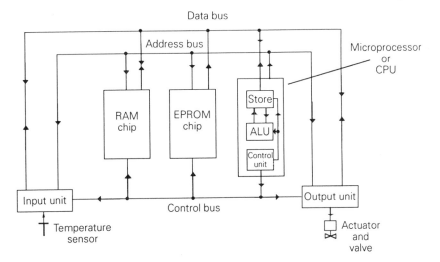

**Fig. 2.7** Bus architecture of an outstation.

be sent on the data bus to the address where it is required. For example, the control bus could carry a signal for a sensor temperature reading to be sent on the data bus to the microprocessor temporary store.

Those systems using three buses to connect the chips are referred to as being designed with a **three-bus architecture**; this is a common architecture for BEMS outstations, and microcomputers generally, although there are other architectures. In the single-board outstation considered here the buses are 'printed' conductors on the single PCB. In outstations using many printed circuit boards the buses are contained within the backplane, or rack, on to which a number of printed circuit boards can be slotted. In this way, an outstation can easily be expanded.

## 2.4 Memory

Much of the data from the sensors and the program instructions are stored in the memory chips. The microprocessor has only a small temporary store (which because of its size operates very fast), so for larger, and consequently slower operating storage, separate memory chips are used. Fig. 2.7 shows the memory chips connected to the bus structure. One chip is a **read only memory** (or ROM) and the other a **random access memory** (or RAM), but more accurately a read and write memory; Fig. 2.8 shows the principle of a memory chip, with its addresses and contents, similar to pigeon-holes. With the details of all the memory positions given filled in Figure 2.8 would comprise a **memory map**. For a typical 8-bit microprocessor (a bit is a *bi*nary digi*t*, a 1 or 0), the address bus is 16 bit which allows $2^{16} = 65\,536$ address locations to be handled.

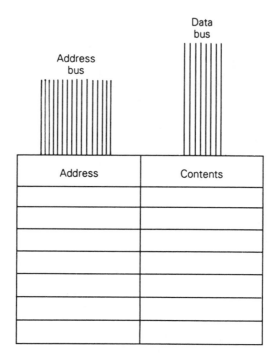

**Fig. 2.8**   Principle of a memory chip.

The ROM chip can send only data or instructions, it cannot receive and store them from other chips in the outstation. In other words, it can only be 'read from' – not 'written to'. The ROM chip therefore contains the manufacturer's program and data which the user cannot alter. The program and data are 'burnt' into the ROM during manufacture. As microprocessors (and computers generally) can deal only with binary signals, where 1s and 0s correspond to high and low voltages, often 5 V and 0.5 V respectively but dependent on the type of chip structure used (many are complementary metal oxide semiconductor, CMOS [4]), then the memories simply have to store 1s and 0s. The ROM, as shown in Fig. 2.9, is an array or matrix of 'switches' that are permanently set open or closed.

These switches are forms of **bipolar** or **field effect transistor** (FET) devices [4]. The absence of a device (here a diode) in Fig. 2.9 will result in a 0 being stored, and the presence of a diode in the storing of a 1. According to the signal on the address bus from the microprocessor, the **address decoder** [6] locates the appropriate row for reading, here only four are shown each with its 4-bit word of data. The decoder is like a set of switches for a particular line. When the switch for a particular line is closed, then the signals from that line appear on the data bus. Buffers (not shown in the diagram), controlled by the control

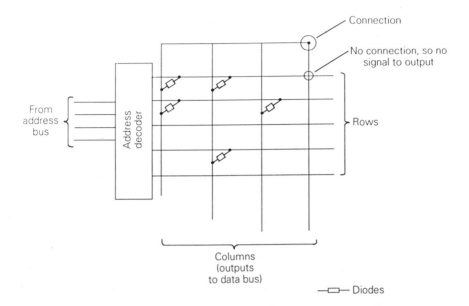

**Fig. 2.9** Section of a ROM.

bus, store the data before it is sent along the data bus. For instance, if the decoder selects the top line of the memory matrix in Fig. 2.9, then the output on the data bus, going from left to right, is 1100. If the memory stores individually accessed bits of data instead of **bytes** (a group of 8 bits which is treated as a unit), then it is necessary to have a decoder for the column of the memory matrix for addressing individual bit memory locations. The storage for a ROM is shown in Fig. 2.9, but for a RAM there are extra connections to the data bus and to buffers for writing data (see references [6] and [11] for further details of memory operation).

Standard control functions for the outstation, such as a time schedule, on/off control, optimiser loops and PID loops (these are all explained in later chapters), are written and stored by some manufacturers in ROM chips. The times for switching on plant, the set points and the control functions, and so on, required from the ROM 'library' that users can set and alter as required are stored in the RAM. Selection of the control functions required in the outstation, the control strategy, is more complex than simply the setting of set points and times, and is often referred to as **configuring** the outstation. Many operators do not get involved with configuration, buying pre-configured outstations. Also some manufacturers do not allow easy access to the configuration. Configuration is dealt with in more detail in Section 2.10.

The control functions, or programs, written in ROM chips are considered as **firmware**, whereas the user's data of set points and times are part of the user 'software' because they can be easily altered, or are soft. Most computer programs that one is familiar with on personal computers are considered to be software, often referred to as **application software**.

The outstation itself and its chips (and generally what can be touched of a computer system) is called **hardware**. Similarly, an outstation's input channels (for sensors, etc.) and output channels (for relays, valves, etc.) are the **hard points**, **real points** or often just the 'points'. The number of them is a measure of the outstation's size. Correspondingly, there are **soft points** (or **pseudo-points**, or **nodes**), relating to calculations and set points for controls.

Although ROMs once manufactured are unalterable, a number of manufacturers actually use Erasable and reProgrammable ROMs, or EPROMs, so that alterations such as improvements in later outstation models can be made using the same memory chips. The EPROMs are erased with low-intensity ultraviolet light and can be programmed with special equipment.

Some of the smaller and cheaper outstations are totally pre-programmed, with the user being able only to put in a rather restricted 'program' of set points and times, etc. in a small RAM memory. The larger outstations have greater memories and tend to have a greater flexibility for setting up (configuring) control strategies by selecting from a menu of various control functions from the EPROM (optimum start, compensation, PID, etc.). The user's particular configuration for the items of plant, with the relevant times and temperature settings, will be stored in RAM; the memory that can be written to by the user, so that times and temperatures can easily be changed when required.

Whereas the elements of the ROM matrix were simple transistor elements, or the absence of them for 0s, in a RAM the matrix is made up of changeable switching elements that need a constant d.c. supply of electricity to maintain their state, the memory contents are 'volatile'. In other words, the program and data stored in a RAM chip are wiped out and lost if mains power to the outstation is cut. To avoid this catastrophe batteries are installed in outstations (Fig. 2.5), to act as a back-up in case the mains supply fails. However, these batteries can be of variable quality and do not last indefinitely, so they need to be regularly checked. Also it is wise to heed the computer maxim always to keep a back-up copy of a program. The outstation configuration (the control strategy program) can be copied on to the larger memory of the central station, and the outstation reprogrammed from the central station copy in the event of loss at the outstation.

Some outstations have **software clocks**, instead of real time clocks, in software rather than dedicated hardware circuits or chips, and these may be stopped if there is no battery back-up when there is a power cut.

It can be appreciated how a RAM chip's memory is volatile as one type, the **dynamic** RAM has a storage element that is based on a charged capacitor. This needs regularly or dynamically to be recharged. A **static** RAM uses 'flip-flop' memory elements that stay in an on or off state as long as there is power to the chip. (References [6] and [11] give further details on the flip-flop and the electronics in a typical microprocessor.)

As we have already mentioned, the central station is often a personal computer and so it is very similar to an outstation except for screen, keyboard and printer. But another significant difference is that the central station also has a considerably larger memory not only in terms of RAM and ROM chips, but in disk storage as well, which is much larger.

As we have also stated, each binary signal, a 1 or a 0, or ON and OFF, is termed a *b*inary dig*it*, or **bit**, and a **byte** is a group of 8 bits which is treated as a unit and stored at a storage location. Many outstations and older PC central stations are built around 8-bit microprocessor chips (common ones being: the Motorola 6800, later improved to 6809; the Intel 8080, later upgraded to 8085; the Rockwell 6500 series; and the Zilog Z80), which work with data and program instructions in 8-bit, or byte, lengths; more commonly, there are 16-bit microprocessor chips (e.g. the Motorola 68 000, the Intel 8086 and 8088, the Zilog Z-8000 and the Texas Instruments 9900), 32-bit and 64-bit chips being used in PCs. The outstations are following, and 16-bit outstations are now also common. A machine that can deal with more bits in a unit, or has a longer **word length**, is a more powerful machine and has more capabilities.

RAM and ROM chips typically can store 1 to 8 kilobytes (Kbytes) each (kilo or simply K here means $2^{10}$, or 1024). To keep down costs most outstations do not have extensive memories, although they vary considerably between manufacturers. Consequently, there is a limit to the data that an outstation can store, just as there is a limit to the number of inputs and outputs and programming that it can handle.

*Example*
Consider an outstation with 8 sensors whose temperatures are logged and stored every 15 min. How much data can be stored in 1 Kbyte of RAM?

*Solution*
If one temperature reading takes up 1 byte of memory, then 32 bytes of data are used every hour, and

$$32 \times 24 = 768 \text{ bytes}$$

are used every day. So 1 Kbyte could hold just over one day's data. If the **log** (the logged data) held hourly readings, then one day's data would be 192 bytes. However, if a control was being set up and tuned, then its sensor could well be monitoring every 15 s, 1 Kbyte would then store:

$$(1024 \times 15)/3600 = 4.267 \text{ h}$$

of temperature readings for just one sensor. Once the memory became full, unless the data were downloaded to the central station's larger memory, then the initial readings would be overwritten by the later readings. Care must therefore be exercised over data stored in an outstation.

## 2.5   Operation of an outstation

An immersion sensor reading the temperature of water in a hot-water cylinder being heated by primary hot water is shown in Fig. 2.10. The primary hot water is controlled by a valve.

A simplified version of how the outstation operates is that the sensor, its own transmitter circuitry powered by the 24 V supply from the outstation, continuously sends back an electrical signal to the input unit of the outstation. The input unit samples this signal and converts it to suitable binary voltage signals for the CPU to work on. Basically the CPU has two operations: **fetching** and **executing**. Executing the relevant program instruction, via its **instruction decoder**, the CPU sends a signal to the input unit to fetch the appropriate converted temperature reading. In fact the input unit may have signalled to the CPU, or interrupted it to inform it, that the unit has data ready for processing. Receiving the signal from the input unit that it has data ready, the CPU locates the address in the small input unit memory, or **buffer**, where the incoming signal is temporarily stored and sends a control signal on the control bus to fetch the binary temperature, on the data bus, to temporary storage in the CPU memory. The next control program step is read by the CPU from the RAM. A program counter in the CPU locates the relevant program

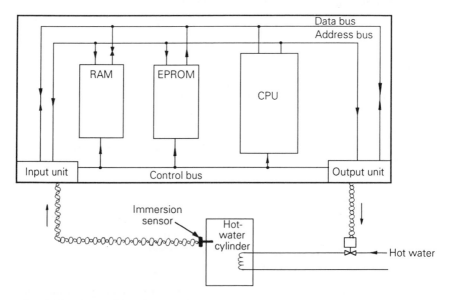

**Fig. 2.10**   Operation of outstation.

step and loads it into the CPU's **instruction register**. By such steps the CPU works through a small control element program from the EPROM, to compare this temperature with a temperature set point in the RAM, previously set by the user. Again, this is all done by fetch and execute operations, each only taking approximately 250 ns to perform.

If the CPU finds that the sensor temperature is now above the set point, then the EPROM program will instruct the CPU to send a binary signal to the correct address of the output unit to switch off the valve. The output unit will have to convert the binary signal to a suitable signal to operate the valve. This is an example of the outstation being used for simple on/off control.

In the middle of all this activity, the CPU may well have executed a program instruction to store the sensor temperature in the RAM at a particular address to form part of a temperature log. Further details on microprocessor operations for control can be found in references [7], [8], [9] and [11].

This whole procedure will take less than 1 s for the microelectronics to perform. In fact the CPU will probably be able to service each input and output point in a matter of milliseconds, although this depends on the number of inputs and outputs the outstation has and the outstation program. The outstation program has a **sequence table**, which is the order in which inputs, outputs and soft points, or control instructions, are serviced by the CPU. For instance, in the example in Fig. 2.10, the sequence table would be:

| Sequence order | Item |
|---|---|
| 1 | immersion temperature sensor |
| 2 | control program |
| 3 | control valve output |

The other inputs and outputs would then be serviced after these. An item can be serviced more quickly by entering it in the sequence table more than once.

The example of the outstation in Fig. 2.5 can accommodate a maximum of 150 sequence steps in its table, and the average **sequence cycle time**, the time taken to execute all the steps, is up to 5 s. This effectively is the **program cycle time**, and it means that each item is served by the CPU in (i.e. each sequence step is):

$$\frac{5}{150}$$

$$\approx 33 \text{ ms}$$

Unlike the example outstation, above, some outstations may have all their program functions (e.g. control, alarm handling, reporting, logging, etc.) in one program sequentially processed. This would produce a program cycle time nearing 20 s [10]. To reduce time the program functions are split up into smaller programs that can be run independently, effectively in parallel at the same time. This is achieved using a **multi-tasking operating system** where the CPU divides its time between the programs or tasks. As the CPU is so fast, each program is effectively as quick as its own program cycle time will allow.

In a multiple-board outstation each card would be served, in turn, by the CPU card. As these are often bigger outstations than single-board versions, then the sequence cycle time will be slightly longer.

The outstation is continuously monitoring the hot-water cylinder temperature, and continuously executing the instructions in the control program. This is an example of **real time** or **on-line computing**, where the microprocessor is interacting and responding to events as they happen. However, when a program and data are loaded into a PC and run, then this is an example of **batch processing**. Most PC central stations' software is a combination of both types, with an **interrupt service routine** (ISR), to interrupt the main PC operating program perhaps to raise an alarm. After the interrupt, the PC returns to its operating program.

Although the outstation is performing real time computing, not every temperature signal from the sensor would be stored for long – only those required for logs at definite times (e.g. every 15 min or as defined by the user) would be stored in the RAM memory.

$\mu P$ = microprocessor

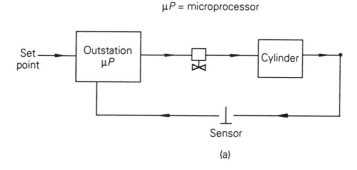

(a)

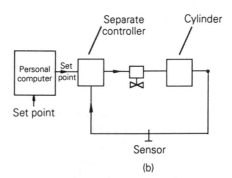

(b)

**Fig. 2.11** Direct digital (a) and supervisory (b) control.

## 2.6 Direct digital control

The signal flow diagram for the outstation control is shown in Fig. 2.11(a). The microprocessor is in complete control, and since it operates with *digital*, or binary, signals, this is termed **direct digital control** (DDC).

However, some manufacturers' standard, stand-alone controls, such as optimisers and compensators, can be interfaced (linked) to personal computers (Fig. 2.11(b)). This is not strictly DDC, but **supervisory control** where the PC can adjust the set point and, in some cases, monitor a sensor reading. But the control cannot be reconfigured or interrogated like an outstation, so it has a rather limited role.

But there is a common feature in the above examples, in that the sensor feeds back the temperature to the controller, an example of **feedback control**, the sensor being in the feedback loop and hence the term 'control loop', or simply 'loop', to describe control programs in outstations.

In the sequence table of the outstation the control loops, with their inputs and outputs, should be listed sequentially, so that the input signal produces an output signal as soon as possible to keep the signals in phase. The time between the input signal being processed and the output signal is the **control loop time**, or 'loop time'. As will be seen in a later chapter, this time should be as short as possible for good control.

## 2.7 Input unit

The input unit, or section, takes signals from sensors, relays, meters, etc. and conditions them such that the microprocessor sees them as digital signals of the correct voltage. For instance, the temperature sensor in Fig. 2.10 is continuously sending back an electrical signal (either a small voltage or current) to the input section of the outstation. This is an **analogue** or continuous signal which needs to be converted into bits and bytes to form a **digital signal** for the CPU to be able to process. The input section therefore contains an analogue to digital (A/D) converter for this purpose.

The outstation can also receive on and off signals from **volt-free contacts**, which are switches, or spare contacts on the relays or contactors of equipment with no voltage – apart from the small voltage signal from the outstation to determine whether the relay is open or closed. The volt-free contacts are opened and closed by coils exerting a magnetic influence on them, the coils being in the equipments' circuit and so being energized when the equipment is switched on. Such contacts are useful for monitoring on/off status of plant or events and counting the units consumed on utility energy meters. As these signals are already in digital form, they do not need to be converted.

With volt-free contacts, the outstation is isolated and protected from any large voltages that are being switched. Other methods of isolation are often used to protect outstations, both at the inputs and the outputs, where large voltage equipment is being monitored and controlled. One method is **opto-isolation**, where a current through a light-emitting diode converts the signal to light to be picked up by a closely coupled **phototransistor** or **photo-diode**.

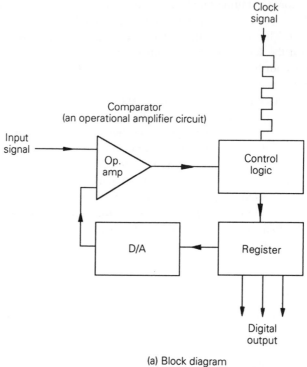

(a) Block diagram

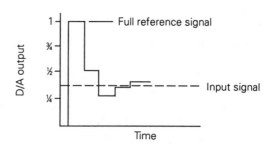

(b) Conversion process

**Fig. 2.12** A successive approximation A/D.

## 2.7.1 Operational amplifier

A major electronics component of outstations themselves and also of A/Ds is the operational amplifier, or 'op amp'. Basically there are two types of amplifier: a **small-signal amplifier** (or voltage amplifier) for amplifying small voltages or currents, which is useful for small sensor signals; and a **power amplifier**, with power transistors and **thyristors** for controlling equipment on the output side of an outstation, such as motors and valve actuators [12], [13]. The op amp is a typical small-scale amplifier which has a high-voltage *gain* (ratio of input to output voltage), often much greater than 1,000. The symbol for an op amp is the triangle, as shown in Fig. 2.12(a); but a commonly used op amp, the 741, is an integrated circuit in an 8-pin DIL package, of which only seven of the pins are required and only three-pin connections are shown in the figure. (The 741 is described in greater detail in references [4] and [14].)

The word 'operational' in an operational amplifier arises from its use to perform mathematical operations such as addition, subtraction, multiplication and division. Hence the operational amplifier, which uses only analogue signals, is the building-block of an analogue computer for solving mathematical equations. In fact this type of computer was the predecessor of the digital computer; it is also a main component of non-digital controls, which are often referred to as 'analogue controls' (the controls that preceded the digital BEMS). As op amps can multiply, integrate and differentiate, it is hardly surprising that a standard control is a proportional plus integral plus differential (*PID*) controller.

Although an operational amplifier performs its operations with a high degree of accuracy and reliability, the output voltage for a given input voltage will change, or 'drift', both with temperature and age. This is one disadvantage of analogue controls – they need recalibrating to offset the drift over time.

## 2.7.2 A/D converters

There are a number of different ways that an analogue signal may be 'digitized' or sliced into a digital signal, but the two commonest A/D converters in use in BEMS will briefly be considered, the **successive approximation** and the **integrating**.

### 2.7.2.1 Successive approximation A/D

The successive approximation A/D has the block diagram of its circuit shown in Fig. 2.12(a), where the input signal is fed into a comparator (an operational amplifier circuit), which compares it to successive half-values of a reference signal, as shown in Fig. 2.12(b). The digital to analogue converter, (D/A) converts the digital signal in the register memory to an analogue value for the

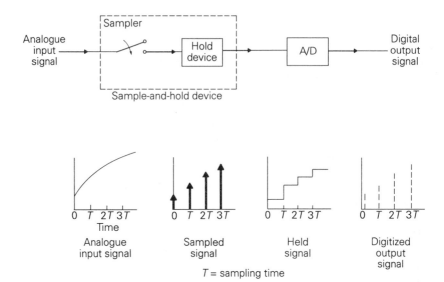

**Fig. 2.13**   Converting an analogue to a digital signal.

comparison process in the comparator. When the two signals are as close together as possible, then the conversion process is complete.

While the A/D is successively approximating to the input signal, any change in the input signal would upset the process. So a **sample-and-hold amplifier** can be used to hold the signal constant until the conversion process is complete. For slowly changing signals this is not necessary. In Fig. 2.13 the input signal is shown as it is processed through the sample-and-hold device and the A/D. Typical conversion times for these A/D converters are around 20 μs.

That the digital signal does not exactly equal the analogue signal is shown in Fig. 2.12(b) and 2.13, although it is fairly close. The resolution of the A/D converter is limited by the word length of the converter.

*Example*
A 0 V to 10 V signal comes in from a water temperature sensor, the lower voltage representing 0°C, the upper 120°C. What is the resolution of an A/D with an 8-bit word length?

*Solution*
Resolution may be defined as the change in the input signal for the digital output to change by the least significant bit (the last bit on the right of a binary number). An 8-bit word can be used to represent in binary the numbers from 0 to 255 ($2^8$ numbers including 0), so the resolution is:

$$10 \text{ V}/2^8 = 39 \text{ mV}$$

or:                                    $120°C/2^8 = 0.469°C$

The resolution of the central station monitor will give graphs a stepped appearance due to the number of lines scanned on the screen. This should not be confused with the A/D resolution.

### 2.7.2.2 Integrating A/D

The second A/D is the **integrating** type. Here the input signal, in the form of a voltage, is compared to the voltage across a capacitor being charged from a constant current source. A high-speed digital counter, controlled by the clock circuit, counts the time until the two voltages are equal. From this, the input signal can be determined in digital form. This is not a precise converter, but is suitable for joystick controllers on PCs used for games.

However, the integrating converter can be made more accurate by altering it to monitor the discharge of the capacitor against a reference negative voltage, with a digital counter digitizing the input signal. A block diagram of this type of A/D which is called a dual slope or dual-ramp converter is shown in Fig. 2.14. Its operation with the capacitor of the integrator charging up for a fixed time and then discharging at a fixed rate against a negative reference voltage, hence the fixed slope, is shown in Fig. 2.15. Once the capacitor has been discharged, the counter stops and the time it has been counting pulses, and therefore the number of pulses, is proportional to the input signal.

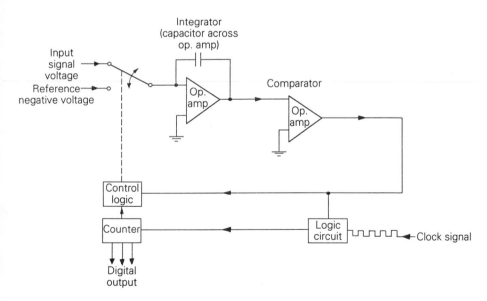

**Fig. 2.14**   Dual slope integration A/D converter.

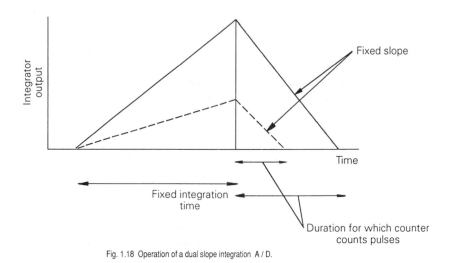

Fig. 1.18 Operation of a dual slope integration A / D.

**Fig. 2.15**   Operation of a dual-slope integration A/D.

Although slow in operation (of the order of a few milliseconds, depending on the input signal), this converter is accurate, but more important, it can integrate a varying input signal (it does not require a sample-and-hold circuit) producing an average value of the signal. If the integration is over 20 ms, the period of the 50 Hz mains supply, then any mains interference on the input signal is averaged to 0. As many BEMS sensor signals do not vary fast (as the temperatures of rooms and water, etc. do not vary much in 20 ms), then the dual-slope A/D is used in many outstations.

To save having an A/D for each analogue input, a **multiplexer** can switch the sensors in turn to the A/D. The multiplexer (MUX) is a circuit that reads or passes on the information from any selected input channel, and Fig. 2.16, shows the principle of it. The early MUXs, as were used on the earliest developments of BEMS, were composed of electromechanical relays, but the ones used in CPU-based outstations are transistor-based (metal oxide semiconductor field effect transistors or MOSFETs, to be precise). The channel is selected by the CPU and the relevant address sent to the MUX on the address bus (see reference [7] for further details). Once the analogue input signal has been converted to a digital signal, it can be stored in a register until the CPU is ready to process it. The CPU will not stay idle while the A/D converter is converting, it can do many operations in this time. Once the conversion is complete, the converter could either send an **interrupt signal** to the CPU, or

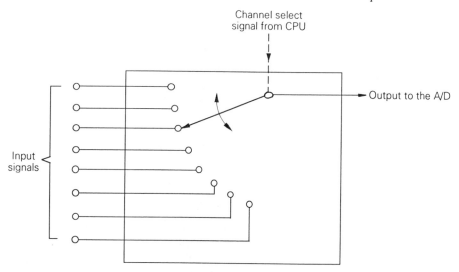

**Fig. 2.16**   The principle of a multiplexer (MUX).

the CPU can regularly 'poll' the multiplexer and other devices, to find any
data that is waiting for it to process.

*Example*
If an outstation has 8 analogue input channels for sensors and it uses one
dual-slope integrating A/D converter with a multiplexer, how often can each
channel be sampled?

*Solution*
The dual slope integrating A/D will probably integrate over 20 ms to avoid 50
Hz mains noise, and it is reasonable to add on another 20 ms for interrupt
signals or polling to take place before the CPU deals with it. So each channel
could be sampled every

$$8 \times 40\,\text{ms} = 320\,\text{ms} \text{ or approx. } \tfrac{1}{3}\,\text{s}$$

However, the outstation also has to run the control program to produce a
control signal as a result of the converted input signal. This program, and its
sequence table, have to be processed before the channel sample can be taken
again and a typical sequence cycle time, already quoted in this chapter, was 5 s.
This does not mean that the time-loop time is also 5 s as typically there are
up to 150 sequence steps for a sequence table, and if a loop has five sequence
steps, then the loop time would be nearer

$$\frac{5}{150} \times 5$$
$$= 0.17\,\text{s} \quad \text{or} \quad 170\,\text{ms}$$

## 2.8  Sampling

From the above example it can be seen that the sampling of the input channels, based on the A/D conversion and signalling time alone, could be as fast as one-third of a second. Is this too fast or too slow for the average building services plant to be adequately controlled? To answer this it is necessary, first, to refer to **Shannon's sampling theorem**. This states that, provided a signal contains no frequency component higher than $f_{max}$, then the signal can be represented by, or reconstituted from, a set of sample values where the sampling frequency is at least twice $f_{max}$. In practice, sampling frequencies ten times the theoretical limit are often used [8].

*Example*
A hot-water heating system mixing valve takes 30 s to go from fully mixing to fully recirculating. Is a sampling period between samples of 5 s adequate for a temperature sensor just downstream of the valve? Is the A/D conversion time satisfactory if the A/D is a dual-slope integrating type?

*Solution*
A mixing valve is a three-port valve often used in compensator control of heating systems to mix boiler water with recirculated water returning from the radiators. (More details on compensator control will be found in a later chapter.) The time from fully mixing to fully recirculating is half a cycle, if the valve were continuously opening and closing, at its greatest frequency. So 30 s from fully open to fully closed is a period of 60 s and a frequency of:

$$1/60$$

$$\approx 0.017\,\text{Hz}$$

Assuming that the temperature of the water varies at the same frequency as the valve, then the sampling frequency for the sensor should be at least twice this, and in practice ten times, giving a frequency of:

$$1/6 \approx 0.17\,\text{Hz}$$

which corresponds to a period of 6 s. So a sampling period between samples of 5 s is adequate.

   As regards the time taken by the dual-slope, integrating-type A/D converter, taken as 20 ms in the previous example, the valve and temperature will not vary significantly during this short time.

In practice, to see how the valve or the rest of the plant is operating, selected sampled values from the input sensors can be stored or logged for later evaluation, most likely at the central station. A graph may be constructed by the central station software from this logged data. The outstation will have limited memory, and the sampling rate for this logged data will have to be carefully selected. Too much data and when the memory becomes full the later data will simply be allocated to memory space occupied by older data; the older data will be overwritten and lost. However, the data will not be lost if it is regularly sent, or downloaded, to the central station for storage, where the storage is much larger. The frequency of downloading depends on the logging frequency.

There are basically two régimes for logging data: one of short term for tuning control loops at the commissioning stage to see whether the control loop settings provide stability (see later); and the other for longer-term monitoring. With both régimes, it is possible to lose information by using too low a sampling rate and a high frequency variation 'aliased' or interpreted as a low-frequency variation, as is shown in Fig. 2.17.

*Example*
An outstation has a memory set aside for each log that it has, capable of holding 96 sampled values from inputs. What should the sampling rate be for: (a) tuning a loop, and (b) long-term monitoring of a temperature?

*Solution*
For tuning a loop (by which we mean setting a loop, for optimum control, discussed in Chapter 6, section 6.7), which can control a valve which can open in 30 s a sampling time of 15 s should be adequate from Shannon's theorem. However, this means that the memory can hold data for a period of:

$$96 \times 5 \text{ s} = 8 \text{ min}$$

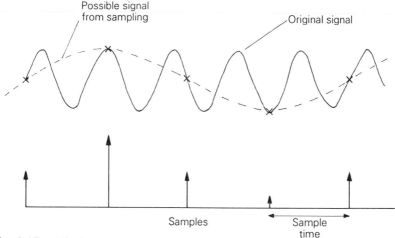

**Fig. 2.17** Aliasing.

For longer-term monitoring daily downloading to the central station should present few problems, so 96 samples spread over a day would give a sampling rate of every:

$$24 \times 60/96 = 15 \text{ min}$$

## 2.9   Output section

Having sensed the temperature of the cylinder via the sensor and the input section, and having put the digitized value through the BEMS control program, then the outstation could well have to send out a signal to alter a valve or switch something. This could be done by simply sending out a pulse. To move a valve by a certain amount a number of pulses will need to be sent to move the valve for a certain time. This is valve movement on an **incremental** basis. This is the most popular method of moving valves.

However, a valve may require an analogue signal to move it to a definite position, in which case a digital to analogue (D/A) converter is required to give a movement on a **whole-value** basis. A schematic diagram is shown in Fig. 2.18 of an 8-bit D/A converter, where the digital signal is sent through a ladder of incremented resistors, with the resultant analogue signal being the output of the summing operational amplifier. This is the reverse of the successive approximation A/D.

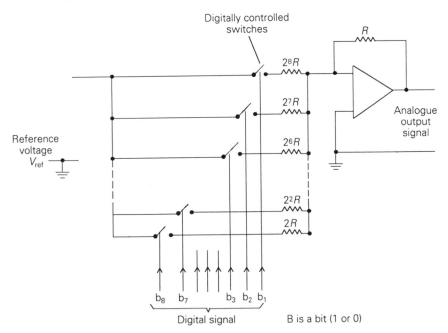

**Fig. 2.18**   A D/A converter.

*Example*
If an 8-bit D/A has a digital signal 01000100, what is the analogue output signal?

*Solution*
Referring to Fig. 2.18, the output signal is:

$$V_{\text{ref}} \{b_8 \, R/2R + b_7 \, R/2^2 R + \ldots + b_1 \, R/2^8 R\}$$

The *R*s cancel out giving:

$$V_{\text{ref}} \{b_8/2 + b_7/2^2 + \ldots + b_1/2^8\}$$

In the given signal only $b_7$ and $b_3$ are 1 with the other bits being 0. So the analogue output signal is:

$$V_{\text{ref}} \{1/2^2 + 1/2^6\} = V_{\text{ref}} \{1/4 + 1/64\}$$
$$= V_{\text{ref}} \{0.266\}$$

The full-scale analogue output would result from the digital signal 11111111, and it would be:

$$V_{\text{ref}} \{1/2 + 1/4 + 1/8 + 1/16 + \ldots + 1/256\}$$

which is:

$$V_{\text{ref}} \{[128 + 64 + 32 + 16 + 8 + 4 + 2 + 1]/256\}$$

or more simply

$$= V_{\text{ref}} \times (\text{value of byte} /256)$$
$$= V_{\text{ref}} \{255/256\}$$

which is almost the full reference voltage. This voltage is small and there is little power in the circuitry to drive equipment, so the signal must be amplified to drive or switch longer voltage circuits to operate equipment, such as values and pumps. Large voltages, a.c. and d.c., can be controlled with relays and contractors. Opto-isolation is often included in the output unit to protect the low voltage microprocessor signal circuitry from any larger voltages emanating from the more powerful driving circuits.

## 2.10 Configuration

The outstation control strategy (the relationship between the inputs and the outputs of the outstation, or the program the outstation follows to enable it to control the plant) is set up, or **configured**, from a library of control elements, or **modules**, in the EPROM. This means that the library of modules is part of the firmware. There are no standard symbols for these modules, manufacturers

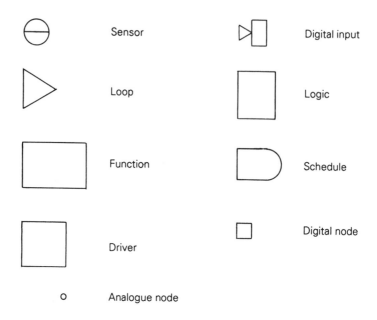

**Fig. 2.19**  Configuration module symbols.

using their own different symbols. The symbols used in this book are shown in Fig. 2.19 (they are used by at least one UK manufacturer). These elements are described further in later chapters with relevant control configurations; here only brief details are given.

The **loop module** is the basic control element providing an output signal after comparing the input signal, from a sensor, with the required set point. Connection to the outstation output is via a **driver module**. Although the loop symbol is a triangle, like the op amp, it should not in fact be confused with the op amp. In the following chapters the op amp is not referred to, so the triangle will relate only to a loop.

The **function module** performs mathematical functions on analogue values. Such functions are averaging, taking the maximum or minimum from a number of inputs, multiplying, adding, dividing, comparing, etc.

For digital values, there are **logic modules** such as the logical AND, NAND, OR, NOR, etc. (explained later in Chapter 5, section 5.8), which can be used for conditional control, for instance, to switch on the heating to a low level for frost protection if the outside temperature goes below zero. The **comparator** function module is often used with these logic modules to apply logic to analogue values.

The **schedule module** selects its output depending on the time of day and is effectively a time switch. It is often associated with the **optimiser** module which determines the latest time to switch on the heating to get up to temperature by the occupancy time (this is examined in Chapter 9).

Sensors and digital inputs are required on **strategy diagrams**, so there are symbols for them as shown in Fig. 2.19. Sequence table numbers are placed above each symbol to complete a strategy diagram.

Comparison with Fig. 2.2, a model of an outstation, shows the loop and the functions in general. The number of each type of module an outstation can use depends on the size of the outstation. For the outstation in Fig. 2.5 with 8 inputs, it can use up to 16 loop modules and 64 function modules, as well as many other modules.

The strategy required by the user is configured by linking up the required modules to storage areas, with specific addresses, in the RAM. This process is referred to as **soft-wiring**. These addressed storage areas, or **analogue nodes**, store the output from a module where it can be read by another module linked to that node. For instance, a temperature sensor connected to a loop and, in turn, connected to a driver is shown in Fig. 2.20.

The analogue nodes are shown as a matrix, with certain rows reserved for certain modules. In Fig. 2.20 the matrix is shown in reduced size (the real matrix having 255 nodes), the top row is for sensors and the second row for loop outputs. The driver outputs (in this case, to open or close a valve) go to **digital nodes**, the small square symbol, which are storage bits in the RAM. Other digital nodes are also stored in a digital matrix similar to the analogue matrix. A digital node is identified as, for instance, byte 7 or bit 0, or just 7,0. Each byte has 8 bits, numbered from 0 to 7.

An outstation is configured from the central station, by going into the configuring part of the software. Here the modules are selected from a **software menu**, or library, and numbered for identification and nodes assigned to the modules. The process is detailed and a number of manufacturers prevent users from doing this configuration, rather configuring the outstations to the client's specification. Others have standard configurations or **macros** which

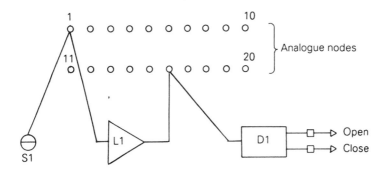

**Fig. 2.20** Strategy configuration.

can be loaded into the outstation, rather than supplying detailed configuration steps. Whatever the manufacturer's procedures, the more the user understands the control strategy, the less there is the likelihood of inappropriate or wrong control strategies being applied. Training courses are provided by most manufacturers to give the necessary understanding.

**References**

[1]   Eyke, M. (1988) *Building Automation Systems – a Practical Guide to Selection and Implementation*, BSP Professional Books, Oxford.
[2]   Scheepers, H. P. (1991) *Supporting Technology for Building Management Systems*, Honeywell Europe, Offenbach, Germany.
[3]   CIBSE (1986) CIBSE Guide, Volume B, Section B10, Electrical power, Chartered Institution of Building Services Engineers, London.
[4]   Diefenderfer, A. J. (1979) *Principles of Electronic Instrumentation*, Holt-Saunders International, Philadelphia, Pa.
[5]   Bentley, J. P. (1988) *Principles of Measurement Systems*, Longman Scientific and Technical, London.
[6]   Morris, N. M. (1983) *Microprocessor and Microcomputer Technology*, Macmillan, London.
[7]   Stoecker, W. F. and Stoecker, P. A. (1989) *Microcomputer Control of Thermal and Mechanical Systems*, Van Nostrand Reinhold, New York.
[8]   Bibbero, R.J. (1977) *Microprocessors in Instruments and Control*, Wiley, New York.
[9]   Houpis, C. H. and Lamont, G. B. (1985) *Digital Control Systems: Theory, Hardware, Software*, McGraw-Hill, New York.
[10]  Scheepers, H. P. (1991) *Inside Building Management Systems*, Honeywell Europe, Offenbach, Germany.
[11]  Money, S. A. (1987) *Practical Microprocessor Interfacing*, Collins, London.
[12]  Morris, N. M. (1983) *Control Engineering*, 3rd edn, McGraw-Hill, London.
[13]  Chesmond, C. J. (1986) *Control System Technology*, Edward Arnold, London.
[14]  Sinclair, I. R. (1988) *Practical Electronics Handbook*, Heinemann/Newnes, Oxford.

# 3
# The BEMS central station

The central station (also sometimes referred to as the supervisor, or slightly confusingly the central processing unit (CPU) is the heart of the BEMS, and the main communication channel for the operator. Here is contained the user software and the main storage of data relating to the plant and buildings controlled. In older BEMS, originating around the late 1970s and early 1980s, the central station was a minicomputer **floor model**, with the electronics chassis robustly encased, standing upright on the floor and integral with the operator's desk, similar to the current **workstations** or **supermicros** but much less powerful. With the advances in chip technology, the central station in most BEMS is now a microcomputer or personal computer (PC).

## 3.1  Central station basics

The PC was made possible by the development of VSLI chips and the first microcomputer (the APPLE microcomputer) was made in 1977 by Wozniak and Jobs.

The central station PC, being microprocessor-based, is very similar to the outstation, except that like any other PC the central station has a keyboard, a screen or monitor, with a much larger **primary memory** of RAM chips, and a large secondary or .**backing memory**, on hard disk and floppy disks (explained later).

The 'QWERTY' keyboard (the top line of letters on a standard keyboard) is similar to a typewriter keyboard, with additionally **function keys**, to perform special operations or routines, cursor movement keys and a numeric pad of keys.

Compared to the outstation, the PC has a much larger primary memory; 256 Kbytes is typical of the older BEMSs, but BEMSs with 32-bit machines typically have 1–4 Mbytes and 64-bit machines are on the way. Central station PCs additionally have large backing memories of 20–200 Mbytes for operator software and data storage.

The primary memory is composed of the ROM and RAM chips and the backing or secondary memory is non-volatile magnetic disks containing the central station's large amount of software. As with the outstation, the central station power is often characterized by its CPU or microprocessor chip, its speed and memory size that the CPU can connect to, as well as the CPU memory, or register size, and the data bus size. These characteristics are shown for a few PCs in Table 3.1.

**Table 3.1**   The characteristics of some PCs

| Chip | Speed (MHz) | Max. memory (bytes) | Data bus size (bits) | Register size (bits) | Example |
|------|-------------|---------------------|----------------------|----------------------|---------|
| MOS Technology 6502 | 1 | 64 K | 8 | 8 | Apple IIe |
| Intel 8088 | 10 | 1 M | 8 | 16 | IBM PC |
| Intel 80286 | 20 | 16 M | 16 | 16 | IBM PS/2 50 |
| Intel 80386 | 25 | 4 G | 32 | 32 | IBM PS/2 80 |
| Intel 80386SX | 20 | 16 M | 16 | 24 | 386 SX machines |
| Motorola 68020 | 25 | 4 G | 32 | 32 | Apple Mackintosh II |

Note: G = Giga = $10^9$

It is not intended here to go into the full details of PCs, their devices, operating systems and software, but to give a brief outline as related to a BEMS. (For further details the reader is referred to Colantonio [1] and other books in the References.)

## 3.2  Secondary memory

For PCs, there are two types of disk: floppy and hard disks. Floppy disks are either 8, 5.25 or 3.5 in in diameter and are made of plastic coated with a magnetic material and contained within a stiff plastic cover having a small slit for the head of the disk drive to read or write to the disk.

The disks may be single sided or double sided – i.e. with storage on one or two sides. Also the magnetic material may be single, double or high density; the greater the density, the greater the storage. The disks are rotated at about 300 revolutions a minute in the disk drive and the information is stored on the disk in sectors of circular tracks on the disk. The size of the sectors is determined when the disk is initially **formated** or programmed in the PC. Typically a 5.25 in disk has a minimum capacity of about 160 Kbytes if a single side is used. (It is worth noting that the information on an A4-size sheet of paper with single-spaced typing would need about 4 Kbytes.) There are disks that use both sides, and also disks with denser magnetic coatings. Hence a double-sided, high-density disk has a capacity of approximately 1.6 Mbytes. Increasingly popular are the robust 3.5-in disks which also have variations in sides used and density, with capacity starting at 400 Kbytes, a high density 3.5-in disk having approximately 1.4 Mbyte.

Hard disks are made from aluminium rather than plastic and because of their rigidity can store more information, closely packed, than a floppy disk. A typical hard disk can hold at least 20 Mbytes. They can also be rotated faster than a floppy disk and so access information quicker. The life of the early hard disks was about 10 000 hours but modern disks have lives of up to 50 000 h. However, it is always wise to back-up a hard disc with floppy disks, just for that awful moment – even though it may take tens of floppies! High speed tapes can also be used for back-up storage using a **tape streamer**.

A **fixed disk** is installed inside the PC and is never handled by the user. A **disk-on-a-card** is a cheaper hard disk (and being a card it can be slotted into an expansion slot on the motherboard inside the PC). A **Bernoulli disk drive**, or Bernoulli box, is a hard disk contained within a plastic cartridge that can be removed from the disk drive like a floppy disk.

On all the above disks the data is stored on concentric, circular **tracks**, which are split into sectors, so that **files** of data and programs can be located.

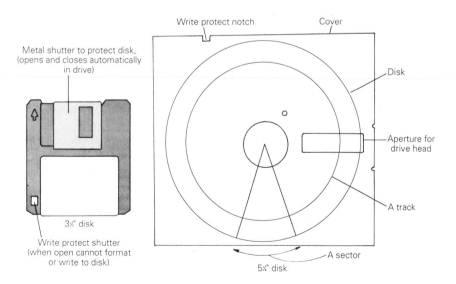

**Fig. 3.1** Floppy disks.

A **disk directory** of all the files contained on the disk is written on the disk and updated each time a file is written or saved. The updating is done by the computer **disk-operating system**. Examination of the disk directory reveals the file names, file types, sizes in bytes, the dates and times they were written and the free space left on the hard disk in bytes.

Other storage devices exist such as **optical disk drives** using compact disk (CD), technology which can store hundreds of Mbytes of data (some at present in read-only form). Hence they are known as CD-ROMs. However, they have yet to make an impact on BEMSs. Another development in data storage has been the **magnetic bubble memory**, which has mostly been used for small amounts of data. One BEMS manufacturer has made a virtue of employing these non-volatile memories instead of RAM, but this has primarily been for outstation use rather than central station secondary storage.

### 3.3  Monitors

A **monochrome text monitor**, or screen, simply displays letters and figures in one colour. Most monochrome monitors can display 25 lines of text, each with 80 characters. The characters are made up of dots, and each occupies a character box, commonly 9 dots wide by 14 dots deep. These dimensions are referred to as the **resolution**.

When there is a need to display graphs a more expensive monitor, a **monochrome graphics monitor**, is needed. This controls each dot or picture element, called a 'pixel', individually, so that graphs, diagrams, charts, pictures, etc. can be displayed. The resolution of a graphics monitor is given as the total number of horizontal dots by the vertical dots – e.g. 320 by 200 pixels. Often the only difference between a graphics monitor and a text monitor is the electronic circuit board or card controlling it.

A **colour graphics monitor**, which most BEMSs now use, can display pictures and text in many colours. The different colours that can be displayed on the monitor is related to the resolution. The total number of colours that can be chosen with which to display a picture is called the 'palette'.

As the monitor is controlled by a **display adapter**, or for monitors with graphics capabilities a **graphics adapter**, one cannot necessarily choose a better monitor without changing the adapter. In some PCs the adapter is part of the main PC circuit board, or motherboard – in which case change may be difficult – but in others the adapter is a separate board that can be easily taken out and replaced. Common display adapters are: Color Graphics Array (CGA), Enhanced Graphics Array (EGA) and Video Graphics Array (VGA).

### 3.4  Printers

A printer is a very useful component of a BEMS central station that produces a **hard copy** of text, figures and graphs (of variable quality depending on the type) on to paper. The most common printer supplied with BEMS is the **dot matrix**. On these the printhead consists of between 7 and 27 pins arranged vertically. Most models have 9 pins but more expensive versions with 18 or 24 pins are increasingly common. The appropriate pins are struck against an inked ribbon and the paper to form the characters. This is for **draft-mode printing**. For slower, higher-quality printing **near letter quality** mode is used, where the printhead strikes the pins twice for each character, each in a slightly different position.

The **daisy wheel** printer consists of a wheel of characters which is rotated for a hammer to strike the selected character against the ribbon. This type of printer is noisier and slower than a dot matrix, and as it cannot produce graphics it is seldom used in BEMSs.

**Ink jet** printers spray small electrically charged drops of ink on to the paper. A varying electric field directs the drops to form the required character. The print is of a high quality and the printing is fast. One distinct advantage is that a number of coloured inks can be used to print in colour.

Superior-quality printing is produced by the **laser** printer, but it is relatively expensive and would rarely be justified for use with a BEMS alone. However, laser printers are increasingly being purchased for use on office LANs where a number of users can access them.

## 3.5 Mouse

A **mouse** is additional to the keyboard as an input device for moving the cursor and for selecting symbols or **icons** on the screen. A thin cable connects the mouse to the PC. The mouse is a small hand-held box with one or more buttons

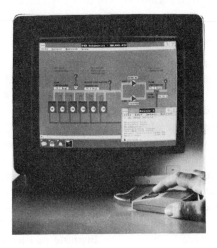

**Fig. 3.2**  A mouse.

on it, and it is slid across the table with the cursor on the screen moving in the same way as the mouse. Selections and operations are made by pressing one or more buttons on the mouse. Originally the mouse was developed to minimize the size of the PC keyboard, and Apple used it as an essential component of their Mackintosh computers. As the mouse proved so useful, especially in making drawings on the screen, it was incorporated by other manufacturers and is now a standard item on most BEMSs; Fig.3.2 shows a mouse.

## 3.6  Expansion

As some outstations can be expanded by adding extra circuit boards or cards, so most PCs have **expansion slots** on their motherboards for additional cards, or for replacing and upgrading existing cards. The expansion slot is a connection to the PC's bus into which boards can easily be inserted. For instance, one could add a graphics adapter card to enable a text monitor to display graphs and pictures. Another card could add more RAM to the PC to run larger programs, whilst a maths-coprocessor card speeds up mathematical computation for large mathematically based programs.

An interesting expansion card is a **network adapter**, which is a sophisicated circuit board for connecting a PC to other PCs in a **local area network**, or LAN. A LAN is the connection by cables of two or more PCs together, so that they can share programs, printers, large high-capacity hard disks and other hardware. This greatly enhances each PC and allows communication between PCs. Although this is not of great inherent use to a BEMS itself, unless there is an existing LAN within the building where the BEMS is located, the linking of outstations to a central station is akin to a LAN and is discussed later.

## 3.7  Parallel and serial connections

To connect the central station PC to an external device, such as a printer or monitor, then an **interface** is required such that the device is effectively connected directly to the 3-bus architecture of the PC's CPU. There are two types of interface: **parallel** and **serial**.

A parallel interface or **parallel port** transmits information, under the control of the CPU, to and from the device a byte at a time. Each bit of the byte is sent simultaneously down its own wire, the wires being in parallel. Actually more than eight wires are needed, eight for each bit, some for controlling the transmission and reception and one wire for a reference ground voltage.

A parallel interface is the General Purpose Interface Bus, (GPIB), developed by Hewlett-Packard to connect laboratory instruments to a PC, and is a standard interface for 16 parallel wires. The Institute of Electronic and Electrical Engineers (IEEE), in the USA, adopted this standard in 1975 as IEEE-488. It was updated in 1978 and is also known as the IEEE Bus. Eight lines are for data and information, five are for general interface management to ensure an orderly flow of information and three are for data transfer control, or **hand-shaking**. Handshaking consists of control signals making it possible for two electronic circuits to synchronize their work or 'talk' to each other. The receiving device, for instance, has to be ready to receive data from the sending computer.

A common PC interface standard for sending information to printers is the Centronics standard, based on one of the first printers made by Centronics Data Computer Corporation. A common Centronics connector has 36 edge-connecting pins and the male connector is held in place by two clips on the edge of the female connector.

These parallel connections are for connecting the PC directly to peripheral equipment, within a couple of metres of it. Any further and parallel interfaced cabling becomes expensive and the signals would need amplification, so that they did not lose their strength. A cheaper cabling system is one that uses serial transmission of information.

A **serial interface** or **serial port** transmits data from the PC one bit at a time, one bit after another. This is slower than parallel transmission, but needs less connections and wiring. Many BEMSs simply use twisted pair cables (like low voltage telephone cable), for local communication. Also because of the limited ways of sending data serially, it has some universal standards. A very popular method or **protocol** (a set of rules) for sending digital information serially is the one that complies with the North American Electronic Industries Association (EIA) standard RS-232-C (which also conforms to the internationally recognized CCITT (Comité Consultatif International Télégraphique et Téléphonique) V.24 standard, except that the on and off pulse shape is different). It was originally introduced in 1960, and revised in 1963 (RS-232-A), in 1965 (RS-232-B) and in 1969 (RS-232-C). The RS-232-C standard specifies the functions and signal voltage levels of the 25 pins in the standard **D-type** connectors. The 'D' shape comes from the thirteen horizontal pins above the twelve pins; a '0' is represented by a voltage of 5–15 V and a '1' represented by a voltage between − 5 to –15 V. Often few of the 25 wires are actually needed. Signals can be satisfactorily transmitted over distances up to 15 m. For greater distances, up to 1000 m, then equipment complying to RS-423-A is required [21].

Most PCs have at least one serial RS-232-C interface or port from the motherboard or expansion slots to a D-type socket on the back of the chassis or case. Most outstations also have RS-232-C ports for connecting to a small portable, lap-top, or notebook PCs, PC or keypads, for local programming and adjustment, if there is not already an integral display and keypad on the outstation.

Another common serial standard is the 20 mA current loop where voltages can range over ± 80 V with the current held constant at 20 mA. But it is mainly due to the RS-232-C standard that many PCs and devices of different manufacture can use the same serial interface. More important, the RS-232-C is very similar to a common standard that defines the handshaking signals used to control standard **modems** by which a BEMS central station can communicate with distant outstations over telephone lines. (For further details on interfacing see references [2], [3] and [21].)

## 3.8  Modems

For communication between the central station PC and a remote outstation in another building, the PC is connected via the RS-232-C port to a modem which modulates the digital signal into an audio signal suitable for transmission over the public switched telephone network (PSTN). There is a modem at the

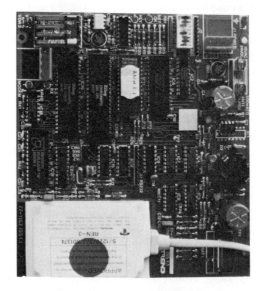

**Fig. 3.3**  A stand-alone modem, and a modem board to go inside an outstation.

receiving end which demodulates the audio signal into a digital signal for the outstation microprocessor. The term 'modem' derives from its function of *mod*ulating and *dem*odulating signals. A modem is shown in Fig. 3.3.

The PC could well have an **internal modem** either on its motherboard or as a separate card on an expansion slot. In this case, the telephone line simply connects to the internal modem through a connection on the back of the PC. An **external modem** is in its own box and needs a separate power supply, and it is connected to the PC via the RS-232-C port.

Just as the central station PC needs a serial interface to a modem, and a modem itself, so the outstation would need an interface card or **communications control card** and modem to communicate with the central station. Often the outstation has **autodial** facilities to enable it to dial automatically the central station's phone number to raise important alarms or to download sensor logs, preferably overnight to save on phone charges, although the downloading is usually initiated by the central station. Similarly, the outstation could be reprogrammed, its set points changed, data examined, and so on, simply over the telephone.

Although ordinary PSTN lines can be used for BEMS's communication, leased telephone lines are available which are reserved exclusively for one organization. These lines are often connected directly and do not suffer noise and attenuation by not being switched at a telephone exchange. There are two-wire and four-wire leased lines, the latter having two wires for transmission each way and therefore saving on modem turn-around time.

Modems are classed by their maximum conversion and transmission rates. Most modems normally used can operate at least at 300 bits per second (bps), or less correctly 300 baud [4], with many modems operating at 1200 bps to 2400 bps and high-speed modems up to 10 000 bps. With a modem operating at 1200 bps, it means that it can send data at 120–150 bytes per second, so that a typed page would take 27–33 s to transmit.

Hayes Microcomputer Products Inc., in the USA, is one of the largest modem manufacturers and it has virtually set an industry standard for the equipment. Because of this 'standard', communications software usually has features specifically for the Hayes Smartmodem and so other manufacturers produce Hayes compatible modems.

If it is required that a BEMS central station should communicate with its outstations over the PSTN, then not only interface cards and modems will be needed, but the BEMS software may have to be altered if it does not already have communications software. One cannot simply connect BEMSs to modems.

With individual bits of data being modulated, sent over the PSTN and demodulated, there is the possibility of stray voltages and interference on the line causing corruption of the data, hence some form of **error checking** is employed. This is often a **parity check** on each byte of data sent.

Seven of the byte's eight bits are used for the information, and another bit is added for the party bit, the parity being either even or odd. The first seven bits sent, from right to left, of the byte below have odd parity, so if an even parity check is used, then the parity bit, the eighth bit at the end, is made a 1 to make the whole byte even:

$$1 \qquad 1 \quad 0 \quad 0 \quad 0 \quad 1 \quad 0 \quad 1$$
parity
bit

The error checking convention could be that all bytes will have odd parity, so the parity bit of the above byte would be 0. Thus the above byte under this odd parity check becomes:

$$0 \qquad 1 \quad 0 \quad 0 \quad 0 \quad 1 \quad 0 \quad 1$$
parity
bit

**Asynchronous transmission** is when the receiver does not know when the transmitter of the information is going to send information. The line is then left at a voltage indicating a 1 (i.e. for the RS-232-C this is $-5$ to $-15$ V [3]), which is interrupted by a *start bit* of a 0 (RS-232-C 5 to 15 V). A **stop bit** is used to indicate the end of the byte. So the above byte will now become as that shown in Fig. 3.4.

**Synchronous transmission** is faster than asynchronous transmission as the transmitter and receiver have synchronized clock signals and do not require the start and stop bits.

The route between the central station and the outstation, whether over PSTN or not, is referred to as a 'channel'. When a message is sent from the central station to the outstation, then as a check the outstation sends a duplicate of the signal it has just received to the central station to appear under the original message on the central station screen. A channel like this sending messages simultaneously in both directions is a **full-duplex channel**. A **half-duplex**

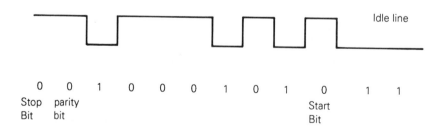

**Fig. 3.4**   Start and stop bits for transmission.

**channel** does not produce this 'echo' and can only transmit in one direction at a time.

For a computer to transmit text as well as numbers, it has to convert them to binary signals. It does this by using the American Standard Code for Information Interchange (ASCII). The central station keyboard characters are also converted to ASCII for the CPU to understand them. ASCII is a 7-bit code developed by a number of manufacturers as a standard code. For instance, the letter E in ASCII is:

$$01000101$$

which is the decimal number 69. See Colantonio [1] for the full ASCII Code.

## 3.9 Networks and buses

Modems can be used for communications over the telephone system for central stations and outstations. However, communications within a building can be made by a simple **twisted-pair cable** (often a number of twisted wires bundled together in one cable like telephone wire), connecting up the BEMS stations. This forms a local area network (LAN), or continuous bus, between the outstations and the central station. Each station needs a **network adapter card** (or **communication node controller**), to link it into the LAN. In most older style BEMSs the central station acts as the master, controlling the communication. In this older, hierarchical arrangement the individual outstations do not communicate with each other, but only with the central station. A small number of manufacturers do supply systems in which each outstation can act as a central station and also communicate with each other, but these outstations are much larger and consequently more expensive.

Generally, a LAN refers to the linking of a number of PCs together in a network to share high-grade, expensive equipment, such as a laser printer or a large hard disk and its large programs, so that all the PCs can use them without the need for each one to have its own dedicated and expensive equipment. Also, the PCs can share data. The PCs are linked to a **LAN server**, which is a more powerful PC. This server can store a number of programs that each PC can access without each one needing to have a large memory like the server. So the LAN enhances the individual PCs by allowing access to expensive equipment on the network.

As BEMS outstations are effectively small computers, then their network can be referred to as a LAN, but the data transfer rate is much lower and can be slower than that required for PCs with large programs and data arrays. But similarly for a BEMS with a LAN, outstations can have the minimum memory and intelligence required, but have access to the central station with more memory and intelligence, as well as access to the other outstations. This is very useful for large buildings, especially air conditioned office blocks, with a number of different zones which often have separate heating and air conditioning systems.

First, consider an industrial site with a heated building used partly as offices, partly for manufacture and partly as a warehouse. One outstation could control each area with its own separate requirements. But only one outstation need have an outside air temperature sensor, solar sensor and wind sensor, as all the other outstations can access these sensors. The central station could be situated in the energy manager's office, separate from any of the outstations, but linked to them on the LAN. There could also be a printer, connected to the LAN, in the gatehouse for printing alarms for a security man; Fig. 3.5 shows such a LAN. The printer would have to have its own network adapter card.

Second, consider a large multi-tenanted office block of many floors. Small outstations, each with say four inputs and four outputs, will control the individual items of plant (often air conditioning fan coil units or variable air volume terminal units) on each floor. Each floor would have its own separate LAN, or **sub-LAN**, for its small outstations. A larger outstation would be master of, or local server for, the sub-LAN and would be joined into the main LAN of the building on which would be the main central station and the other sub-LAN masters, as is shown in Fig. 3.6.

Each floor's sub-LAN would control that floor's heating and air conditioning system and could monitor its energy consumption for that particular tenant. In identifying each outstation, outstations could be given **attributes**, such as the floor that each is situated on and those that are in south-, north-, east- and

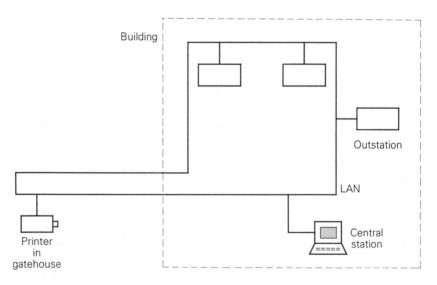

**Fig. 3.5** Local area network or LAN.

west-facing zones controlling air conditioning equipment. This would allow for better control, for instance, reducing the heating in synchronization with the sun's movement around the building when there is significant solar gain.

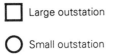

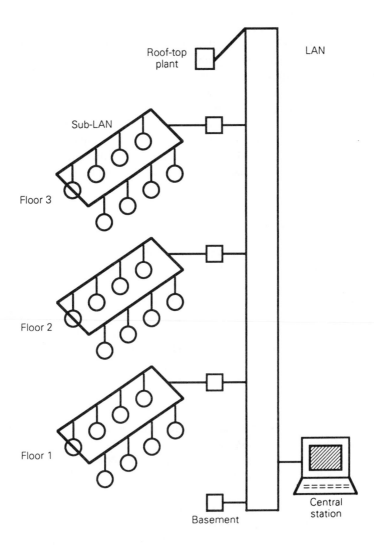

**Fig. 3.6**  A large building with sub-LANs.

Small outstations are now being produced which control individual items of plant, so that the plant itself becomes intelligent. The equipment manufacturers (or OEMs, other equipment manufacturers, as distinct from the BEMS manufacturers) can then put the outstations on their plant at the factory and test and commission them before they are sent to the site. Then at site the outstation needs simply to be connected to the LAN. Even temperature sensors, switches and relays will become intelligent (**smart sensors**, switches, etc.), with their own microprocessor and communications link on to a bus around the building.

There is the possibility of fire detection systems and security systems also linking in to BEMS systems, although failures on one system must not affect any other, making the building unsafe in an emergency.

With this potential for communication between systems, and with outstations becoming smaller and cheaper, so that individual items of plant can become intelligent and communicate on the BEMS LAN, 'intelligent' buildings may soon be a reality. However, there is still the problem of communication between different manufacturers' intelligent equipment and different BEMSs. At present, BEMS manufacturers can have widely different LAN topologies, as well as other incompatibilities, but this is discussed in more detail later.

## 3.10  Network topology

The way that the stations are positioned on a LAN is called the **topology**. Generally BEMS LANs are similar to those that link up PCs, except that there is much less information for BEMS outstations to communicate than PCs, which for instance are required to exchange software programs and large amounts of data. So BEMS LANs are often scaled-down versions of PC LANs with smaller and cheaper twisted-pair connections. There are basically three topologies for LANs, all three being shown in Fig. 3.7:

(i)   star
(ii)  bus
(iii) ring

In the star all outstations are connected to the central, message-switching station (CS). The advantage of this topology is that is requires most of the communication intelligence to be at the central station and less at the outstations. However, it does depend crucially on the central station at the centre of the star.

With the bus topology, all stations have the potential to communicate independently with each other. Information is sent along the bus in **packets** or **frames**, often eight bits long, with a receiver identification 'tag' on it. All stations are 'listening' for messages but the tag will identify which station it

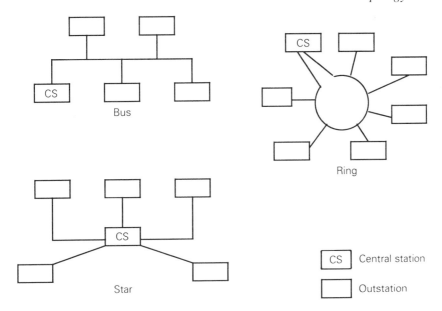

**Fig. 3.7** Network topology.

is for. One advantage of this topology is that new stations can be inserted by simply tapping into the bus cable. The disadvantage is that information between various stations can travel in opposite directions and collide. So a **carrier sense multiple access** (CSMA) protocol is needed that requires each station to 'listen before speaking' and to transmit when there are no other messages being sent. The protocol is much simpler if the central station controls the bus and it also saves hardware and software at the outstations.

In a ring topology the network cable is connected to each station, in turn, and the information travels round the ring in one direction only. Ring topologies often use the **token-passing** protocol, where a token (a pattern of bits) is transmitted around the ring from one station to the next. Only the station with the token is allowed to transmit if it wishes, and it does so by attaching a target address and its information to the token. The token and information is then passed to the next station on the ring which copies it and re-transmits it. Only the addressee station will make use of the information. The message format for a BEMS network using the ring topology for a message from station A to station B is shown in Fig. 3.8.

The message can be up to 100 ASCII characters long. The outstations, modems, central stations, printers and other devices are physically connected to the ring through their node controllers or network adapter cards. The ring itself is a two-wire, 20 mA current loop. If the sending node sees its message go round the ring ten times without being accepted, then it removes it and tries

| To :   A. | From   B. |
|-----------|-----------|
| MESSAGE : | |
| | |
| | |
| | |
| | |
| | |
| | |
| ERROR   CHECK | END |

**Fig. 3.8**   Message format.

again later. The LAN in Fig. 3.5, discussed earlier, is an example of a ring type.

Just as sub-LANs are connected to a main LAN, via a larger master outstation, as shown in Fig. 3.6, so LANs themselves can be connected together to

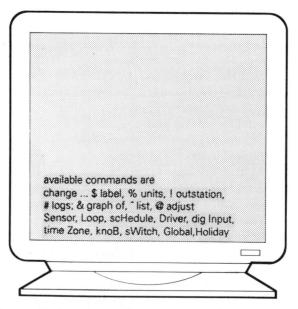

**Fig. 3.9**   Screen display of typical menu commands.

form a **supernet** or **internet**. If two LANs have different protocols, then they can be connected together by a **gateway** which converts the protocols. With a single manufacturer's BEMS, a gateway would only be necessary to connect to another manufacturer's system. For more details on LANs see references [4], [6], [7] and [21].

## 3.11 Central station software

A BEMS, like all computer systems, needs a set of instructions, or a program, to tell it what to do. The actual chips, circuit boards and the physical parts of the BEMS are referred to as the hardware, whereas the programs, which are not physical objects, are referred to as software. Programs written on ROM chips are referred to as firmware as these programs are contained within hardware, and are actually a part of it.

The microprocessor, the electronic chip at the heart of all BEMSs' central station PCs and outstations only operates with digital, on/off signals. Such signals form a **low-level programming language**, or **machine language**, which consists of binary numbers representing instructions for the microprocessor, as well as data and memory addresses. Machine language instructions consist of two parts, an **operation code**, or 'opcode', which is the operation to be performed, and an **operand**, the number or address on which the operation is to be performed. Most CPU instructions can be summarized as fetch and execute operations. There are surprisingly few instructions for a CPU. The Intel 8088, used on many of the early IBM PCs, has a set of about 100 basic instructions. The instruction to add is simply:

00000101

**Assembly code**, or assembly language, is slightly easier than machine code, as easy-to-remember mnemonics are used for the instructions instead of binary digits. For instance, the add instruction would now be:

ADD

and substract would be:

SUB

The mnemonic instructions still have to be converted into machine code, though, and a program written in assembly code has to be run through another special program called an **assembler** to translate it into machine code. The program before translation is referred to as the **source code**, and after translation it is referred to as the **object code**. When an outstation has a keypad on it, a code similar to assembly code is used to communicate with the outstation CPU.

Both machine code and assembly code deal with the CPU at its closest or lowest level, and are consequently referred to as low-level languages. Low-level languages are difficult to use and are often specific to particular PCs. So easier **high-level** languages, such as BASIC, Pascal, C and FORTRAN were developed for writing programs, with a short **statement**, or instruction, in the language representing a lot of machine-coded instructions. Also these high-level languages are not machine specific and mathematical symbols and words are used in the statements.

The high-level languages have to be translated to machine code, just as the low-level languages have to be. There are two types of translator. An **interpreter** translates and runs one instruction at a time, allowing the programmer to see the results, and any errors instantly. A **compiler** translates the entire program and so the resulting code runs much faster.

BASIC, developed in 1965, is the most popular language for PCs and some early BEMSs used it. But it primarily uses an interpreter translator, although compiled versions are now available, and it is slow. So most BEMSs now use Pascal and FORTRAN, which employ compilers.

This does not mean that a BEMS user has to learn a programming language such as Pascal because most BEMS use **application software** or an **application package** where the programming is hidden and a non-specialist can use it. An example of application software is a word processing package. It is through such software that PCs have become so popular. The programming in such software is hidden by a **user interface** which brings up a 'menu' of commands for the user to select. Figure 3.9 shows a typical menu that would appear on a BEMS monitor, and although this type of program is now rather basic, it does show the essential details of BEMS software.

To get a graph of, say, the inside temperature from an outstation sensor, then one types:

&   [return or enter]

or using a mouse clicks on the '&' and the central station screen comes up with:

Graph of...?

to which one types in the sensor number of the inside temperature sensor. Then a graph will come up on the screen. Such a graph is shown in Fig. 3.10, with the boiler flow water temperature graph as well.

To see the actual temperatures being read by the sensors, then 'Sensors' in the menu indicates that the sensors' readings are brought up on the screen by typing:

S   [return or enter]

to which the central station responds:

sensor...?

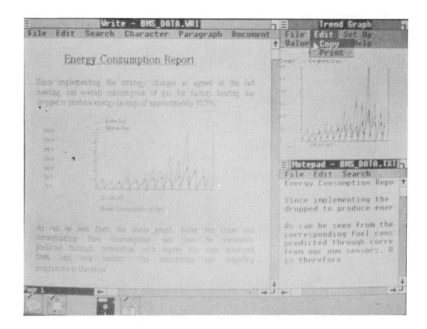

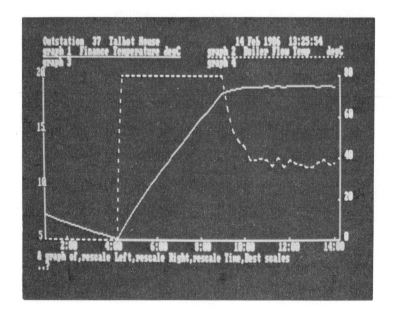

**Fig. 3.10** Graphical outputs.

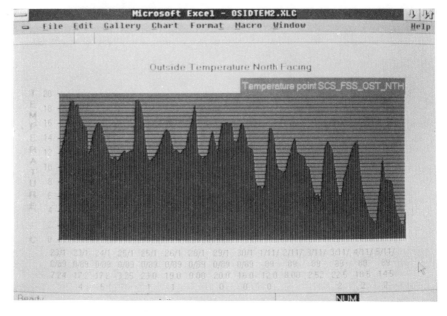

**Fig.   3.10 c.**

to which one types in the appropriate sensor number:

1   [return or enter]

would bring up on the screen the list of all ten sensors' readings, as shown in
Fig. 3.11:

This is a static menu, but some BEMSs have **pop-up menus**, which are
called up on command. **Pull-down menus** are associated with software which
uses a lot of graphics, and the menu items can be selected with a mouse
pointing an arrow to the required menu command.

Instead of displaying just a list of sensor temperatures, many BEMSs have
software which can display graphics and plans of plant rooms can be drawn
on the screen and the relevant temperatures of, for instance, the flow and
return temperatures can be shown. Fig. 3.12 is an example of this.

This type of software is now becoming dated as it is replaced by BEMS
software using a **windowing environment**, where the screen can be divided
into a number of different boxes or windows shown in Fig. 3.12, together with
a separate program or diagram shown in it, on top of the main window. With
this type of program, the basic method of presentation of information is in
schematic diagrams using colour graphics. Associated with such a program
are **icons**, small pictorial symbols, often at the bottom of the screen. For
instance, the icon for an alarm program is a bell, and that for the password

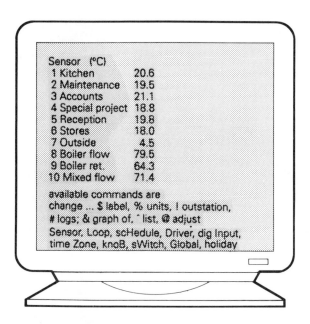

**Fig. 3.11** Screen display of sensor temperatures.

program is a padlock, open when the correct password has been entered and closed otherwise. A mouse is the primary input device, moving a pointer around the screen to select the required icon, or a small box on a diagram, called a **click box**. Clicking the mouse, sometimes with a double click, on a click box produces another window of graphic information. The mouse can also be used to enlarge and reduce windows and move them around the screen.

Microsoft's Windows package, which is regularly upgraded and improved as a newer version, like most good software, is now used on most modern BEMSs which makes operation much easier, although it requires more memory than the program with the menu at the bottom of the screen.

Microsoft Corporation, founded in 1975 by William Gates and Paul Allen, has written much of the **operating system** software used by many PCs, of which perhaps the best known is MS-DOS. The operating system is a set of programs, that controls the PC's hardware and manages its use of software, making the PC easier to use. It acts as an interface between the user and the PC, and sets up the PC for use when it is switched on.

BEMS software may include a **computer-aided drawing** (CAD) package to aid the drawing of plant schematics, as that in Fig. 3.12, as well as a word processing package for writing reports, and it will most likely have a **spreadsheet package**, for manipulating data, doing numerous calculations and producing various graphs. Spreadsheets, or worksheets, are basically tables of

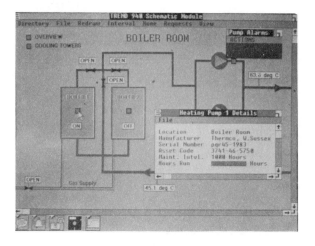

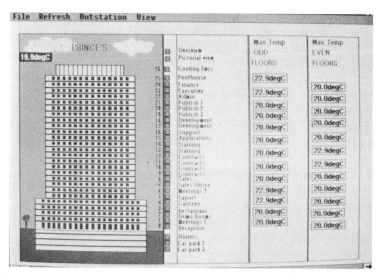

**Fig. 3.12**   Plant room and building schematics.

rows and columns of data that can be manipulated by formulae and easily turned into graphs by the spreadsheet software. These packages can be very useful for monitoring and targeting energy consumption (they are discussed in more detail in Chapter 10 on monitoring and targeting). Examples of spreadsheet packages are: Lotus 1-2-3, SuperCalc and Microsoft Excel. Fig. 3.13 shows an example of a spreadsheet of oil consumption from a large site.

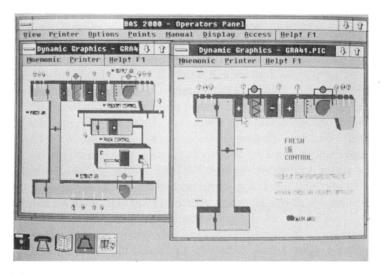

**Fig. 3.12 c.**

## 3.12 Compatibility, communications and standards

One of the great drawbacks of a BEMS is that once one has bought a system, other manufacturers' equipment such as outstations, sensors and software cannot be connected to it without a great deal of programming effort and information from the relevant manufacturers. This is not so much a manufacturers' ploy as simply the result of the numerous possible ways of writing a piece of software (including the different languages) and the different ways of storing data in an outstation (including the different memory sizes and the relevant area of memory for, say, temperature sensor logs to be stored), as well as different types of equipment. So this results in one manufacturer's BEMS being able not to communicate with another manufacturer's.

Part of this communication problem stems from the computer industry where there are many different protocols (sets of rules for governing com-

Name;  Atkins House
Address;  Sabiri Way, Milestown.

Account No;  53476  Oil  35 second.  Supplier; Fiddlers.

| Date | Stored | Delivered | Price p/litre | Cost of delivery | Litres used | Oil YRT | Del. cost YRT |
|---|---|---|---|---|---|---|---|
| 03-May-92 | 30594 | 40922 | 15.08 | 6,171.04 | 55651 | 645300 | 97,324.51 |
| 31-May-92 | 55301 | 54532 | 14.63 | 7,978.03 | 29825 | 629120 | 97,358.27 |
| 05-Jul-92 | 44868 | 13640 | 15.63 | 2,131.93 | 24073 | 625304 | 97,104.60 |
| 02-Aug-92 | 26957 | 0 | 15.63 | 0.00 | 17911 | 623281 | 93,043.12 |
| 06-Sep-92 | 32549 | 27280 | 15.63 | 4,263.86 | 21688 | 621450 | 93,237.71 |

**Fig. 3.13**  Spreadsheet output.

munication) for PCs, which means that PCs from different manufacturers cannot easily communicate. To try to resolve this standards are being developed. An all-encompassing communications standard for many different types and makes of computer and equipment will be very complex, but to try to describe proposed standards and what the network hardware and software do the International Standards Organization (ISO) developed *The Reference Model of Open Systems Interconnection* (the OSI model) [10], [11].

To understand the model it is worth considering our own methods of communicating. When we speak to someone near to us, we have to establish initial contact, probably by looking at them and saying their name. Then we send the message which consists of words in the language we are using, which are so ordered to obey the rules of grammar and syntax. If the person is a foreigner who does not speak our language, then he or she will indicate in some way that they do not understand and that the communication has not been understood. Likewise, PCs and BEMS have different languages and grammars, although they share binary signals, as we share the same alphabet as, say, Frenchmen and Germans.

For a group of people at a meeting there has to be a protocol for speaking, we cannot all speak at once. This is similar to outstations on a LAN.

When we phone someone, we have to dial their number first. For a local number in inner London it may be 928 8298. If we are in inner London, this suffices; but if we are in outer London, then we have to add 071, so that the phone system can route our call to inner London. If we are in another country, we have to add further numbers to route the call to the UK. Our phone conversation, then, requires various layers of numbers, or protocols, sent prior to contacting the other person. We do not have to understand how the call is routed or how the message is sent (whether as an analogue or digital signal). The system is 'transparent' to us, and as far as we are concerned the person to whom we are talking could almost be standing next to us. We are 'virtual' users.

The OSI model defines the various layers of protocol which have to be added to messages to be sent between computers and computer equipment which are communicating. The model is split into seven layers, or protocol levels, as shown in Fig. 3.14. The figure shows two computer systems, X and Y, which could well be two manufacturers' central stations, connected together perhaps on a LAN. Each system has hardware and software layers conforming to the OSI model, so that they can communicate.

The layers divide the model into smaller, more manageable segments. Each layer isolates the lower layers from the higher ones and adds values to the services provided by the lower layers. Figure 3.15 shows this addition of protocol **headers** and **tailers** to the basic message, similar to the addition of digits in our telephone example.

Layers 1–4 are called the 'transfer service' as they are responsible for

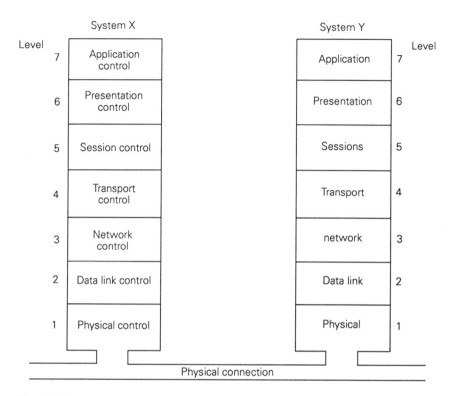

**Fig. 3.14** The OSI seven-layer model.

moving information from one point to another. Layers 5–7 are known as 'user layers' as they give users access to information on the network.

Layer 1 is the 'physical layer', and defines the physical connection between the computer and the network – i.e. the actual connectors, cables and signalling voltages. This is like the RS-232-C standard. LANs for PCs with large-

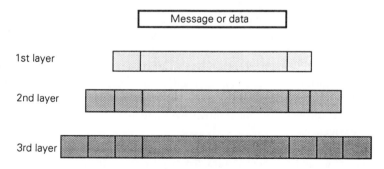

**Fig. 3.15** The addition of headers and tailers.

scale data transmission would use coaxial cables, proprietry cables such as Ethernet cables or fibre optics.

Layer 7 is the application layer and in a BEMS is the central station application software, for instance, producing plant diagrams and temperature graphs in a windows environment. Although many BEMS manufacturers are now using Microsoft Windows as the basic central station software, there is a lot of variation in its application and the underlying software.

Much of the compatibility work for BEMSs centres on layer 7, so the other five layers will not be considered further. For more details on the OSI model and computer communications the reader is referred to references [2], [4], [5], [8], [10], [11] and [21].

One example of BEMS incompatibility is in how the outstation software stores sensed data from outstation sensors, and how information on the actual sensors is stored, as well as their role in the control configuration. The fact that manufacturers will use different sensors is another complication. Consider the transmission of data from an outstation to a central station.

The central station may need the last day's outside temperature readings from an outstation's sensor. Once the central station has established contact with the outstation, the central station needs to know the address for this information in the outstation's memory and the command or code to send the information to the central station. The temperature data may be stored as voltage readings to be converted when required, or stored as already converted temperatures. The outstation may store all temperature sensors' data in one memory block and have a protocol that sends the whole block of data, rather than individual sensor's data, to the central station. The error checking routines (e.g. a parity check) may also differ from manufacturer to manufacturer. So there are many possibilities for the protocols and, in effect, each manufacturer's protocol will be unique. Of course this protocol, as well as the other BEMS software, is of great commercial importance to the manufacturer as it will have cost many man-years to develop. In fact there will be few people in the company who actually know and have access to the whole protocol.

However, there is an instance in the UK where a number of manufacturers have released protocols, in confidence, to a software house which produces energy monitoring software. Having obtained the protocols, much time and effort had to be expended in writing software to interface the protocols, but now its monitoring software can be used with a number of manufacturers' BEMSs. In a very few isolated cases, clients have been given access to BEMS protocols and software and have unwisely made alterations with rather disastrous consequences.

A successful integration of three different manufacturers' BEMSs by one client was managed by West Sussex County Council. It needed a mainframe computer and considerable programming effort to get the BEMSs' data and commands into one common format. This enabled all three BEMSs to be accessed from one computer terminal.

At the London Stock Exchange an older-generation central station was replaced by a new **head-end computer**, which communicated with the old outstations and additional ones of a different manufacturer. Communication was facilitated by using Public Host Protocol developed by US BEMS manufacturer, American Autometrix.

Another approach to compatibility is that rather than adapt the head-end computer, one goes to the sensor end of the system [20] and uses a common bus with an open protocol to connect together different manufacturers' smart

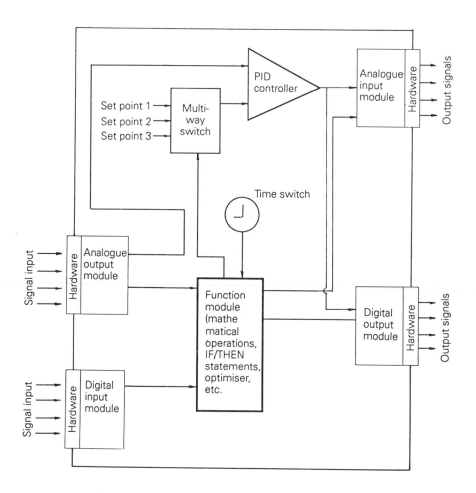

**Fig. 3.16**  BEMS centre model of an outstation.

or intelligent equipment. The 'smartness' comes from employing common interface chips. A number of head-end and bus systems are described below.

### 3.12.1   Development of a BEMS communications standard

The BEMS Centre at Building Services Resarch and Information Association (BSRIA) has produced a report on the development of a communications standard for BEMS [9]. The standard relates to the applications software of BEMS and is just concerned with layer 7 of the OSI Model. The BEMS Centre proposed standard considers a model of a typical BEMS outstation (Fig. 3.16) and the data required to define its control configuration, inputs and outputs and the data it stores.

It proposes that the data be stored on a spreadsheet program basis, with separate sheets for outstation details, sensors, sensed data, control loops, control configurations, etc. (Fig. 3.17). The main point is that the spreadsheet would be a common format for all manufacturers' BEMSs which would great-

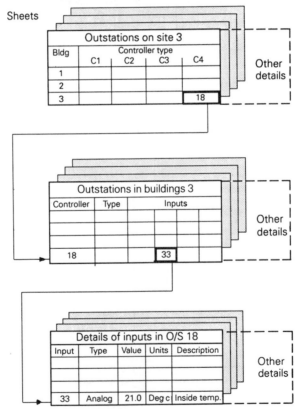

**Fig. 3.17**   Spreadsheet basis for storing BEMS data.

ly ease the accessing of data between different systems. However much work still has to be done to implement this proposed standard.

### 3.12.2 The FND Standard

Much work on a BEMS communications standard has been done in Germany. Two projects have been established: FND (Firm Neutral Datatransmission), promoted by German public authorities who own 50% of all large buildings in Germany; and PROFIBUS (PROcess FIeld BUS), sponsored by the German government.

The FND is effectively a gateway between BEMSs' LANs. Its specification was published in 1988, and conformance tests in 1990. The FND specification and conformance testing papers will appear as a German DIN standard [12]. In relation to the OSI Model, the FND standard has layers 4–6 empty, with layer 1, the physical layer, using the CCITT (Comité Consultatif Internationale de Télégraphic et Téléphonique) X.21 standard. This is a more sophisticated type of RS-232-C standard for intercomputer communications. Layers 2 and 3 of FND use the CCITT X.25 standard [9]. Layer 7, the applications layer, contains the FND protocol. Communications between different BEMSs in the FND concept is like communications between islands, containing a particular manufacturer's central station, and an overall central station centre. Each island [IZ] has an island central standard interface adapter (IZ-SSA), which communicates with the central through the central interface adapter (LZ-SSA). This communication between two different manufacturers' BEMSs is shown in Fig. 3.18.

The manufacturer's communication system is converted to FND through all

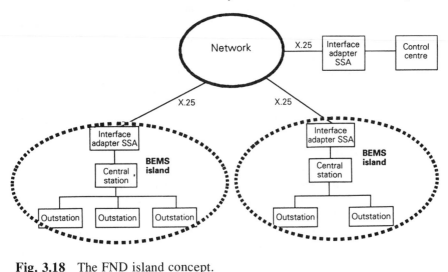

**Fig. 3.18** The FND island concept.

7 layers, starting at the physical layer up to the application layer, where the manufacturer's data and messages are also converted to FND for transmission. The FND protocol is centred on data points, digital inputs being Message Points, analogue inputs being Measuring Points, analogue outputs being Set Points and digital outputs being Switch Points. There are also high and low limits and totalizer points.

In December 1989 a Landis and Gyr Visonik 400 was connected to a Honeywell Delta 2000 and a Honeywell EXCEL, all controlling exhibition halls in Berlin. This involved a great deal of engineering effort in setting up the FND data points for the IZ- and LZ-SAs and the island central and main central parts of the system [12]. The FND concept of linking BEMS islands, as was done in Berlin, is shown in Fig. 3.18.

### 3.12.3   The PROFIBUS fieldbus

PROFIBUS is an example of a **fieldbus** and relatively low-tech, intended for small-and medium-sized buildings. Fieldbus is the name given by the International Electrotechnical Commission (IEC) to a proposed international standard for a low-level industrial data bus [9]. It has wider application to the manufacturing industry besides BEMSs. Fieldbus networks are intended to connect actuators, sensors, controllers and similar devices at a low level of communication rather than allow for distributed computation and large data communications as in a computer LAN. Hence fieldbuses do not need the full 7-layer architecture of the OSI model [18].

Whereas FND is for complete BEMSs to communicate, PROFIBUS is for outstation to outstation (or controller to controller) communication. Layer 1, the physical layer, is based on the RS-485 standard using shielded twisted-pair cables. The maximum length between outstations is 1200 m, and up to 4800 m with repeaters. Layers 3–6 are empty. The application layer (layer 7) is divided into two sub-layers. The upper layer is a Fieldbus Messaging Service (FMS) and is tailored to suit other fieldbus applications.

The PROFIBUS project was sponsored by the German government with thirteen companies and five research institutions participating. It was started in November 1987. A PROFIBUS User Group was founded in 1989 and took over the running of the project. The structure of the fieldbus, with **active** and **passive participators**, is shown in Fig. 3.19.

The active participators are on a decentralized token ring and the passive participators are on a centralized, polling, bus. When one of the active participators has the token, then it may poll the passive, slave, participators for information, as well as transmitting to other active, master, participators. Once an active participator has the token, then it is master of the whole bus. The passive participators need less hardware and software and can be used to keep the cost of the system down [9].

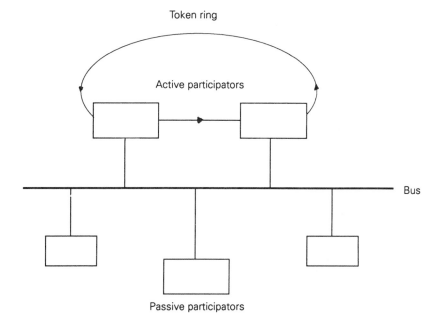

**Fig. 3.19** The PROFIBUS structure.

### 3.12.4 The ASHRAE initiative

ASHRAE (American Society of Heating, Refrigerating and Air Conditioning Engineers) formed a standards committee to develop a standard communications protocol in 1987 for building energy management and control systems (EMCS). A draft standard was issued in 1991, and it is anticipated that the standard will be issued by the end of 1992.

The name chosen for the protocol is BACnet (Building Automation and Control Networks). The draft protocol may be understood by considering it as two separate but closely related parts; a model of the information in the BEMS, in terms of **objects**, and the functions or 'services' used to exchange it [19]. Like the FND standard, BACnet will interface between BEMSs with their own manufacturers' (or vendors') internal design. It will model the design with 20 standard **object types**, examples of which are listed in Table 3.2.

Each of the objects in Table 3.2, then, has defined properties; those for the binary input object are given in Table 3.3 [19].

The functions or **applications services** provide commands for accessing and manipulating information. In the draft standard there are five groups of application services, as shown in Table 3.4.

The object access services provide the means to read from and write to the properties of objects, and to create or delete them. The virtual terminal ser-

**Table 3.2**  Some objects that may comprise a typical BEMS device

| |
| --- |
| Control loop |
| Analogue input |
| Analogue output |
| Analogue value |
| Binary input |
| Binary output |
| Binary value |
| Schedule |
| Group |

**Table 3.3**  Properties of the binary input object

| | |
| --- | --- |
| Object identifier | Polarity |
| Object type | Inactive text |
| Present value | Active text |
| Description | Change-of-state time |
| Status flags | Elapsed active time |
| Reliability | Change-of-state count |
| Override | Time of reset |
| Out-of-service | |

**Table 3.4**  The five groups of applications services

| |
| --- |
| Alarm and event |
| File access |
| Object access |
| Remote device management |
| Virtual terminal |

vices allow a monitor and keyboard to interact with the system as if it were directly connected to the system, the communication and protocols all being dealt with 'unseen' by the user.

It is considered by ASHRAE that three networking methods will meet the needs of BEMSs; Ethernet, Arcnet (both already developed as LANs) and a **master–slave/token-passing** (MS/TP) network, being defined by ASHRAE but relying on the EIA-485 (formerly RS-485) physical layer standard. Before the ASHRAE draft came out, some companies in the USA had published their protocols in the hope that this would be the way forward.

### 3.12.5  The Public Works of Canada Protocol

The Public Works of Canada (PWC) is claimed to be the largest landlord in the world [9]. It has developed a protocol for standardizing the man–machine interface – i.e. what comes up on the screen of the central station or display of the outstation. This would greatly help staff training and would enable greater staff redeployment. The main feature of the PWC proposal is the Standard Operator Interface Console (SOIC). The PWC do not specify the communications system a manufacturer must use, provided that the BEMS can be interfaced to a PWC LAN or WAN (Wide Area Network).

### 3.12.6  EIBUS

Although communications between BEMSs and outstations has been considered above, communications systems between smaller devices, such as lights, light switches, security contacts, etc., are rapidly being developed. These are small, cheap buses using twisted-pair cabling, with custom made chips connecting the small devices to the bus. The buses could well be used in small buildings where a conventional BEMS would be too costly.

Such a bus is the European Installation Bus (EIB or EIBUS), originally developed by Siemans of Germany but now Pan-European. It is a simple, twisted-pair cable carrying both signals and power (a nominal 28 V d.c.) to the connected devices. It would appear that up to 800 devices could be connected to the system but this is unlikely as it is intended for small sites. It could well be that the bus is connected in to a larger system using PROFIBUS. Although the EIBUS will implement all the 'key' layers of the OSI 7-layer model, they will not all be externally accessible [13]. This is due to the difficulties of implementing the full model on a small controller. Devices should be on the market by 1992 [17] with an EIB trademark. Siemens are manufacturing EIBUS chips.

### 3.12.7  BATIBUS

BATIBUS is another small system bus similar to EIBUS, and like the latter, it was developed by a company making electrical switchgear and control equipment for electrical panels. BATIBUS is French-based and has been developed by Merlin Gerin, a large switchgear and electrical components manufacturer. Although it originated from work on a bus for communication between electrical components, it was then extended to a bus for building control. *Bâtiment* is the French for 'building', hence BATIBUS.

Merlin Gerin say that the concept is that BATIBUS should be easy to install by general electrical contractors, multifunctional, able to control heating, lighting, intruder and fire detectors, and easily configured by building users [14]. It has been designed to be economic for buildings up to 10 000 m$^2$. The BATIBUS cable is a single twisted pair which can be laid in a bus, star or ring topology [15]. Figure 3.20 shows a system with a combination of these topologies.

Communication between devices on the bus is operated under CSMA/CA (carrier sense multiple access with collision avoidance) control. Up to 1000

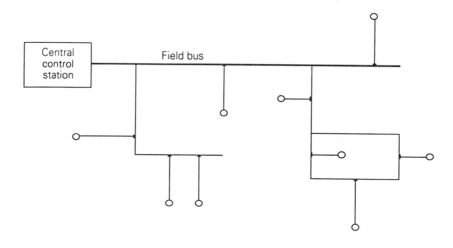

O Intelligent sensors and actuators

**Fig. 3.20**   The BATIBUS system.

devices can be connected to the bus, with up to 75 powered directly from the bus, at 15 V d.c. Adjustment of two code wheels on each device gives 240 different settings of the microprocessor circuits to give devices unique addresses. If there are more than 240 devices on the bus, then similar devices would presumably have to share an address. Although up to 1000 devices may be connected to the bus, with a twisted-pair cable using wires of 0.75 mm² diameter the maximum length of cable is 1500 m and the maximum distance between the central control station and the furthest device is 200 m.

How compatible BATIBUS is to the OSI 7-layer model is unclear, but the system is fully open to members of the BATIBUS Club, formed in 1989. In 1990 there were over 70 manufacturers in the Club [14]. Approved products have the BATIBUS trademark, and Intel and NEC are manufacturing BATIBUS chips.

South Link Business Park, in Oldham, Lancashire, has ten office blocks with the BATIBUS system controlling the electric heating. The blocks and their heating systems are designed to the guidelines of the Electricity Association's Energy Efficient Design (EED). One office block is split into two BATIBUS networks, each with its own central control unit and two output modules to switch the heater contactors.

### 3.12.8  Intelligent Room Bus

Honeywell in Germany has been involved with FND and PROFIBUS, but this has not stopped it from developing its own small bus sytem, which like similar systems is not OSI compatible. The small bus developed is the Intelligent Room Bus, or R-Bus. It uses a three-wire 1.5 mm$^2$ unshielded cable providing 24 V d.c. and signals to and from actuators; the maximum cable run is 200 m. Typical modules that can be connected to the bus are given in Table 3.5.

**Table 3.5**  Modules that can be connected to the R-Bus

| |
| --- |
| Room temperature controller |
| Local set point |
| Control output |
| Analogue output |
| Unit control |
| Local command |
| Variable air volume |

The system uses a current loop bus limited to 3.5 mA current with a data transfer rate of 1200 bps [16]. Up to 16 modules can be connected to an R-Bus, controlled by a **multicontroller module**, which contains the application software. The multicontroller has interfaces to control two buses.

### 3.12.9  Summary

Although work is progressing on standardization, many standards are being developed. If the BEMS industry resembles the process control industry, which went down this 'bus' route about five years earlier, then there will probably evolve a small number of tried and tested commercial standard buses.

However, for large buildings many buses of varying sizes will be required to service all the intelligent devices, and a **backbone bus** will be necessary to connect them. These will be controlled by the PC-type central station, rather than the bus controller, and for these central stations there will be communication links governed by another communication standard, or standards, such as FND or ASHRAE.

## References

[1]  Colantonio, E. S. (1989) *Microcomputers and Applications*, D.C. Heath, Lexington, Mass.

[2]  Money, S. A. (1987) *Practical Microprocessor Interfacing*, Collins, London.

[3]  Sayer, M. *RS-232 Made Easy*, Prentice-Hall, Englewood Cliffs, NJ.

[4]  Jesty, P. H. (1985) *Networking with Microcomputers*, Blackwell, Oxford.

[5]  James, M. (1989) *Low-cost PC Networking*, Heinemann, London.

[6]   Clare, C. P. (1984) *A Guide to Data Communications*, Castle House

[7]   Deasington, R. J. (1982) *A Practical Guide to Computer Communications and Networking*, Wiley, New York.

[8]   Williams, T. J. (1984) *The Use of Digital Computers in Process Control*, Instrument Society of America, NC.

[9]   BEMS Centre, BSRIA (1989) The development of an application level communications standard for building management systems, BSRIA, Bracknell.

[10]  Zimmerman, H. (1980) OSI Reference Model – the OSI model of architecture for open systems interconnection, *IEEE Transactions on Communications*, COM-28(4).

[11]  Houldsworth, J. (1990) *OSI Handbook*. International Computers Ltd, London.

[12]  Fischer, P. (1990) FND and PROFIBUS. Standard communications in building automation systems Communications Standards for BEMS, BEMS Centre Colloquium, Birmingham.

[13]  Colebrook, P. (1990) EIBUS. Communications Standards for BEMS, BEMS Centre Colloquium, Birmingham.

[14]  Joseph, D. (1990) BATIBUS Communications Standards for BEMS, BEMS Centre Colloquium, Birmingham.

[15]  Joseph, D. (1990) Catching the right bus. *Electrical Design*, October.

[16]  Fischer, P. (1990) Intelligent Room BUS. Communications Standards for BEMS, BEMS Centre Colloquium, Birmingham.

[17]  Dymott, J. (1990) Don't miss the bus. *Building Services* (CIBSE), **12**, December.

[18]  Pimentel, J. R. (1989) Communications architectures for fieldbus networks. *Control Engineering*, October.

[19]  Bushby, S. T. and Newman, H. M. (1991) The BACnet communication protocol for building automation systems. *ASHRAE Journal* (Atlanta), April.

[20]  Wilkins, J. and Wills, S. (1990) What are smart sensors? *Building Services* (CIBSE), **12**, December.

[21]  da Silva, E. (1986) *Introduction to Data Communications and LAN Technology*, Collins, London.

# 4
# Sensors and their responses

As has been seen in earlier chapters, a BEMS outstation is basically a microprocessor processing digital electrical signals. But most plant equipment controlled by a BEMS is controlled on temperature, pressure or flow, rarely on electrical signals. So these non-electrical parameters must be measured and converted to electrical signals, invariably a voltage. This measurement and conversion is the function of the **sensor**, **transmitter** and **transducer**. The sensor responds to the change in the measured parameter (e.g. the temperature), the transducer changes the sensor signal to an electrical signal (e.g. a pressure into a voltage) and the transmitter is the electronic circuitry to enable a suitable strength voltage proportional to the sensed parameter to be sent to the outstation. Often the sensor transmitter and transducer are integral in a measuring device and it is difficult to separate them, so that sensors are commonly referred to as 'transducers'.

Many of the details of measuring devices relate to their electronic circuitry and the use of operational amplifiers. Such aspects are not dealt with here, but references [1]–[4] will provide further details.

## 4.1 Binary and pulse inputs

Although detailed devices are required for an outstation to measure, say, temperature, some inputs to the outstation are just open or closed, high or low or on/off signals, (i.e. binary signals) which do not need A/D converters, but may need to be conditioned to the appropriate voltage level for the outstation and, in the case of pulses, need to be of sufficient duration for the outstation to detect them during the sequence cycle time.

One form of binary input is from a **status sensor** which is usually an electrical relay or switch that is open or closed. Status sensors can monitor, for instance, whether boiler burners are operating or electric motors are running. Although energized by the burner or motor to its relevant state, the sensor must have volt-free contacts, so that no large voltages and currents are connected to the outstation. This is done either by using volt-free auxiliary contacts on the appliance or by using a relay energized by the appliance, as explained in Chapter 2.

A second form of binary input is from a **pulse sensor** or **event counter** which sends a pulse to the outstation each time an event occurs. A common event that is sensed is the rotation of a utility's energy meter, so that the BEMS can count the rotations and hence monitor energy use. The utilities now provide meters which are serially interfaceable to BEMSs, which produce pulsed output as the meter moves. Event counting is also useful for **condition-based maintenance** by monitoring the number of times that plant and equipment is switched on and used. (This is discussed further in Chapter 10 on monitoring and targeting.)

## 4.2  Temperature sensors

By far the most used sensor for a BEMS is the temperature sensor. There are a number of different types, as detailed below, with different cost and accuracy implications. Fielden and Ede [5] point out that sensors are likely to provide the greatest source of failure and maintenance problems in a BEMS.

### 4.2.1  Platinum resistance thermometer

Platinum resistance thermometers are the more expensive and accurate temperature sensors used in BEMSs. They rely on the fact that platinum, like other metals, increases its resistance as it gets hotter; the relationship is of the form:

$$R_t = R_0(1 + \alpha t + \beta t^2 + \Gamma t^3)\qquad(4.1)$$

where   $R_t$ = metal resistance at temperature $t°C$ ($\Omega$);
   $R_0$ = metal resistance at 0°C ($\Omega$);
   $t$ = temperature (°C);
   $\alpha$ = temperature coefficient ($K^{-1}$).

$\beta$ and $\Gamma$ are constants which are very small and usually neglected, so that equation (4.1) becomes:

$$R_t = R_0(1 + \alpha t)\qquad(4.2)$$

Table 4.1 shows the values of $\alpha$ for some common metals.

**Table 4.1**  Values of $\alpha$ for some common metals

| Metal | $\alpha \times 10^3$ (K$^{-1}$) |
|---|---|
| Nickel | 6.7 |
| Iron | 4 |
| Copper | 4.3 |
| Platinum | 3.91 |
| Silver | 4.1 |

Due to its highly linear, repeatable relationship of resistance against temperature over a wide temperature range and its chemical inertness, platinum is the most widely used metal for resistance thermometers. The metal in the form of a wire is traditionally wound on a mandril and the resistance determined by passing a constant current through it and measuring the voltage across it. Due to the purity of platinum that can be achieved, there is a low statistical variation in the resistance between similar samples, and there is a British Standard for platinum resistance thermometers (PRTs): BS 1904. A typical platinum element has [1]:

$$R_0 = 100.0 \, \Omega$$

resistance at 100°C, $R_{100} = 138.5 \, \Omega$
resistance at 200°C, $R_{200} = 175.83 \, \Omega$

$$\alpha = 3.91 \times 10^{-3} \, \text{K}^{-1}$$

$$\beta = -5.85 \times 10^{-7} \, \text{K}^{-2}$$

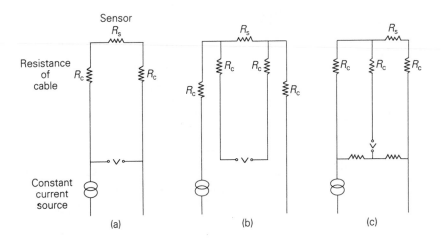

**Fig. 4.1**  Voltage measurement across a sensor using (a) 2-wire, (b) 4-wire and (c) 3-wire cable.

A Wheatstone bridge circuit is often used to determine the sensor's resistance to great accuracy [7], [4].

To avoid voltage drops through the two wires connecting the sensor to the outstation four wires are used, as shown in Fig. 4.1. Since four wires are rather expensive, a compromise of three wires, as shown in the figure, is sometimes employed.

Tolerances of $\pm 0.075\,\Omega$ at 0°C are specified in BS 1904 for Class 1 elements and $\pm 0.1\,\Omega$ for Class 2. Bentley [1] states that in a typical element 10 mW of electrical power dissipated in the element as $I^2R$ heating causes a temperature rise of 0.3°C.

Modern BEMS platinum resistance thermometers (PRTs) use platinum films on a substrate about 1 mm². The thin film of platinum is accurately trimmed by laser. Often-used PRTs are standard PT100 PRTs, which conform to the BS 1904 Class B standard. A chip sensor [6], which actually uses a nickel iron alloy film, 10 μm thick, to avoid the expense of platinum is shown in Fig. 4.2, which still provides moreover a linear and stable sensor. The sensing element is the laser-trimmed square spiral on the silicon substrate, with a resistor network around it.

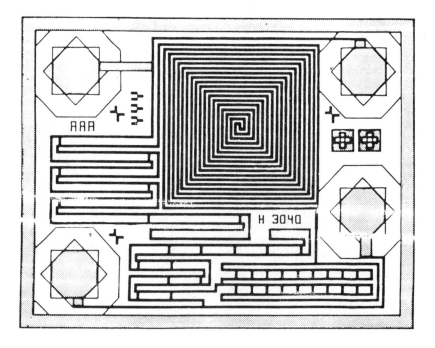

**Fig. 4.2** Layout of 1.0 × 1.3 mm² laser-trimmed chip with photochemically etched resistor network; 10 μm thick square spiral constitutes sensing element.

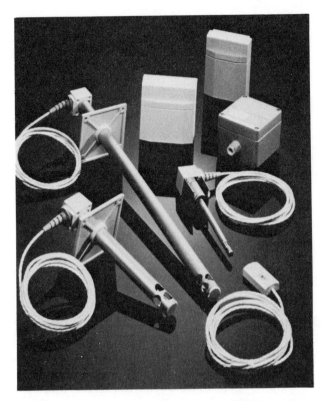

**Fig. 4.3**  Sensors.

The sensor chip, as with other types of sensor elements, is installed in a suitable plastic case for internal and external air temperature measurement and in a probe for ducted air and piped water measurement, as shown in Fig. 4.3.

The duct sensor element (Fig. 4.3) consists of a platinum element sensor positioned at the end of the probe, with four wires connecting it to the transmitter in the box at the probe end. The transmitter is an electronic circuit supplied with 24 V d.c. from the outstation which amplifies and conditions the sensor signal for sending to the outstation, which could be quite distant from the sensor element. The signal from the transmitter is sent along a two-wire cable, as a signal current of 4–20 mA. The current is proportional to the temperature sensed, with an offset of 4 mA.

### 4.2.2  Thermistors

A cheaper sensing element is the **thermistor**, a ceramic material made by sintering mixtures of metal oxides into whatever shape is required: bead, disc or rod. The size can be quite small, which gives it a distinct advantage. Copper

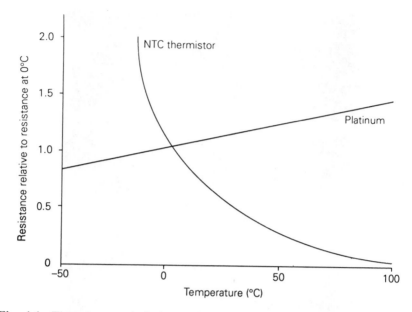

**Fig. 4.4**   Thermistor and platinum sensor resistance changes.

leads are connected to the thermistor element, encapsulated in a vitreous material.

Thermistors are a form of semiconductor and their resistance depends on their composition. A minority have positive temperature coefficients (PTCs), where resistance increases with increasing temperature. The majority have negative temperature coefficients (NTCs), their resistance falling with increasing temperature. Although the change in resistance with temperature is larger than that for platinum, the resistance changes non-linearly with temperature, as is shown in Fig. 4.4.

The relationship between resistance and temperature for a NTC thermistor is given by:

$$R_t = R_\infty \exp(\beta/T) \qquad (4.3)$$

where $R_t$ = thermistor resistance at temperature t°C (Ω);
   $R_\infty$ = resistance that thermistor tends to at high temperatures (Ω);
   $\beta$ = thermistor material constant (K);
   $T$ = absolute temperature (K).

A more practical and commonly used alternative to equation (4.3) is:

$$R_t = R_{25} \exp \beta \, [1/t - 1/25] \qquad (4.4)$$

where the resistance at 25°C is taken as the reference point. A typical thermistor has an $R_{25}$ of 12 kΩ with β 3750 K. The tolerance on such a thermistor is

± 7% of $R_{25}$ and I²R heating of 7 mW raises the read temperature by 1°C, so thermistors cannot be expected to be as accurate as PRTs. In fact the **field accuracy** of one BEMS manufacturer's thermistor is ± 1°C, whereas the thermistor element itself has an accuracy of ± 0.2 °C.

### 4.2.3 Semiconductor circuit sensors

Silicon semiconductor diodes and transistors are sensitive to temperature changes and the junction voltage of these devices changes by about 2.2 mV per degK over a temperature range − 55°C to 150°C. These can be made up into integrated circuit devices, which are effectively current sources which produce a current proportional to temperature, and very linear. The temperature sensitivity of 1 µA/K is amplified by an operational amplifier circuit in the transmitter to a level suitable for the 4–20 mA standard signal. A resistor in the transmitter circuit can be adjusted to vary the temperature range. Figure 4.5 shows the output from the transmitter of a BEMS semiconductor sensor.

The current signal to the BEMS from the sensor can be converted to a voltage signal for processing in the BEMS by simply putting an accurate resistor in series with the semiconductor sensor (Fig. 4.6).

It is interesting to note that semiconductor circuits in parallel yield the average sensed temperature, and when in series the minimum sensed temperature. Most BEMS manufacturers who use semiconductor sensors, however,

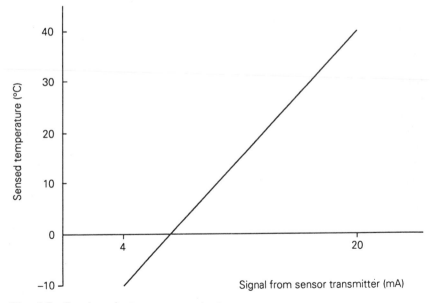

**Fig. 4.5** Semiconductor sensor output.

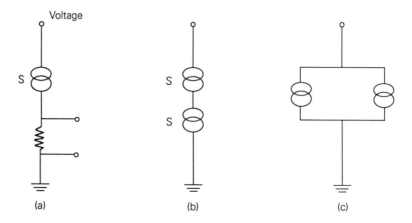

**Fig. 4.6** Semiconductor sensor, S, to give (a) a voltage, (b) a minimum sensed temperature and (c) the average sensed temperature.

would not complicate their sensor range with series and parallel sensors, but would use separate sensors and calculate the average, minimum or maximum by using outstation logic function modules.

## 4.3  Setting up sensors

When a sensor is measuring a temperature, its transmitter is sending a signal, proportional to the sensed temperature, to the BEMS outstation. The outstation needs to know what range of temperature the sensor is measuring; is it a room temperature range of, for example, 0°C–40°C, or a hot-water temperature range of, for example, 0°C–100°C, etc.? Often different sensors are used with different ranges – e.g. immersion sensors for water pipes, duct sensors, inside air temperature sensors, outside air temperature sensors and surface contact clamp-on sensors, as shown in Fig. 4.3.

In the EPROM of the outstation, discussed in Chapter 2, there is a **sensor module**, and a sensor-type module, that read the signals from the sensor. First, the signal (for this outstation 4–20 mA) is converted to a voltage of 1–5 V by a **signal conditioning circuit** and it is then converted to a digital signal by an A/D converter. All this is done in the input unit by the **analogue input interface**.

Initially, the outstation has to be **configured** as to the type of sensor connected to a particular input and its corresponding analogue node, say, node 1 for sensor 1 at input 1, node 2 for sensor 2 at input 2, etc., and the relevant alarm levels set. This is done through the sensor module.

The **sensor-type module** converts the standard digital signal, from the sensor module, to the relevant engineering units, for a temperature sensor (°C).

A number of different sensor types can be set up in the outstation RAM to accommodate different sensors, room, duct, water, etc. But once a room temperature sensor type has been set up, for example, then it defines the temperatures from the corresponding conditioned voltages for a standard room temperature sensor.

To set up the outstation modules in RAM one has to get into the **configuration mode** of the outstation. This is not a routine operation for a site caretaker or boilerman, so entry to the configuration mode will be password-protected at a high security level. Entry, for most outstations, will be via the central station or a local portable PC. Figure 4.7 shows the kind of information that has to be entered in to the central station to set up the sensor-type module in the outstation's RAM.

The capital letters in Fig. 4.7 indicate the key to type on the central station keyboard to enter the relevant value – e.g. T is for the top of the sensor temperature range corresponding to 20 mA (or 5 V), and B is for the bottom of the sensor temperature range, corresponding to – 5 and – 20 mA. The upper and lower limits to the working range set limits to the signal to be expected, normally the temperatures corresponding to 4 mA and 20 mA. Outside these limits, an **out-of-limits** alarm is raised, indicating that the sensor may be malfunctioning.

*Example*
For an outside air temperature sensor $B = -151°C (-5 V)$, and $T = +51°C$ $(+5 V)$. What typically are the signals sent back to the outstation from the sensor, and what is the corresponding range of temperature (U and L)?

*Solution*
Knowing that the signal from the sensor will most likely be 4–20 mA, then it is better to consider currents than voltages. So – 5 V corresponds to – 20 mA and + 5 V to + 20 mA. Assuming that the sensor is linear, then $B$ and $T$ are two points on a straight-line graph:

$$y = mx + c \qquad (4.5)$$

where $y$ = the temperature axis (°C);
$\quad x$ = the current signal axis (mA);
$\quad m$ = the slope (°C mA$^{-1}$);
$\quad c$ = the intercept (°C).

Bottom of range =
Top of range =
sensor Upper limit to working range =
sensor Lower limit to working range =

**Fig. 4.7** Information of sensor-type module.

Substituting in the two values gives:

$$-151 = -20\,m + c \tag{4.6}$$

$$51 = 20\,m + c \tag{4.7}$$

from equations (4.6) and (4.7) the following is derived:

$$y = 5.05x - 50 \tag{4.8}$$

The sensor's transmitter sends a signal between 4 and 20 mA, so using equation (4.8):

$$L = -29.8$$

$$\approx -30°C$$

and $\qquad\qquad U = 51°C$

To configure the outstation input for this sensor one would type the responses:

$$? \; B \; -151$$
$$? \; T \; 51$$
$$? \; U \; 51$$
$$? \; L \; -29.8$$

The example data, above, defines the outside air temperature type of sensor and stores it in the outstation RAM. This type of sensor we can define as Y1, using the capital notation, and the sensor type module has been set up for Y1-type sensor.

Still in the configuration mode the sensor module is then selected to set the relevant outstation input channel, say, the third input channel, as the input for the outside air temperature sensor, consequently defined as S3. Typing in the relevant commands to the central station allows the outside air temperature sensor S3 to be set up.

S3 will be configured as a type Y1 sensor, as defined in the sensor-type module set up above, but also the desired high and low sensor alarms can be set, the sensor labelled, e.g. 'outside air temp.', and a **sensor alarm delay** of a few minutes set to ensure that the sensor alarms will not operate unless it is a genuine alarm, not just a fluke, transient reading from a sensor, perhaps due to interference. Sensor alarms should not be too tight otherwise alarms may inundate the central station. On one user's BEMS, which had no alarm delay software, alarms were reported via a modem to the maintenance depot printer and men sent out to rectify the problems. Often just as someone had been dispatched the printer would report that the alarm was no longer present, it had been of short duration!

Once the sensor type and sensor modules have been set up, the outstation has all the information it needs to define the sensor and calibrate the mA signals to temperatures for control and logging.

## 4.3.1 Non-linear sensors

The sensor type considered above was a linear sensor, where the voltage and temperature were related by a simple, straight-line equation. Unfortunately a commonly used sensor is the thermistor, a non-linear device. When the thermistor's output is converted to a digital voltage for the outstation CPU to process, due to the thermistor's non-linear characteristic, the digital voltage will also be non-linear.

There are two methods of tackling this problem, either linearize the thermistor over a small temperature range by placing an accurate resistor in series or parallel with the thermistor or use a **look-up table** of temperatures corresponding to voltage signals. With the former method a standard sensor type module can be used, but for the latter method the look-up table replaces this module.

*Example*
It is proposed to use a thermistor for an air temperature sensor, for both internal and external use. Compare the two methods for using this for a BEMS outstation, employing another resistor and using a look-up table. The data on the thermistor resistance is given below:

| Temperature (°C) | Resistance (Ω) |
|---|---|
| − 10 | 55 340 |
| 0 | 32 660 |
| 10 | 19 990 |
| 20 | 12 490 |
| 25 | 10 000 |
| 30 | 8 058 |
| 40 | 5 326 |

*Solution*
The first method is to put a resistor in series or parallel with the thermistor. Looking at the temperature range, at 25°C the resistance of the thermistor is 10 000 Ω. It would be quite easy to obtain an accurate resistor of this value and it would make the calculations easy if the thermistor were linearized around this temperature. With a 10 000 Ω resistor in series with the thermistor, then the voltage across it is:

$$V_{meas} = V_{supp} \frac{R}{R + R_{th}}$$

where $R$ = constant resistance (Ω);
  $V_{meas}$ = measured voltage signal across R (V);
    $R_{th}$ = thermistor resistance (Ω);
  $V_{supp}$ = voltage supply to the sensor (V).

The term $R/(R + R_{th})$ is much more linear than $R_{th}$ itself as is shown in Table 4.2 and Fig. 4.8. This has normalized $R_{th}$ around the $R_{25}$ value (10 000 $\Omega$), at a value of 0.5 to compare with the combined term.

**Table 4.2**   Resistance ratios

| Temperature (°C) | $\dfrac{R}{R + R_{th}}$ | $0.5 \times \dfrac{R_{25}}{R_{th}}$ |
|---|---|---|
| − 10 | 0.15 | 0.09 |
| 0 | 0.23 | 0.15 |
| 10 | 0.33 | 0.25 |
| 20 | 0.44 | 0.4 |
| 25 | 0.50 | 0.50 |
| 30 | 0.55 | 0.62 |
| 40 | 0.65 | 0.94 |

If a 10 000 $\Omega$ resistor is placed in parallel with the thermistor, then when a voltage is applied the current can be measured (or the voltage across another resistor in series). The current signal from the parallel resistors is:

$$I_{meas} = V_{supp} \frac{R + R_{th}}{R\,R_{th}}$$

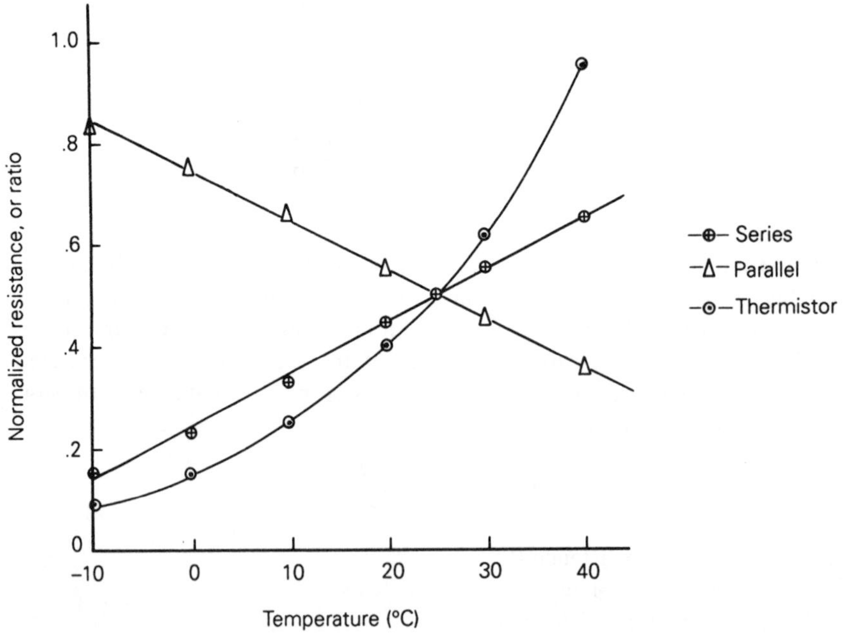

**Fig. 4.8**   Resistance ratios.

Again, the resistance ratio produces a reasonably linear relationship, as the normalized values in Fig. 4.8 show.

The second method, the look-up table, could be done by applying a constant current source to the thermistor and measuring the voltage across the thermistor. There would then be a direct non-linear relationship between temperature and voltage. A look-up table could then be calculated and put in the EPROM. But rather than have a table of every possible voltage and temperature, a more compact way is to approximate the non-linear relationship to a number of straight lines. Five straight lines, each spanning 10 K, from − 10°C to 40°C would be satisfactory. Then intermediate voltages can be converted into temperatures by a sensor type module, as used for linear sensors.

Reference [8] examines interfacing a thermistor to a microcomputer, and determines a look-up table, as well as the A/D, the program for conversion and the display of a temperature.

## 4.4  Block diagrams of the sensor

This configuration process can be seen in terms of the block diagram, much used in control theory and textbooks. The sensor and transmitter can be represented by the block diagram shown in Fig. 4.9.

The semiconductor sensor changes its current flow in relation to the temperature change it senses. The temperature current relationship is described by the **static gain**, $K_s$, which is the slope of the temperature current line shown in Fig. 4.10 and the intercept $c_s$:

$$I = K_s t + c_s \tag{4.9}$$

where  $I$ = sensor current (μA);
$\quad K_s$ = slope or $dI/dt$ (μA $K^{-1}$);
$\quad t$ = temperature (°C);
$\quad c_s$ = intercept (μA).

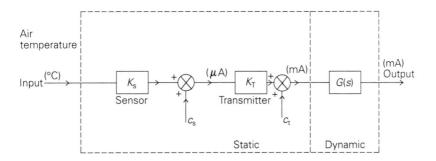

**Fig. 4.9**  Block diagram of sensor and transmitter.

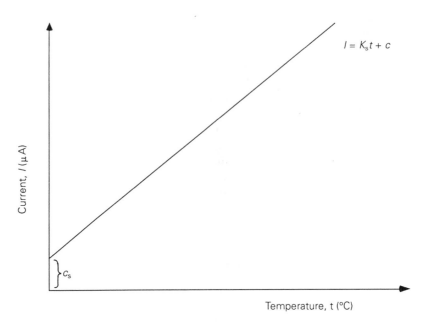

$$I = K_s t + c$$

Current, $I$/($\mu$A)

$c_s$

Temperature, t (°C)

**Fig. 4.10**  The static gain of a sensor.

The circular symbol with the cross inside is used in block diagrams to represent addition, (+) or subtraction (−). The static gain is that gain when the current and temperature are not varying with time (time does not appear in the temperature current equation) and the sensor is in equilibrium. The term **steady state gain** is sometimes used instead of 'static gain'. The **dynamic** or time-dependent characteristic of the sensor and transmitter is represented by the $G$ [$G(s)$] block, where $s$ is a complex variable:

$$s = \sigma + jw$$

where  $j = \sqrt{(-1)}$;
  $\sigma$ = real part of $s$;
  $w$ = imaginary part of $s$.

This dynamic block, and the operator $s$, are discussed in more detail in Chapter 5, and Section 5.5 on Laplace transforms. It is worth noting that sensors can be non-linear (like the thermistor), and also suffer from hysteris and age [1] which makes the sensor relationship and block diagram of Fig. 4.9 more complicated.

If the sensor has a negligible value of $c_s$, then the sensor and transmitter blocks can be combined, as shown in Fig. 4.11. The configuration is simply the process of defining the static gains, $K_s K_t$, and the intercept, $c_t$, of the sensor–transmitter combination. This is done by inputting two prescribed

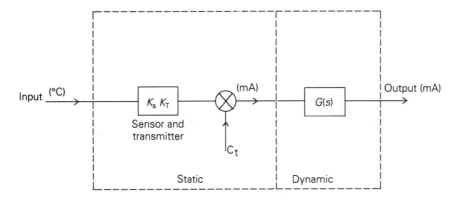

**Fig. 4.11**   Sensor and transmitter combined.

points of the linear relationship into the outstation. It also shows the elementary beginnings of manipulating block diagrams to simplify control analysis.

## 4.5   Interference

Interference is defined as the picking up of a **deterministic signal**, such as a sinusoidal signal at 50 Hz from a power cable, affecting the required transmitted signal. There are also **random signals** due to random motions in electronic devices, and these are referred to as **noise**.

The greatest problem for BEMSs is external interference and noise, often from other plant in the plant room. Nearby a.c. power circuits operating at 240 V, or 415 V, 50 Hz, can produce sinusoidal interference signals referred to as mains **pick-up** or **hum**. d.c. Circuits are less likely to produce interference, but when these or a.c. circuits are switched, then transient noise can be produced. Lighting from fluorescent and other discharge lamps is another common cause of interference, with the arc of the lamp occurring twice per cycle. However, lamp interference occurs only with malfunctioning of the luminaire or poor design.

Interference is picked up by the BEMS equipment by **inductive coupling, capacitive coupling** or **multiple earths**, or combinations of these three [1]. The first two refer to the interferring circuit and the BEMS circuit having a mutual inductance or a mutual capacitance. Multiple earthing arises from connected pieces of equipment being separately earthed and the local earth not being at zero potential. This is often due to large electrical equipment upsetting the potential locally.

As mutual inductance and capacitive coupling are inversely proportional to the distance between the circuits, then it is sensible to keep the BEMS and its sensors and cabling as far away from interfering equipment as possible.

But this is not always practicable, especially for sensor cables which are often quite long. Here the inductive coupling can be reduced by twisting the sensor cables in pairs to produce the required number of wires in the cable as **twisted pairs**.

To avoid capacitive coupling the BEMS equipment can be contained in an earthed metal screen or shield. Ideally the equipment should be insulated from the screen. This is not so much of a problem for the outstation in its electrical cabinet, but it is not so easy for the sensor and its cable. The latter can be screened by having a light metal lattice around the twisted pairs, just under the plastic sheath, similar to that on coaxial cable.

In general, BEMSs manufacturers take additional precautions against interference as such small signals are used by the microprocessor which can easily be contaminated by interference. Such measures can be the use of op amps as differential amplifiers for signals to reject a lot of the interference. The **common mode rejection ratio** (CMMR) is a measure of an amplifier's performance, the CMMR being as high as possible, a typical value being $10^5$ or 100 dB.

Another subtle ploy is to use an integrating A/D which integrates over 20 ms, the period of the 50 Hz mains cycle. Being a sine wave, the positive part of the interference signal cancels out the negative half-cycle during integration. Filtering and averaging of sensor readings are other methods to obtain better signals.

## 4.6  Sensor dynamic response

We have considered the static gain of the sensor, above, but the sensor also has a dynamic response, represented in Fig. 4.9 by the G-block. This dynamic response comes from the sensor having its own thermal mass which takes time to heat up and cool down as the air or water whose temperature is being measured changes. This is described by the following equation:

$$\begin{array}{l}\text{Rate of change of}\\\text{heat into sensor}\end{array} - \begin{array}{l}\text{Rate of change of heat}\\\text{out of sensor}\end{array} = \begin{array}{l}\text{Rate of change of}\\\text{heat stored in sensor}\end{array} \quad (4.10)$$

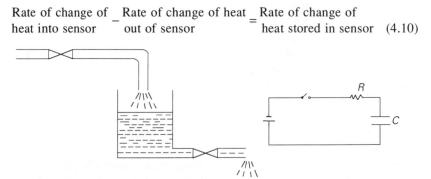

**Fig. 4.12**  Water and electrical analogies.

A useful way of understanding equation (4.10) is to consider a couple of analogies: a cylinder with a hole in it (or more exactly an open pipe and valve in the bottom), and an electrical resistor capacitor circuit with a battery and switch, as shown in Fig. 4.12.

Table 4.3 shows the analagous quantities.

**Table 4.3**   Electrical, thermal and liquid analogies

| quantity | electrical charge (C) | thermal heat (J) | liquid volume (m$^3$) |
|---|---|---|---|
| potential | voltage (V) | temperature (°C) | height (m) |
| flow | current (A) | Watt (W) | (m$^3$ s$^{-1}$) |
| | (charge per second) | (Joule per second) | |
| resistance | ($\Omega$) | (KW$^{-1}$) | (s m$^{-2}$) |
| $\left(\dfrac{\text{potential}}{\text{flow}}\right)$ | | | |
| capacity | (F) | (JK$^{-1}$) | (m$^2$) |
| $\left(\dfrac{\text{quantity}}{\text{potential}}\right)$ | | | |

From the table it can be seen that the previous equation can be rewritten as:

Heat flow into sensor − heat flow out of sensor
= rate of change of heat stored in sensor                    (4.10)

which is analogous to the flow of water in the cylinder and charge in the capacitor. It is interesting to note that temperature is analogous to voltage for electricity and to height for water. Temperature is the driving potential for heat transfer.

The best way of examining the response of a sensor is suddenly to change the temperature of the fluid it has been measuring for some time and with which it is in equilibrium. One could effect the same response by plunging a BEMS water temperature sensor into a tank of hot water from a tank of cold water. This instantaneous step change in the water temperature causes the sensor temperature to change, but as the sensor takes time to heat up or cool down it does not instantaneously achieve the new water temperature. Figure 4.13 shows this for a sudden increase in the fluid temperature.

When the sensor is suddenly plunged into a hotter fluid, then it will gain heat and there will be no heat loss term. It is assumed that the sensor takes a negligibly small amount of heat from the bulk of the fluid, so that the fluid's temperature is unaltered. So equation (4.10) becomes:

$$h_s A(t_{\text{fluid}} - t_s) = MC_p \frac{dt_s}{dT} \qquad (4.11)$$

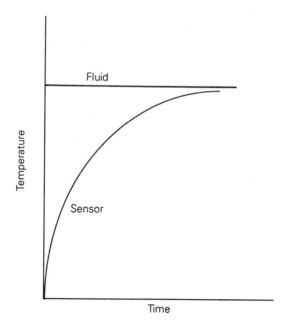

**Fig. 4.13**   Sensor heating up.

where   $M$ = mass of the sensor (kg);
$\quad C_p$ = specific heat capacity of sensor (J kg$^{-1}$ K$^{-1}$);
$\quad t_s$ = sensor temperature at time $T$ (°C);
$\quad t_{so}$ = sensor temperature at time $T = 0$ s (°C);
$\quad t_{fluid}$ = fluid temperature (°C);
$\quad T$ = time (s);
$\quad h_s$ = heat transfer coefficient to sensor (W m$^{-2}$ K$^{-1}$);
$\quad A$ = area of sensor (m$^2$).
Rearranging equation (4.1) to solve it yields:

$$\frac{dT}{\tau} = \frac{dt_s}{(t_{fluid} - t_s)} \tag{4.12}$$

where $\tau$ = sensor time constant (s), given by:

$$\tau = \frac{MC_p}{h_s A} \tag{4.13}$$

The $\tau$ equation, above, can be verified by dimensional analysis:

$$\left[\frac{MC_p}{h_s A}\right] = \left[kg \, \frac{J}{kg \, K} \, \frac{m^2 K}{W} \, \frac{1}{m^2}\right] = \left[s\right]$$

The larger the mass of the sensor, the larger the time constant and the slower the response. The sensor casing also adds to the mass, as does a sensor pocket or well, as is shown in Table 4.3 for a thermistor.

Integrating equation (4.12):

$$\int_0^T \frac{T}{\tau} = \int_{t_{s \text{ initial}}}^{t_s} \frac{dt_s}{(t_{\text{fluid}} - t_s)} \tag{4.14}$$

where it is assumed that the step change in fluid temperature has occurred at time $T = 0$ s after which the fluid temperature immediately becomes $t_{\text{fluid}}$ and the sensor temperature rises from its original value of $t_{s \text{ initial}}$ at time $T = 0$ s to $t_s$ at time $T$ s; equation (4.12) becomes:

$$T = \tau \ \{ -\ln(t_{\text{fluid}} - t_s) - [-\ln(t_{\text{fluid}} - t_{s \text{ initial}})] \}$$

Note that the minus sign is due to the $-t_s$ in the denominator of the integral. Rearranging the equation gives:

$$T = -\tau \ \ln\left[ \frac{(t_{\text{fluid}} - t_s)}{(t_{\text{fluid}} - t_{s \text{ initial}})} \right] \tag{4.15}$$

Another common form of this is:

$$\frac{(t_{\text{fluid}} - t_s)}{(t_{\text{fluid}} - t_{s \text{ initial}})} = \exp(-T/\tau) \tag{4.16}$$

*Example*
A hot-water temperature sensor in a pipe has an initial temperature of 10°C. A valve then opens up and allows water through the pipe from the boiler at 80°C. What is the sensor temperature 1 min later? The sensor time constant, $\tau$, is also 1 min.

*Solution*
The sensor temperature, $t_s$, is obtained explicitly from equation (4.16) as:

$$t_s = t_{\text{fluid}} - \exp(-T/\tau) \ \{ t_{\text{fluid}} - t_{s \text{ initial}} \}$$

subtracting $t_{s \text{ initial}}$ from both sides simplifies it to:

$$t_s - t_{s \text{ initial}} = \{ t_{\text{fluid}} - t_{s \text{ initial}} \} \ [1 - \exp(-T/\tau)] \tag{4.17}$$

Here $t_{s \text{ initial}} = 10\,°C$;
$\qquad t_{\text{fluid}} = 80\,°C$;
$\qquad\quad T = \tau = 60$ s.
So that:

$$t_s - 10 = \{ 80 - 10 \} \ [1 - \exp(-1)]$$

$$t_s = 10 + 70[1 - 0.368]$$

$$t_s = 54.2\,°C$$

### 4.6.1   Time constants

The above example shows that it takes some time for the sensor temperature to rise, the time constant of the sensor being the determinant factor. This was defined by the sensor parameters in equation (4.13) but it can also be measured as the time for the sensor temperature to rise to 63.2% of its full temperature rise. Equation (4.17) can be used to demonstrate it. When $T = \tau$, equation (4.17) is:

$$t_s - t_{s\ initial} = \{t_{fluid} - t_{s\ initial}\}\ [1 - \exp(-1)]$$

$$= \{t_{fluid} - t_{s\ initial}\}\ [0.632]$$

The rise in $t_s$ from its initial value, $t_{s\ initial}$, is 63.2% of the temperature difference between the fluid temperature, $t_{fluid}$ (the temperature the sensor is approaching) and the initial sensor temperature, $t_{s\ initial}$.

Typical time constants for various sensors are shown in Table 4.3, which has been taken from reference [9]. The velocity of the fluid in which the sensor is placed also affects the sensor time constant as the heat transfer coefficient reduces at low velocity. For instance, when the water velocity around a sensor is below 0.2 ms$^{-1}$, the time constant increases significantly [9].

**Table 4.3**   Typical sensor time constants

| Sensor element | Time constant (min) |
| --- | --- |
| Thermistor in water | 0.2 |
| Thermistor in pocket in water | 0.6 |
| Thermistor in still air | 2.4 |
| Resistance thermometer bulb in water | 1.0 |

From a log of the water temperature sensor in a pipe in the above example, a BEMS would produce a graph like that shown in Fig. 4.13 when the sensor was plunged into the hot water: this is a graph of a **first-order system**.

If a tangent is drawn on the first-order curve at time $T_1$ and it crosses the final temperature which the sensor is trying to achieve, $t_{fluid}$ in the example, at $T_2$, then as is shown in Fig. 4.14:

$$T_2 - T_1 = \tau$$

This can be demonstrated from equation (4.17):

$$t_s - t_{s\ initial} = \{t_{final} - t_{s\ initial}\}\ [1 - \exp(-T/\tau)] \qquad (4.17)$$

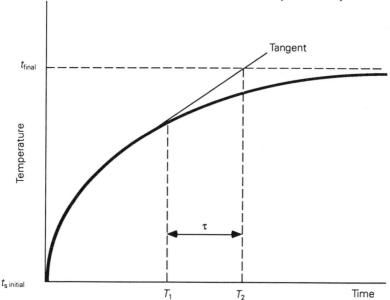

**Fig. 4.14**   Determination of the time constant of a first-order system.

where $t_s$ = sensor temperature (°C);

$t_{s\ initial} = t_s$ at time $T = 0$;

$t_{final}$ = final temperature which the sensor is trying to achieve;

$\tau$ = cylinder time constant (s).

Differentiating equation (4.17) to obtain the slope of the tangent gives:

$$\frac{\mathrm{d}t_s}{\mathrm{d}T} = \frac{1}{\tau}\ \exp\left(-T/\tau\right)\ \{t_{final} - t_{s\ initial}\} \qquad (4.18)$$

The equation of the tangent line at the point $T_1$ is:

$$t_s = \left[\frac{1}{\tau}\exp\left(-T_1/\tau\right)\ \{t_{final} - t_{s\ initial}\}\right]T_1 + c \qquad (4.19)$$

where $c$ = intercept of line (°C).

The line has the two points on it at $t_s$ and $T = T_1$ and $t_{final}$ and $T = T_2$. So from equation (4.19):

$$T_2 - T_1 = \left[\frac{1}{\tau}\exp\left(-T_1/\tau\right)\ \{t_{final} - t_{s\ initial}\}\right]^{-1}\ \{t_{final} - t_s\} \qquad (4.20)$$

From equation (4.16) it can be seen that:

$$\frac{t_{final} - t_s}{t_{final} - t_{s\ initial}} = \exp\left(-T_1/\tau\right)$$

which when substituted into equation (4.20) gives:

$$T_2 - T_1 = \tau \qquad (4.21)$$

It is worth noting that $t_{\text{final}}$ is the hot-water temperature, and that the sensor temperature will approach it very closely, although specifically it will not exactly equal it. However, in practical terms when $T = 2\tau$;

$$t_s - t_{s\text{ initial}} = 0.86 \ \{t_{\text{final}} - t_{s\text{ initial}}\}$$

and when $T = 3\tau$:

$$t_s - t_{s\text{ initial}} = 0.95 \ \{t_{\text{final}} - t_{s\text{ initial}}\}$$

and when $T = 4\tau$:

$$t_s - t_{s\text{ initial}} = 0.98 \ \{t_{\text{final}} - t_{s\text{ initial}}\}$$

In other words, after $2\tau$ the sensor temperature has risen to within 86% of $t_{\text{final}}$, 95% and 98% after $3\tau$ and $4\tau$, respectively.

### 4.7  Measurement errors

The dynamic response of a sensor affects how quickly it approaches the measured fluid temperature. Until the sensor is in equilibrium with the fluid, there will be some error in the sensed temperature.

An even greater factor in the error of a sensor's temperature measurement, especially for water temperature measurements, is how well the sensor is in contact with the fluid it is measuring. To measure the temperature of hot water in a pipe, for instance, the sensor could be inserted as part of a probe into the pipe, with a mechanical seal to allow removal.

Another more popular method is to place the sensor into a **pocket**, or well, which has already been screwed or welded into the pipe. The sensor can then readily be taken out for maintenance or replacement.

An easier way, especially for BEMS installations on existing plant, but more prone to error, would be simply to strap the sensor to the pipe. This method is frequently employed on domestic hot-water cylinders and calorifiers, the sensor casing being held in place by a band around the calorifier. Such sensors are referred to as **strap-on sensors** or **surface contact sensors**, or simply **contact sensors**.

Wherever sensors are used to measure water temperature, it is unlikely that they will be in direct contact with the water. Pockets or wells will be installed into which the sensors can be placed. The sensor will then be measuring the inside surface temperature of the pocket, whereas the outside surface of the pocket is in contact with the water. Provided that the pocket is made of a material of good conductivity (brass and stainless steel are suitable and commonly used materials), then the thermal resistance will be small.

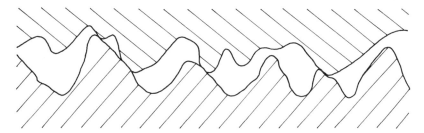

**Fig. 4.15**   Two surfaces in contact.

Unfortunately, there will be more resistance between the surface of the sensor and the inside surface of the pocket. This is due to the two surfaces being rough on a microscopic scale and making contact at relatively few points of small area. Microscopically it is like putting the profile of Switzerland on top of that of Scotland. Figure 4.15 shows this contact between two surfaces.

Where contact is made, the area is often small and it forms a **constriction resistance** to heat flow, like three lanes of motorway traffic being funnelled in to one lane, with the resultant hold up or resistance to flow. Holm describes the original work on constriction resistances in relation to electrical contacts in his seminal book [10], but the theory is very similar for thermal contacts. Holm's model is of a contact point being replaced by a small sphere of radius $r$, where $\pi r^2$ is equal to the contact point area (Fig. 4.16).

The sphere has infinite conductivity and the resistance to heat flow through one of the contacting surfaces is:

$$R_{\text{th constr}} = \frac{1}{\pi r k}$$

where $R_{\text{th constr}}$ = thermal constriction resistance (m² K W⁻¹);
    $k$ = conductivity of the contact member (W m⁻¹ K⁻¹);
    $r$ = sphere radius (m).

Sphere of infinite conductivity

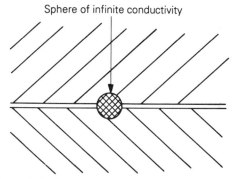

**Fig. 4.16**   Holm's model of a constriction resistance.

A more elaborate model gives the more correct:

$$R_{\text{th constr}} = \frac{1}{2ak} \tag{4.22}$$

where $a$ = radius of the circular contact area (m).

For two surfaces in contact, each will have a constriction resistance of $1/4ak$, and the combined resistance will be the two constriction resistances in series, $1/2ak$. There will be convection and radiation heat transfer across the gaps between the surfaces [16], but it is assumed that the resistances of these two modes is much greater than that of the constriction resistance.

So for a sensor in a pocket, there is the small resistance due to the metal of the pocket itself and a larger constriction resistance due to the contact area of the sensor and pocket. To reduce the constriction resistance the area of contact needs to be increased. This can be done by putting some silicon grease or oil into the pocket to fill in the gaps and so increase the area of contact. The conductivity of the fluid is much larger than the air it replaces and it therefore shorts out the constriction resistances. To retain the oil or grease the pocket must be positioned vertically.

The need to put oil and grease in pockets is an additional maintenance requirement which inevitably may be forgotten. So, to ensure that there is good thermal contact between a sensor and its pocket, springs can be put at the sensor tips to ensure there is adequate pressure, and consequently good contact, with the pocket. Even with this, there is still the influence of the pipe wall and its heat loss that can affect the sensor's reading [2]. With all these factors, errors of 20% or more below the fluid temperature can be made.

Compared to the sensor in a pocket, the strap-on sensor is even more subject to error. This is because it is measuring the outside surface temperature of the pipe, or calorifier, not the water temperature itself. The pipe surface temperature can be considerably lower than the water within it due to radiation and convection losses, depending on the level of insulation. However, the insulation has to be stripped off around the sensor location for access to the pipe surface. Conduction can then occur through the sensor, its case and wires. Constriction resistances are invariably higher as well, due to the curved surface of the pipe. Hence serious errors can occur with strap-on sensors.

*Example*
A surface-mounted sensor has only $10^{-5}$ of its surface area making contact with a 25 mm copper hot-water pipe:

(a) What effect has this on the temperature read by the sensor?
(b) What happens when a heat transfer fluid is inserted between the sensor and pipe?
   Assume that there are no convection or radiation losses.

*Solution*

(a) The actual effect is difficult to quantify as little work has been done to measure thermal constriction resistances [16]. The fraction of the actual area of contact used in this example has been taken from measurements between flat surfaces in contact [17], under a pressure of approx. 9 kPa.

Assuming the constriction resistance to be due to a single circular contact, then if the surface area is $A$, the radius of actual contact, $r$, is:

$$r = \left[ \frac{10^{-5} \times A}{\pi} \right]^{0.5}$$

So the constriction resistance is:

$$R_{\text{th constr}} = \frac{1}{2k} \left[ \frac{\pi}{10^{-5} \times A} \right]^{0.5} \tag{4.23}$$

and with $k = 390 \text{ W m}^{-1} \text{ K}^{-1}$ [19]:

$$R_{\text{th constr}} = 0.72 \, (A)^{-0.5}$$

This has units of $\text{K W}^{-1}$, not the usual units.

Taking the thickness of the copper pipe to be 1.2 mm [18], and the sensor head to which the thermistor or PRT is attached to be of equal thickness and conductivity, the resistance of the pipe (and the sensor), $R_p$, is:

$$R_p = \frac{1}{kA}$$

$$= \frac{1.2 \times 10^{-3}}{390A}$$

$$= 3.1 \times 10^{-6} \, \text{A}^{-1}$$

which is substantially below the constriction resistance. For instance, if the nominal contact area were 4 cm$^2$, the ratio of the constriction resistance to the pipe and sensor resistance would be:

$$\frac{R_{\text{th constr}}}{2 \times R_p} = 2.3 \times 10^3$$

So, if the water in the pipe were at 80°C and the sensor read 70°C, the temperature drop across the constriction resistance would be:

$$\frac{R_{\text{th constr}}}{2R_p + R_{\text{th constr}}} \times 10$$

$$= 9.99 \, \text{K}$$

(b) Taking the conductivity of the heat transfer grease to be $0.1 \text{ W m}^{-1} \text{ K}^{-1}$, and the separation of the sensor and pipe surface to be $2 \text{ μm}$ (dictated by the surface roughness), the resistance of the grease, $R_g$, is:

$$R_g = \frac{2 \times 10^{-6}}{0.1 \times 4 \times 10^{-4}}$$

$$= 0.05 \text{ W K}^{-1}$$

This compares with a constriction resistance of $35.85 \text{ W K}^{-1}$. As the constriction resistance and the grease resistance are in parallel, the combined resistance is that due predominantly to the grease, i.e. $0.05 \text{ W K}^{-1}$. So if the heat flow through the resistances to the sensor remains the same with the grease, then without the grease the temperature drop reduces from 10 K to:

$$\frac{10}{R_{\text{th constr}}} (R_g + 2R_p)$$

$$= \frac{10}{35.85} (0.05 + 0.015)$$

$$= 0.018 \text{ K}$$

Effectively the temperature difference, and error, has disappeared with the introduction of the grease. But this is a simplified, idealized example, to illustrate the importance of good contact between the sensor and pipe.

## 4.8  Comfort

Constriction resistances do not affect air temperature sensors as they are surrounded by air, but there are two other problems. Both relate to inside temperature sensors. The first is how representative the sensor reading is of the bulk air temperature in the room. Warm air will come from an emitter which may well be the other side of the room to the sensor and there will be a **distance/velocity lag** before the sensor senses the warm air. Also the sensor may be in a stagnant area with little air movement, unrepresentative of the bulk of the air. This is not a sensor error, but rather a positional error.

But the more important problem is that an air temperature sensor is not measuring comfort, even though a principal aim of a BEMS is to control the building services plant, so that the building is reasonably comfortable for the occupants. A measure of the thermal comfort of a room is the **dry resultant temperature** in that room. The dry resultant temperature takes account not only of the air temperature, but also of the radiant temperature. One only has to sit near a large single glazed window in winter or on a sunny day to appreciate the radiant component of comfort. The dry resultant temperature for a typical room with air speeds of the order of $0.1 \text{ m s}^{-1}$ is approximated to [11]:

$$t_{res} = \tfrac{1}{2} t_r + \tfrac{1}{2} t_{ai} \tag{4.22}$$

$t_r$ is the temperature measured by a thermometer at the centre of a blackened globe, 100 mm in diameter. Section A5 and A9 of the CIBSE Guide ([12], [13]) refer to $t_{res}$ at the centre of a room, giving it the symbol $t_c$. Both sections state that at the centre of the room $t_r$ approximates to the mean surface temperature of the room, $t_m$:

$$t_m = \frac{\Sigma \, (A t_{surf})}{\Sigma \, A}$$

where $A$ = area of a surface of the room (m$^2$), and
    $t_{surf}$ = temperature of a surface of the room (°C).
    It would be inpracticable for a BEMS sensor to be housed in a 100 mm blackened globe in the centre of a room. Also most BEMS room temperature sensors predominantly measure the air temperature. There is little published data to support this statement, but there is a little more data on room thermostats ([14], [7]), which have similar housings to BEMS room temperature sensors and serve a similar purpose. Letherman [7] quotes the steady state response of a thermostat to air temperature and radiant temperature to be:

$$t_t = \Gamma t_{ai} + (1 - \Gamma) \, t_{surroundings} \tag{4.23}$$

where   $t_t$ = thermostat sensor temperature (°C);
        $t_{ai}$ = air temperature (°C);
$t_{surroundings}$ = mean surface temperature of surroundings (°C);
        $\Gamma$ = dimensionless factor relating thermostat sensitivity to air and radiant temperatures.
    For a ventilated casing to the thermostat, a mean value for $\Gamma$ is quoted as 0.9 and for an unventilated case 0.67. Presumably the second term on the right of equation (4.23) includes the effect of the influence of the internal wall on which the thermostat is positioned. An internal wall is often chosen for positioning thermostats and BEMS sensors as opposed to the inside surfaces of external walls as the latter can be quite cold and much lower than the room air temperature.
    To relate the air temperature to the dry resultant temperature the type of heating has to be considered. Different types of heating give out differing proportions of radiant and convective heat which result in different values of $t_{ai}$ and $t_m$. The CIBSE Guide relates $t_{ai}$ and $t_c$ by the ratio $F_2$ and provides tables of values of $F_2$ for various heating systems (radiators, convectors, radiant panels, etc.) [13]. The ratio is defined as:

$$F_2 = \frac{t_{ai} - t_{ao}}{t_c - t_{ao}}$$

where $t_{ao}$ = outside air temperature (°C).

*Example*

A factory is heated by forced warm-air heaters. The system is designed to provide a dry resultant temperature of 19 °C when it is − 1 °C outside; $F_2$ is 1.17 and $t_m$ is 15.8 °C. What is the BEMS room sensor reading if it is in a ventilated case?

*Solution*

Equation (4.23) for the thermostat can be used with $t_m$ put in as an approximate value for $t_{surroundings}$. In fact the latter will probably be slightly higher than $t_m$ as it is closer to a warm inside wall. $t_{ai}$ is required for equation (4.25), and this can be obtained from the $F_2$ ratio:

$$1.17 = \frac{t_{ai} - (-1)}{19 - (-1)}$$

giving

$$t_{ai} = 22.4\,°C.$$

Putting the values into equation (4.23):

$$t_t = (0.9 \times 22.4) + (0.1 \times 15.8)$$

$$= 20.16 + 1.58 = 21.74\,°C$$

So to maintain $t_c$ at 19 °C and $t_{ai}$ at 22.4 °C, the BEMS sensor must control to 21.7 °C.

To alleviate the problem of obtaining a representative inside temperature of a building, where some rooms will inevitably be colder than others, due to the heating system being unbalanced or having wrong emitter sizes, a number of sensors can be employed. Their outputs are then addressed to an **averaging function module** which produces a signal of the average value for the relevant control loop. Typically one average module can have up to four sensors, but a number of modules can be combined in parallel to increase the number of sensors.

**Minimum** and **maximum function modules** can also be used in parallel with the average module to identify the extreme rooms to indicate how unbalanced the heating system is.

### 4.8.1 'Monday morning blues'

As most BEMSs' internal temperature sensors are predominantly air temperature sensors, then when the building is warming up on a Monday morning after the heating has been switched off over the weekend the BEMS will switch off or modulate the heating when the required air temperature is met. This could mean that the fabric, which takes much longer to heat than the air, has not got very warm, so the radiant temperature, and hence the dry resultant temperature, would be low and the building still uncomfortably cold.

Chapter 9 on optimiser control deals with preheating, but there is an interesting example there that demonstrates the difference in time to heat the air and the fabric. Figure 4.17 shows the single-storey office building used in that example.

Table 4.4 shows the heat stored in the various elements of the building, and Table 4.5 shows the individual time constants of the elements (the latter are derived in Chapter 9 on optimiser control).

**Table 4.4** Heat stored in the elements of the building

| Element | Heat stored | |
|---|---|---|
| | (MJ) | Fraction of total (%) |
| Window | 13 | 1 |
| Air | 59 | 4 |
| Brick | 100 | 8 |
| Block | 229 | 17 |
| Roof | 340 | 25 |
| Partitions | 614 | 45 |
| Total | 1355 | 100 |

**Table 4.5** Time constants of the elements of the building

| Element | Time constant, $\tau(h)$ |
|---|---|
| Brick | 5.8 |
| Block | 5.1 |
| Window | 0.7 |
| Roof | 4.5 |
| Partitions | 6.7 |
| Air (1 air change per hour) | 1.0 |

From these tables it can be seen that the air can heat up much quicker than the fabric elements. Although there is heat exchange between the air and the fabric, which will limit large temperature differences, there is still a distinct possibility that the air temperature will rise well ahead of the fabric temperature. The BEMS sensor will respond to the air temperature and control the heating accordingly. This gives rise to a low, dry resultant temperature, especially on a Monday morning when the fabric has lost heat over the weekend, hence the term 'Monday morning blues'.

Some BEMSs manufacturers recommend that a sensor is placed within an internal wall to control the preheating on the internal fabric temperature. However, this will effectively give the sensor a long time constant, necessitating the use of another sensor to measure the air temperature inside the room for controlling the heating when the building is up to temperature.

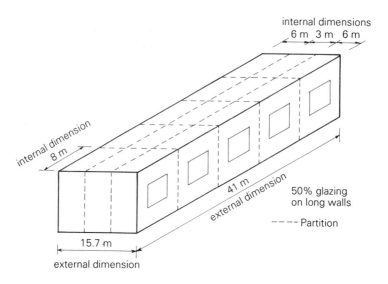

**Fig. 4.17** Example building.

### 4.9 Smart sensors

A laser-trimmed thin film sensing element on a silicon substrate is shown in Fig. 4.2. It would be possible to add on to the same chip a CPU to make it intelligent. With an A/D converter, a communication section and some memory to store look-up tables and the sensor type module then one has the basics of a **smart sensor**. The A/D would allow a digitized signal to be transmitted to the outstation and the CPU would enable more sophisticated signal processing to be carried to avoid interference. A smart sensor would also be able directly to control a valve actuator or relay, etc. Figure 4.18 shows the concept of a smart sensor, where the boxes do not represent areas on the chip, but merely discrete functions of the chip in its DIL package.

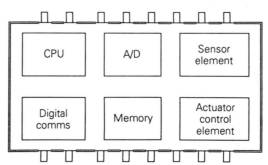

**Fig. 4.18** Concept of a smart sensor.

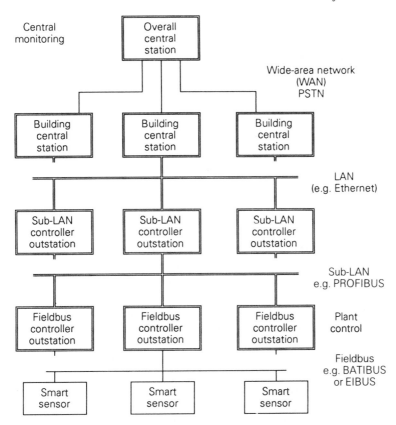

**Fig. 4.19** Possible architecture for a BEMS with smart sensors.

One chip containing these specialized functions, for one sensor type, would render manufacturing of it expensive. However, by putting a limited range of sensor elements on to the chip, it is rendered multi-purpose, thus widening the market and reducing cost [15]. Users would then select which sensing element they required to use. Using smart sensors would tie in with small outstations for controlling individual items of plant, and also the use of field-buses. A probable architecture for a BEMS using smart sensors is shown in Fig.4.19.

## References

[1] Bentley, J. P. (1988) *Principles of Measurement Systems*, 2nd edn, Long-man, London.
[2] Stoecker, W. F. and Stoecker, P. A. (1989) *Microcomputer Control of Thermal and Mechanical Systems*, Van Nostrand Reinhold, New York.

[3] Chesmond, C. J. (1982) *Control System Technology*, Edward Arnold, London.

[4] Diefenderfer, A. J. (1979) *Principles of Electronic Instrumentation*, 2nd edn, Holt-Saunders, Eastbourne.

[5] Fielden, C. J. and Ede, T. J. (1982) *Computer-based Energy Management in Buildings*, Pitman, London.

[6] Hencke, H. (1989) The design and application of Honeywell's laser-trimmed temperature sensors. *Measurement + Control*, **22**, October.

[7] Letherman, K. M. (1981) *Automatic Controls for Heating and Air Conditioning Principles and Applications*, Pergamon, Oxford.

[8] Martin, G. (1982) *Microprocessor Appreciation Level III*. Technician Education Council Hutchinson, London.

[9] CIBSE (1986) Guide, CIBSE Volume B, Section B11, Automatic control, Chartered Institution of Building Services Engineers, London.

[10] Holm, R. (1958) *Elektrische Kontakte*, Springer–Verlag, Berlin.

[11] CIBSE (1986) CIBSE Guide, Volume A, Section A1, Environmental criteria for design, Chartered Institution of Building Services Engineers, London.

[12] CIBSE (1986) CIBSE Guide, Volume A, Section A5, Thermal response of buildings, Chartered Institution of Building Services Engineers, London.

[13] CIBSE (1986) CIBSE Guide, Volume A, Section A9, Estimation of plant capacity, Chartered Institution of Building Services Engineers, London.

[14] Fitzgerald, D. (1969) Room thermostats, choice and performance. *Journal of the Institution of Heating and Ventilating Engineers*, **37**.

[15] Wilkins, J. and Willis, S. (1990). What are smart sensors? *Building Services* (CIBSE) **12**, 12.

[16] Holman, J. P. (1989) *Heat Transfer*, McGraw-Hill, New York.

[17] Bowden, F. P. and Tabor, D. (1971) *Friction and Lubrication of Solids: Part 1*, Oxford University Press, Oxford.

[18] CIBSE (1986) CIBSE Guide, Volume B, Section B16, Miscellaneous Equipment, Chartered Institution of Building Services Engineers, London.

[19] CIBSE (1986) CIBSE Guide, Volume C, Section C7, Units and Miscellaneous Data, Chartered Institution of Building Services Engineers, London.

# 5
# Basic control

Having considered the basic elements of a BEMS in previous chapters, in this chapter we examine the basics of control: this involves the system that the BEMS is controlling, and its interaction with the BEMS.

## 5.1 The need for control

Initially, it is worth considering the need for control in order to have some appreciation of its importance. Consider a boiler and heating system for a building. The system is sized on the inside, dry resultant temperature required, $t_c$ (also $t_{res}$, but the subscript c refers to the centre of the room) and the design outside air temperature, $t_{ao}$. The CIBSE Guide gives design values for both $t_c$ and $t_{ao}$ ([1], [2]).

Most heating systems are not sized to the exact building heat loss, but are oversized to get the building quickly up to temperature in the morning. Typically systems are 20% oversized, although Section A9 of the CIBSE Guide suggests a larger margin [3].

The Guide states that the design value of $t_{ao}$ should be $-3\,°C$ in London to provide a safety margin of 20% oversizing of the heating plant for a lightweight building ('lightweight' refers to the thermal capacity of the structure, which is discussed further in Chapter 7 on building heat loss and heating). Between 1957 and 1976, in London, on only one occasion in the heating season did the 24-hour mean $t_{ao}$ fall below this temperature [2]. For heavyweight buildings with 20% oversizing the recommended $t_{ao}$ is $-1.8\,°C$, for which there were only two occasions in the heating season in which the 48-hour mean $t_{ao}$ fell below this temperature. The longer time average for the heavyweight building reflects the fact that such a building would not be influenced so much by short-term temperature fluctuations.

*Example*
What is the average heat output from a heating system during the heating season for a lightweight office in London? The system is 20% oversized and produces little difference between $t_c$ and the inside air temperature, $t_{ai}$ (i.e. $F_2 = 1.0$).

*Solution*
For an office the CIBSE Guide recommends $t_c$ should be 20°C. From the CIBSE Guide (Section A2) the average $t_{ao}$ for the 30-year average period 1941–70 (October to April) is 7°C. The design inside to outside temperature drop is:

$$t_{c\ design} - t_{ao\ design} = 20 - (-3)$$
$$= 23°C$$

However, the heating system is 20% oversized, so the temperature drop from inside to outside that it can maintain is:

$$23 \times 1.2 = 27.6°C$$

Therefore the heating is capable of maintaining 20°C inside under favourable conditions when it is $-7.6$°C outside. The heating system produces $t_c$ close to $t_{ai}$, so the heat output from the heating system can be taken as proportional to the temperature difference. The ratio of the average to design heat output is:

$$\frac{20 - 7}{20 - (-7.6)} = 47\%$$

This calculation, like the heating design calculation, does not include the internal heat gains (heat from people, equipment, lighting and the sun [4]) that occur and will further reduce the heat requirement during the day. So the control of the heating system must match the heat requirement, otherwise there will be potential waste of heat and energy. The energy consumption through the heating season should be approximately proportional to:

$$t_c - t_{ao} = 20 - 7$$
$$= 13\ K$$

A 1 K rise in $t_c$ through the heating season would increase the consumption by:

$$\frac{1}{13} = 7.7\%$$

Energy consumption will be fully discussed in Chapter 10 on monitoring and targeting.

## 5.2 On/off control

The simplest and most common control is **on/off** control. As is shown in Fig. 5.1 an on/off controller sends an 'off' signal when the temperature reaches the upper level, $t_u$, and sends an 'on' signal when the temperature drops to the lower level, $t_l$.

Using the water analogy, mentioned in Chapter 4, of the cylinder being filled with water while water flows out from a pipe in the bottom, the supply valve is shut off at the upper level, $h_u$ and opened at the lower level, $h_l$, as shown in Fig. 5.2.

The water level is measured by a sensor in the base of the cylinder, which is pressure sensitive, and sensitive to the level of water above it. This sends a signal to the BEMS outstation which then controls the valve. The valve is either fully open or fully closed, there is no modulation.

The gap between $t_u$ and $t_l$ (also $h_u$ and $h_l$) is the **differential**, sometimes referred to as the **overlap** or **hysteresis**. In Fig. 5.3 it can be seen that halving the differential (from 2D to D) will halve the period (from $2\tau_p$ to $\tau_p$) and double the frequency (from $f$ to $2f$) as:

$$f = \frac{1}{\tau_p} \tag{5.1}$$

For accurate control a small differential is required. Too small a differential and the frequency of cycling will be high and the controlling device, the valve

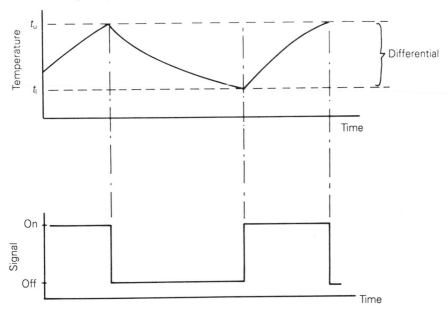

**Fig. 5.1** On/off control.

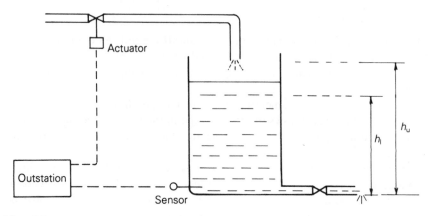

**Fig. 5.2**  On/off control of water flow.

in the water cylinder example, will get increased use and wear. So a compromise between close control with low device life and looser control with longer device life is required. Often, if on/off control is used, the accuracy of

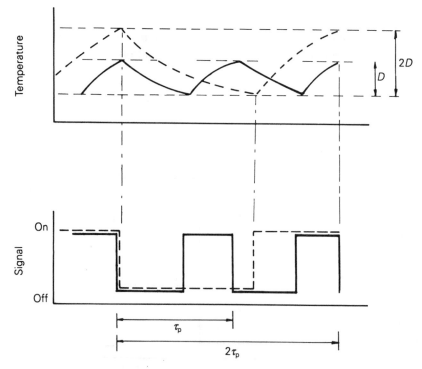

**Fig. 5.3**  Effect of halving the differential.

control needed is not high, otherwise a more sophisticated and expensive control would be used. Also the application determines the accuracy of control.

For instance, a boiler supplying hot water to a radiator heating system will have controls, such as room thermostats and even perhaps thermostatic radiator valves, controlling the heating system. So the boiler thermostat does not have to have too small a differential as there is control further along in the system. A differential of 5 K is generally considered adequate for the boiler, although at low loads a wider differential is more efficient. However, the room thermostat needs a closer differential than 5 K as this would mean the room could vary from hot to cold – e.g. 22°C to 17°C. A differential of 1 K to 2 K would be more appropriate. Although the differential of thermostats cannot easily be altered, on/off control with a BEMS, employing a temperature sensor and an output channel for sending on/off signals, does have an easily adjusted differential.

### 5.3 Binary drivers

An example of on/off control with a BEMS is shown in Fig. 5.4. Here hot water is pumped around a radiator heating system. A temperature sensor in one of the heated rooms is connected to an outstation which monitors the temperature. When the temperature reaches the upper temperature, say 21°C, then the outstation switches off the pump. This is a simple example used for illustrative purposes but is a typical control system for a house, except that a thermostat would be used instead of a BEMS.

The BEMS configuration diagram for this control strategy is shown in Fig. 5.5. The hardware, such as the A/D converter, has been missed out for simplicity. The **loop controller**, the triangle in the diagram, converts the sensor reading, already conditioned by the sensor and sensor-type module, to a value between 0% and 100% depending on how near or far the temperature is to the required set point. If the set point were 21°C, then the signal would be 0%. (Further details on the loop controller and its operation are given in Chapter 6.)

The loop controller, or loop module, sends this output to an address where the **binary driver** is programmed to take the value at this address as an input. A driver, like the loop module, is a software module, or program, that is used to drive plant in response to an input signal. The binary driver is a driver where the 'on' ($t_l$) and 'off' ($t_u$) signals can be individually set by the operator to correspond to any value of input signal between 0% and 100%, as shown in Fig. 5.6. In other words, the on/off differential can be fully adjusted. If the differential were set to zero, then noise on the input would cause the driver to operate randomly. The binary driver sends a signal to the relay in the pump circuit to close and start the pump if the value is at or below %$t_l$. If the value

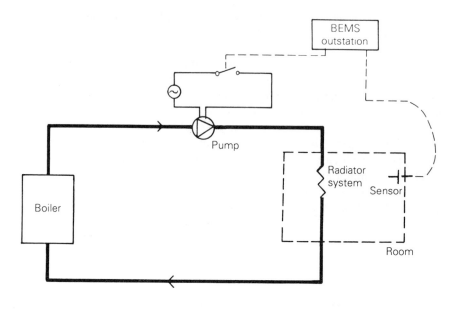

—  —  — BEMS low-voltage wiring

**Fig. 5.4**   On/off control of a heating pump.

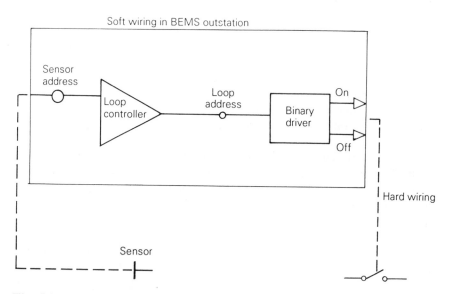

**Fig. 5.5**   BEMS configuration for on/off control of a pump.

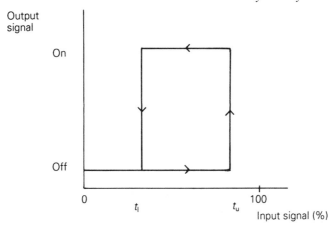

**Fig. 5.6** Binary driver signals.

is at or above $\%t_u$, then a signal is sent to open the relay to stop the pump. In between these two values no signal is sent.

## 5.4 System dynamics

In order to be able to set up on/off differentials, as well as more sophisticated controls, it is useful to understand how the system being controlled responds. Fig. 5.7 shows a simplified block diagram of the on/off control considered above.

All the variables in the block diagram are functions of time, shown by $(T)$; $r(T)$ is the set point, $t_u$, at which the pump is switched off; and $y(T)$ is the output from the system, the temperature in the room. The sensor measures this temperature and sends back a signal to the outstation which gives a temperature in the outstation of $\hat{y}(T)$, an approximation or estimate of $y(T)$. The estimate is often very close to the actual value but measurement and approximation errors may occur, as mentioned in Chapter 4. At the summing point (the circle), the **error**, $e(T)$, is determined by subtraction from the set point:

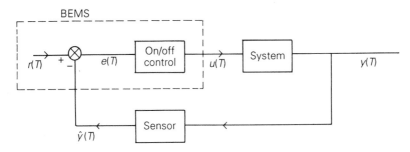

**Fig. 5.7** Block diagram of BEMS on/off control.

$$e(T) = r(T) - \hat{y}(T) \qquad (5.2)$$

Although it is commonly used for $e(T)$, the term error is a misnomer, in that it is not due to an inaccuracy of a poor sensor, but simply the difference between the sensor reading and the required set point.

When the error is zero, the on/off control in the BEMS (the loop controller and the binary driver) sends a signal, $u(T)$, which switches off the pump. The pump will not come on again until the error has increased to equal the differential:

$$e(T) = t_u - t_l$$

The sensor block in Fig. 5.7 represents the static sensor and transmitter blocks of Fig. 4.9, as well as the dynamic block $G(s)$. Included in the sensor block of Fig. 5.7 is the outstation hardware, such as the A/D converter, so that $\hat{y}(T)$ is the measured room temperature. If the sensor and outstation are of good quality and accurate, then the static gain terms of the sensor block in Fig. 5.7 have a combined value close to unity. The dynamic response block of Fig. 4.9 will still be present in the sensor block of Fig. 5.7, however, whatever the quality and accuracy of the sensor to describe the sensor response.

The loop with the sensor in it is the **feedback loop**, feeding the result of the control action of the on/off control in the BEMS back to the BEMS, so that the error of the action can be determined. If the sensor and BEMS hardware are fast-acting with good accuracy, then it feeds back virtually the true value and is a **unity feedback loop**.

The system block in Fig. 5.7 represents the pump and the rest of the heating system that goes to produce the resultant temperature output in the room. It should be noted that the arrowed lines in the block diagram represent signals

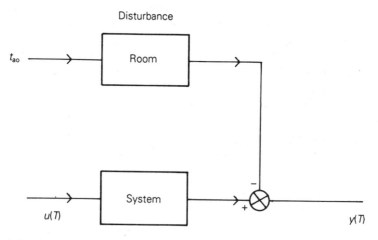

**Fig. 5.8** The inclusion of a disturbance.

or information flow, not heat flow, although heat is present in the system. If the influence of the outside temperature, $t_{ao}$, were to be included in Fig. 5.7, then it would be as a **disturbance**, shown as another block introducing a disturbing signal after the system, as Fig. 5.8 shows.

The system block represents the pump, pipework, hot water, radiators and the boiler. These systems have dynamic responses just as sensors do. If the devices' responses can be described mathematically by expressions like equations (4.10) and (4.11), for a sensor:

$$\text{Heat flow into sensor } - \text{ heat flow out of sensor}$$
$$= \text{rate of change of heat stored in sensor} \qquad (4.10)$$

$$h_s A(t_{\text{fluid}} - t_s) = MC_p \frac{dt_s}{dT} \qquad (4.11)$$

with a first-order differential term, as on the right of equation (4.11), and with no higher differential terms in the equation describing a system, then that is a **first-order system**. The electrical resistor (R) capacitor (C) circuit analogy, mentioned in Chapter 4, is also an example of a first-order system with a time constant of RC. The time constant for the sensor was $(MC_p/h_s A)$.

The radiators in our heating system can be approximated to first-order systems. Adams and Holmes [5] give the time constants for radiators, a few values of which are shown in Table 5.1.

**Table 5.1**   Time constants for radiators (min)

| Water flow rate (kg s$^{-1}$) | Single-pipe circuit | Two-pipe circuit |
|---|---|---|
| 0.014 | 5.5 | 8.0 |
| 0.032 | 2.9 | 3.6 |
| 0.068 | 1.5 | 1.9 |

## 5.5  Laplace and z-transforms

When there are a number of components comprising a system, as in our pumped heating system, there will be numerous differential equations to describe the dynamic response of the system. So the Laplace transformation is used to simplify and transform the differential equations into algebraic equations. The Laplace transformation is defined by:

$$+ [f(T)] = \int_0^\infty f(T) \exp(-sT) \, dT \equiv F(s)$$

where + is the symbol for the Laplace operator giving the transformation of a function. The transformation is used for transforming functions such as

$f(T)$, which are functions of time $T$, into functions of the complex variable, $s$, $F(s)$. There is a limitation that $f(T)$ is zero for $T < 0$, so the transformation is useful for examining sudden changes to the system such as a step change at $T = 0$. The complex variable, $s$, is:

$$s = \sigma + j\omega \tag{5.3}$$

where $j = \sqrt{(-1)}$;
   $\sigma$ = real part
   $\omega$ = imaginary part.

Using the Laplace transformation, differentiation becomes:

$$+ \left[ \frac{d f(T)}{dT} \right] = sF(s) - f(T)\big|_{T=0} \tag{5.4}$$

where $f(T)\big|_{T=0}$, or $f(0)$, is the value of $f(T)$ at $T = 0$. Unless there is any discontinuity in the function at $T = 0$ and the initial conditions are zero, then $f(0) = 0$, so that equation (5.4) is simplified to:

$$+ \left[ \frac{d f(T)}{dT} \right] = sF(s) \tag{5.5}$$

With the time constant, $\tau$, in equation (4.11), it becomes:

$$t_{\text{fluid}} - t_s = \tau \frac{dt_s}{dT} \tag{5.6}$$

Performing a Laplace transformation on equation (5.6), with the initial conditions at zero, gives:

$$t_{\text{fluid}} - t_s = \tau\, s t_s$$

or:

$$t_s(s)\,(\tau s + 1) = t_{\text{fluid}}(s) \tag{5.7}$$

Here $t_s(s)$ has not been changed to the normal notation of $T_s(s)$ for the Laplace transform of $t_s(T)$, to avoid confusion with $T$ representing time. The dynamic response of the sensor in the block diagram in Fig. 4.9 was given as $G(s)$. The $s$ here is the Laplace complex variable and $G(s)$ is the **transfer function** of the sensor, the ratio of the Laplace transform of the output from the sensor to the Laplace transform of the input, with the initial conditions at zero, i.e.:

$$G(s) = \frac{F_{\text{output}}(s)}{F_{\text{input}}(s)} \tag{5.8}$$

where $F_{\text{output}}(s) = $ Laplace transform of the output, and $F_{\text{input}}(s) = $ Laplace transform of the input.

For our sensor with its equation (5.7), the transfer function is:

$$G(s) = \frac{t_s(s)}{t_{\text{fluid}}(s)}$$

$$= \frac{1}{1 + \tau s} \qquad (5.9)$$

This lends itself well to the block diagram, as is shown in Fig. 5.9, where $F_i(s)$ and $F_o(s)$ are the input and output, respectively.

Table 5.2 shows the Laplace transforms of common functions.

**Table 5.2** Laplace transforms of some common functions

| Function of time: $f(T)$ | Laplace transform: $F(s)$ |
|---|---|
| $\dfrac{df(T)}{dT}$ | $sF(s) - f(T)\big|_{T=0}$ |
| Unit impulse $\delta(T)$ | $1$ |
| Unit step $u(T)$ | $\dfrac{1}{s}$ |
| Unit ramp $T$ | $\dfrac{1}{s^2}$ |
| Sine wave $\sin wT$ | $\dfrac{1}{s^2 + w^2}$ |
| Exponential decay $\exp(-aT)$ | $\dfrac{1}{s + a}$ |
| Exponential growth $1 - \exp(-aT)$ | $\dfrac{a}{s(s + a)}$ |
| Time delay of time $T$ | $\exp(-sT)$ |

If a unit step change in fluid temperature $t_{\text{fluid}}$, in our example, with a Laplace transform of $1/s$

$$+ (t_{\text{fluid}}) = \frac{1}{s} = F_{\text{input}}(s)$$

is applied to the sensor with its transfer function

$$G(s) = \frac{1}{1 + \tau s}$$

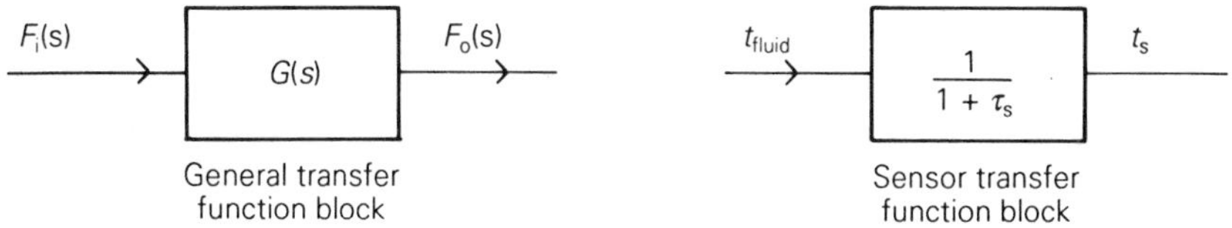

**Fig. 5.9** Transfer functions.

then:

$$\mathscr{L}(t_s) = F_{output}(s) = G(s)\,F_{input}(s)$$

$$= \frac{1}{s}\frac{1}{1+\tau s} \tag{5.10}$$

To convert this back to the **time domain**, converting $F_{output}(s)$ back to $t_s$, denoted by:

$$\mathscr{L}^{-1}(F_{output}(s)) = t_s \tag{5.11}$$

From Table 5.2 we can see that:

$$\mathscr{L}(1 - \exp[-aT]) = \frac{a}{s(s+a)} \tag{5.12}$$

Equations (5.12) and (5.10) are equivalent if:

$$a = \frac{1}{\tau}$$

So the output from the sensor, $\mathscr{L}^{-1}\{F_{output}(s)\}$, or $t_s$, is:

$$1 - \exp[-T/\tau] \tag{5.13}$$

Equation (5.13) is not exactly the same as the sensor equation in Chapter 4.

$$t_s - t_{s\ initial} = \{t_{fluid} - t_{s\ initial}\}\,[1 - \exp(-T/\tau)] \tag{4.17}$$

This is because the Laplace transformation required the initial conditions to be zero. So the **boundary conditions**, (i.e. at the boundary $T = 0$) have to be fitted to the inverted equation. Part of these boundary conditions in the example in Chapter 4 was that the actual step change was not unity or 1 K, but was from 10°C to 80°C, a step change of 70 K. The Laplace of this step change would be:

$$\frac{70}{s}$$

Also for the sensor $\tau = 60\ s$, so the transfer function of the example sensor is:

$$G(s) = \frac{1}{1 + 60\ s}$$

As can be seen in Table 5.2, the Laplace transform of a unit impulse is 1, so the response of a system to a unit impulse is simply the transfer function:

$$G(s) = \frac{F_{output}(s)}{F_{input}(s)} \quad \text{and} \quad F_{input}(s) = \mathscr{L}\{\delta(T)\} = 1$$

so:

$$F_{\text{output}}(s) = G(s)$$

The overall transfer function of the sensor must also include the steady state gains. As the transfer function is concerned only with the dynamic response, when things change at $T = 0$, then the change in time of the steady state gain, or the slope of the steady state equation, although of little significance to the dynamics, is required. As the sensor and transmitter constants, $c_s$ and $c_t$, do not change with time, they become zero when the steady state equation is differentiated with respect to time to determine the slope. So the overall transfer function is:

$$K_s K_t G(s) \ \text{mA K}^{-1}$$

$G(s)$, being derived from the ratio of the output to the input, has the units of inverse time, for the first-order system, so the steady state gains effectively act as scaling factors. Often these steady state gain units are not shown in block diagrams as working through a feedback control loop, one starts at the required temperature, works through the blocks and comes back with the feedback temperature. The blocks' units have cancelled each other out.

It is also often assumed that the sensor introduces no error or approximation into the measurement, i.e. that $\hat{y}(T) = y(T)$

Further details of the Laplace transform and transfer functions, and their use in control theory, can be found in Marshall [6] and other texts such as [12].

The Laplace transformation is useful for simplifying and solving differential equations but the algebraic transformation equation itself can be used for determining the stability of a controller without transforming back to a function of time, $T$, as will be shown later.

But before any transfer function can be determined, one must first have a differential equation, or equations, describing the system. Where these are unknown, one can try to identify the system empirically by switching it on and off, or by changing the set point, $r(T)$ to simulate step functions and observing the response. In Chapter 6 the response of a system to various control changes is used to set up the controller for optimum performance. Another method of identification is to examine the system's response to a sine wave. For a linear system, the output will also be a sine wave, but compared to the input wave, it will be of different **amplitude** (i.e. height of the wave), and **phase** (i.e. the peak of the output wave appearing later or earlier than the input wave). The change in amplitude and phase are plotted in different graphical forms as **Nyquist**, **Bode** or **Nichols plots** [6]. However, it is difficult to subject heating systems and buildings to sinusoidal changes, although small electrical sinusoidal waves of suitably long periods can be injected into actuators once the BEMS's control has been disconnected (the loop opened), but with the BEMS's sensor logging the response. Needless to say, there is little such data from building services plant, although the mathematics of Laplace transforms and these various plots make good exam questions!

So far, we have considered the use of Laplace transforms to solve differential equations, where the functions are analogue and continuous in time. But BEMSs and microprocessors deal with discrete, sampled signals. For these there are **difference equations** rather than differential equations, and the $z$-transform rather than the Laplace. (Here it is not intended to deal with these in great depth and the interested reader is referred to references [13] and [14].)

The difference equation arises as the digital data is sampled, say, every $T$ seconds. So the analogue signal $y(T)$ becomes:

$$y(0), y(1), y(2), \ldots, y(kT), \ldots y(\infty T)$$

where $k$ represents an integer. Usually the function is not of interest up to infinity, but to some general time $kT$. Hence the **discrete-time signal** is referred to as $y(kT)$, or simply $y(k)$. To appreciate a difference equation, first, consider an expression like equation (5.6) for a first-order system:

$$x - y = \tau \frac{\mathrm{d}y}{\mathrm{d}T} \tag{5.14}$$

where for simplicity $x$ and $y$ have replaced $t_{\text{fluid}}$ and $t_{\text{s}}$ respectively. For a discrete-time function, the differential can be replaced by the **backward difference** term:

$$\frac{\mathrm{d}y}{\mathrm{d}T} = \frac{y(kT) - y((k-1)T)}{T} \tag{5.15}$$

Substituting equation (5.15) into equation (5.14) along with $x = x(kT)$ and $y = y(kT)$ gives:

$$y(kT) = y((k-1)T) - \frac{1}{\tau} T \{y(kT) - x(kT)\} \tag{5.16}$$

This is a difference equation, derived from the backward difference method. The forward difference method, rarely used in practice [14], employs $y((k+1)T$ and $y(kT)$ instead of $y(kT)$ and $y((k-1)T)$ respectively in equation (5.15).

From equation (5.16) the $z$-transform can be obtained:

$$Y(z) = z^{-1}Y(z) - \frac{1}{\tau} T \{Y(z) - X(z)\} \tag{5.17}$$

where $Y$ and $X$ indicate that they are the $z$-transforms of $y$ and $x$, as is the similar notation for the Laplace transforms. Notice, by comparing equations (5.16) and (5.17) that $z^{-1}$ acts like an operator on $Y(z)$, shifting it back to the previous sample. The discrete-time transfer function for the first-order system is:

$$G(z) = \frac{Y(z)}{X(z)} = \frac{T}{[\tau(1 - z^{-1}) + T]} \qquad (5.18)$$

Comparing this with the Laplace transfer function in equation (5.9), $z$ is related to $s$, for backward difference equations, by:

$$s = \frac{1 - z^{-1}}{T} \qquad (5.19)$$

One distinct advantage of the $z$-transform is that the coefficients for a more complex transfer function than a first-order system (and most real items of plant are more complex than first-order systems), can be identified directly by numerical techniques on a computer. One such technique is that of **recursive least squares**. The basis of the least squares method is dealt with in Chapter 10 on monitoring and targeting, and references [15] and [16] cover its use for identification.

## 5.6 Dead time and distance velocity lag

So far, we have considered first-order, simple systems like the sensor in Chapter 4. However, the heating system in Fig. 5.4 is more complex. The block diagram method implies that the block and transfer function for each system element, such as the pump, pipework and radiators can be combined to form the overall system transfer function, as shown in Fig. 5.9. Indeed the simplification of complex systems into cascaded first-order systems can be a useful step in analysing complex systems. Stoecker and Stoecker illustrate this by examining a temperature sensor bulb containing a liquid [11].

Generally combining and cascading transfer functions and blocks is satisfactory, provided that there is no **interaction** or **loading** between the blocks. In thermal systems the interaction is relatively small but one must be aware of its possibility. Nagrath and Gopal [7] illustrate interaction by considering two electrical RC circuits (first-order systems) (Fig. 5.10).

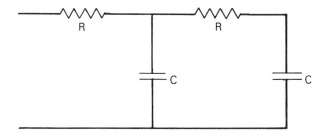

**Fig. 5.10** Two electrical circuits.

One would expect the combined transfer function to be:

$$\frac{1}{(1 + \tau s)} \frac{1}{(1 + \tau s)}$$

whereas more correctly it is:

$$\frac{1}{(\tau^2 s^2 + 3\tau s + 1)}$$

Gille, Pelegrin and Decaulne [8] advocate using transfer matrices where inter-action is considered likely.

To examine a more complex system (but not as complex as a heating system) consider a domestic hot-water, DHW, storage calorifier, heated by primary hot water from a boiler flowing through a coil in the calorifier to heat up the secondary stored water (Fig. 5.11).

If the stored DHW is initially cold and the valve is opened to let in primary hot water from the boiler at time $T = 0$, then the primary hot water takes a short time to get to the coil and the coil temperature, $t_c$, does not immediately respond (Fig. 5.12). This is an example of a **distance–velocity lag**. The coil then has to heat up, and as it can be regarded as a first-order system, it gives rise to the first-order response or **exponential lag**. The water in the calorifier then has to heat up and eventually the sensor begins to warm up and register a temperature change. As shown in Fig. 5.12, there is quite a time lag between the hot-water valve opening and the BEMS temperature sensor responding. There is a **dead time** before the sensor shows any perceptible change in temperature.

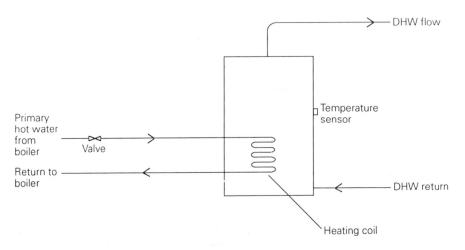

**Fig. 5.11** Temperature measurement of domestic hot water.

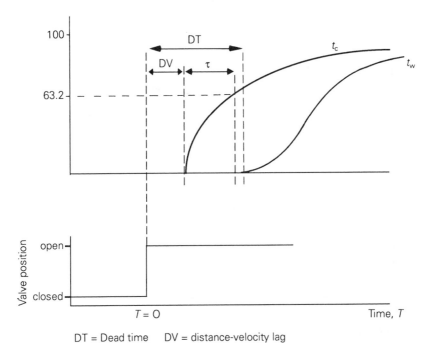

DT = Dead time    DV = distance-velocity lag

**Fig. 5.12**  Responses and time lags.

On a practical note, the temperature that the coil is trying to heat the water to is around 80°C, the primary water temperature from the boiler. This temperature is too high for domestic hot water and would waste energy. A temperature of 55°C is more appropriate (see reference [9] for further details and CIBSE Technical Memorandum 13 for information on minimizing the risk of legionnaires' disease [10]). Consequently, the BEMS would cut off the supply of hot water from the boiler by closing the valve when $t_w$ reached 55°C.

The overall response of the system (calorifier, valve, primary and secondary water and sensor), as measured by the sensor, is of many (say, $n$) first-order systems interacting to form an $n$th order system. An $n$th order system has $n$ time constants and is described by a differential equation with differential terms up to $d^n t$.

As Fig. 5.12 shows, and Fig. 5.13 shows in greater detail for a fifth-order system ($n = 5$), there is a very slow initial rise in temperature which contributes to the dead time. However, the fifth-order system can be approximated to a first-order system with a dead time, as (Fig. 5.13).

All these dead times and distance–velocity lags in systems contribute to poor control as will be shown later. It suffices to mention here that for on/off control the BEMS will not switch on or off at the required limits as the sensor

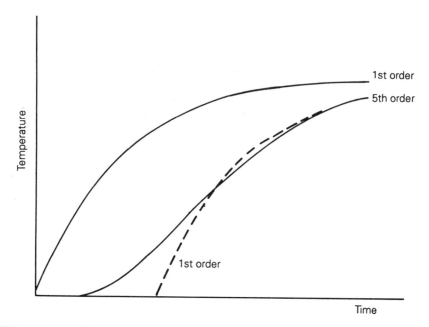

**Fig. 5.13**  A fifth-order system.

is lagging behind the controlled system due to system and sensor lags and responses. As is shown in Fig. 5.14, this will result in a wider differential than intended.

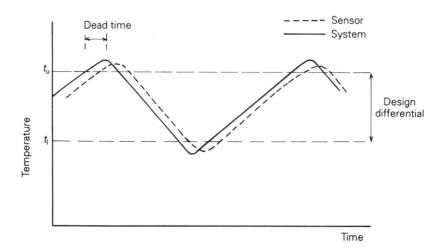

**Fig. 5.14**  The effect of time lags.

## 5.7 Reaction rate and cycling

At low loads the dead times and lags can produce considerable overshoot of the upper differential limit, as the rise in temperature is very steep. This rise in temperature is the **process reaction rate**, or simply the reaction rate.

This reaction rate can be observed with a BEMS by logging the appropriate temperature sensor and displaying the logged data as a graph. The reaction rate is simply the slope of the on/off temperature curves displayed. The steepness of these slopes gives an idea of the heat load and the heat supply. This may be quantified by considering a first-order system, and using the familiar first-order equation:

$$\text{Heat flow into system} - \text{heat flow out of system}$$
$$= \text{rate of change of heat stored in system} \tag{5.20}$$

$$= MC_p \frac{dt}{dT}$$

where $M$ = mass of the system (kg);
$C_p$ = specific heat capacity of the system (kJ kg$^{-1}$ K$^{-1}$);
$t$ = temperature of the system (°C);
$T$ = time (s).

If we consider the DHW storage calorifier which we have discussed earlier, shown in Fig. 5.15, then equation (5.20) becomes:

$$MC_p \frac{dt_w}{dT} = Q_{in} - Q_{out} \tag{5.21}$$

where $t_w$ = DHW temperature (°C);
$Q_{in}$ = heat supplied from the boiler (W);
$Q_{out}$ = heat requirement of the DHW load (W).

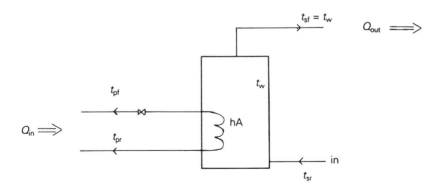

**Fig. 5.15** DHW cylinder.

During the heating process the slope is given by $dt_w/dT$. This is often referred to as the process reaction rate, the term having its origins in the process control industry.

If $Q_{in}$ and $Q_{out}$ are almost equal (i.e. there is a large DHW load), then $dt_w/dT$ will be small and there will be a shallow temperature rise. If $t_w$ is within the differential, then there will be little cycling on and off, as is shown in Fig. 5.16. When $Q_{in}$ is much greater than $Q_{out}$, $dt_w/dT$ and the process reaction rate will be high; this could lead to significant cycling (Fig. 5.16).

If there is no DHW load (i.e. no outflow of DHW), and ignoring the heat losses, then $Q_{out} = 0$ and all the heat gets stored in the cylinder. Putting in more detail about the heat exchange from the cylinder coil gives:

$$MC_p \frac{dt_w}{dT} = hA \left[ \frac{t_{pf} + t_{pr}}{2} - t_w \right] \qquad (5.22)$$

where $h$ = heat transfer coefficient for coil (W m$^{-2}$ K$^{-1}$);
    $A$ = area of the coil ($m^2$);
    $t_{pf}$ = temperature of primary hot-water flow from the boiler (°C);
    $t_{pr}$ = temperature of primary hot-water return to the boiler (°C);
    $\dfrac{t_{pf} + t_{pr}}{2}$ = the mean temperature of the coil (°C).

The temperature rise will be a first-order curve as shown in Fig. 5.17 with a time constant of $\tau = MC_p/hA$. The slope of the temperature rise will be:

$$\frac{dt_w}{dT} = \frac{(t_m - t_w)}{\tau} \qquad (5.23)$$

where $t_m = \dfrac{t_{pf} + t_{pr}}{2}$ (°C)

Once the temperature of the stored water, $t_w$, reaches 55°C, the valve shuts off the primary hot water. Although heat losses from the calorifier were

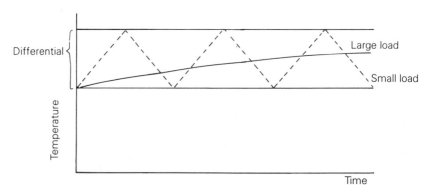

**Fig. 5.16**   Process reaction rates.

ignored earlier, there will be losses, which will make $Q_{out}$ non-zero. The slope of the subsequent cooling down process will be:

$$\frac{dt_w}{dT} = \frac{Q_{out}}{MC_p} \qquad (5.24)$$

The form of $Q_{out}$ will be similar to the heat exchange term from the coil, in that it will be proportional to the temperature difference between the hot water, $t_w$, and the ambient inside air temperature, $t_{ai}$:

$$Q_{out} = h_{loss} A_{cal} (t_w - t_{ai})$$

where $h_{loss}$ = heat transfer coefficient for the heat losses from the calorifier
$\qquad$ (W m$^{-2}$ K$^{-1}$);
$\qquad A_{cal}$ = area of the calorifier (m$^2$)
So the calorifier water will cool down as a first-order curve with a time constant of $\tau = MC_p/h_{loss} A_{cal}$, as is shown in Fig. 5.17.

The valve will open for the primary hot water to flow through the coil when $t_w$ has dropped through the on/off differential, $t_{diff}$. $t_{diff}$, typically 5 K, is small in comparison to the overall temperature rise of the calorifier water from cold, say, 10 K, to 55°C. Hence the heating up and cooling down curves, or process reaction rates, can be approximated to straight lines over the small range of $t_{diff}$, with the lines having constant slopes, $dt_w/dT$ having two constant values, one for the 'on' state and the other for the 'off' state.

The time that the primary hot water is flowing, or the heating is 'on' is:

$$T_{on} = \frac{dT}{dt_w} t_{diff}$$

$$= \frac{t_{diff} MC_p}{Q_{in} - Q_{out}} \qquad (5.25)$$

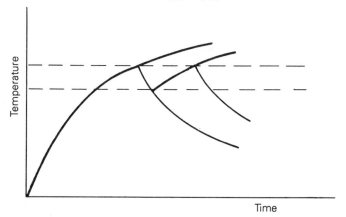

**Fig. 5.17** First-order system cycling.

Here the outflow and heat losses, $Q_{out}$, have been included for completeness. $Q_{out}$ will vary according to the load; the water drawn off from the secondary system and the supply of cold water. $Q_{in}$, however, will be relatively constant as the mean primary hot-water temperature in the coil, $t_m$, will be fairly constant and $t_w$ will be limited by the differential. Relating $Q_{in}$ and $Q_{out}$ by a load factor, $\Phi$, $Q_{out}$ being regarded as the load here:

$$Q_{out} = \Phi Q_{in} \tag{5.26}$$

where $0 \leq \Phi \leq 1$, equation (5.25) can be recast into:

$$T_{on} = \frac{t_{diff} M C_p}{Q_{in}(1 - \Phi)} \tag{5.27}$$

The time that the hot-water flow is off, $T_{off}$, is:

$$T_{off} = \frac{t_{diff} M C_p}{\Phi Q_{in}} \tag{5.28}$$

The period of cycling is given by:

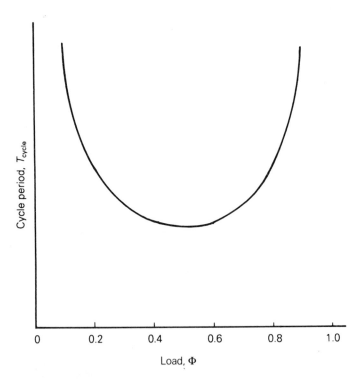

**Fig. 5.18**   The variation of cycle period with load.

$$T_{cycle} = T_{on} + T_{off}$$

$$= \frac{t_{diff} MC_p}{Q_{in}} \left[ \frac{1}{(1 - \Phi)} + \frac{1}{\Phi} \right]$$

$$= \frac{t_{diff} MC_p}{Q_{in}} \left[ \frac{1}{(1 - \Phi)\Phi} \right] \tag{5.29}$$

A graph of this equation is given in Fig. 5.18. It should be noted that the graph is flat-bottomed, with a minimum cycling period at $\Phi = 0.5$ of:

$$T_{cycle} = 4 \frac{t_{diff} MC_p}{Q_{in}} \tag{5.30}$$

It is interesting that the cycling is not proportional to the load, with increasing cycling at low loads, as is commonly thought.

With a BEMS, one has the capability of observing the cycling of plant and the ability of setting the optimum differential. Also the effects of dead times and lags will show up and may lead to remedial work to reduce excesses.

*Example*
The DHW calorifier considered above would probably have the secondary DHW being circulated and used. This was ignored in the calculations above. How would it affect the response of the calorifier?

*Solution*
Assuming the heat loss from the calorifier to be negligible compared to the heat in the used DHW, then:

$$Q_{out} = \dot{m} \, C_p \, (t_{sf} - t_{sr}) \tag{5.31}$$

where   $\dot{m}$ = mass flow rate of DHW (kg s$^{-1}$);
$C_p$ = specific heat capacity of the system (DHW) (kJ kg$^{-1}$ K$^{-1}$);
$t_{sf}$ = temperature of secondary, DHW, flow water = $t_w$ (°C);
$t_{sr}$ = temperature of secondary, DHW, return water (°C).
So the heating-up process is given by equation (5.21), now including the loss term in equation (5.31):

$$\frac{MC_p \, dt_w}{dT} = hA \, (t_m - t_w) - \dot{m}C_p \, (t_w - t_{sr})$$

or:

$$\frac{dt_w}{dT} = \frac{1}{\tau} \, (t_m - t_w) - \frac{\dot{m}}{M} \, (t_w - t_{sr}) \tag{5.32}$$

If $t_{sr}$ is the temperature of the feed water to the calorifier and it is constant, then taking the Laplace transform of equation (5.32) gives:

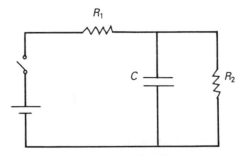

**Fig. 5.19**   Electrical analogy of DHW calorifier with flow.

$$st_w(s) = \frac{1}{\tau}\left(t_m(s) - t_w(s)\right) - \frac{\dot{m}}{M} t_w(s)$$

$$t_w(s)\{s\tau + 1 + \beta\} = t_m(s) \tag{5.33}$$

where $\beta = \dot{m}\tau/M$.

This can be cast into the same form as a first-order equation:

$$t_w(s)\{s\tau^* + 1\} = \frac{1}{(1+\beta)} t_m(s) \tag{5.34}$$

where $\tau^* = \tau/(1+\beta)$.

In effect, the time constant, $\tau$, has been reduced and $t_w$ will not tend towards $t_m$, but a reduced value of it, $t_m/(1+\beta)$. If the DHW cylinder was of diameter $D$ and height $h$ and the pipe through which the water flowed was of diameter $d$ and the water flowed with a velocity $v$, then:

$$\beta = \frac{\dot{m}\tau}{M} = \frac{d^2 v}{D^2 h}\tau$$

The electrical equivalent is an RC circuit with another resistance across the capacitor, as shown in Fig. 5.19.

## 5.8  Condition and logic control

Apart from on/off control, BEMS outstations can use the logic potential in their CPUs to perform useful control functions. Consider the heating system shown in Fig. 5.4 with a boiler and a pump. Control is by switching off the pump when the room temperature sensor reads a higher temperature than the set point.

This could be done by a **conditional** statement quite easily in a BEMS which has programmable soft points, as opposed to the function modules mostly discussed up to now. The statement would take the form of:

IF $t_{ai} > 21$ THEN boiler off

In plain English, this means that if the inside air temperature is greater than 21°C, then switch off the boiler. A differential could be introduced with the statement:

IF $t_{ai} < 20$ THEN boiler on

Although this is much easier than having a loop module (a driver or interface to the actuator is still required), there is a problem of the initial heat up of the room. When $t_{ai}$ first rises through 20°C, before it has yet reached 21°C, the boiler is already on and the absence of a condition may create problems. Another conditional statement could solve this by indicating that the boiler was already on.

But whether a loop module or a programmable soft point is used, a condition statement can independently add to the heating control by switching off the boiler when it is warm outside, on a warm spring or autumn day. The existing control just switches off the pump when the room is up to temperature, leaving the boiler to idle, keeping its own thermostat warm. With an external air temperature sensor, the boiler can be switched off when it is mild:

IF $t_{ao} > 15$ THEN boiler off

For a BEMS using function modules, the conditional control is done by means of a **hysteresis comparator** module and a digital driver, similar to the binary driver, above, but receiving a digital input signal, not an analogue one. A hysteresis comparator module is shown in Fig. 5.20, A being the input from the sensor analogue node, and C being the hysteresis band either side of the set point B.

The hysteresis band stops any oscillation in output when the temperature is exactly at the set point. For our heating example, B could be set to 14°C and C to 2 K. The boiler would then be switched off when $t_{ao} = 15$°C and on again when $t_{ao} = 13$°C.

It is assumed in this control that when $t_{ao}$ is 15°C, then with internal gains in the room (lighting, occupants, equipment and solar), $t_{ai}$ will be around 21°C. To make sure that this is so another hysteresis comparator can be configured to the address node of the $t_{ai}$ sensor and the outputs from the two comparator modules given as the inputs to a logic **AND module**.

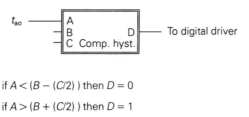

if $A < (B - (C/2))$ then $D = 0$

if $A > (B + (C/2))$ then $D = 1$

**Fig. 5.20** Comparator hysteresis module.

150   *Basic control*

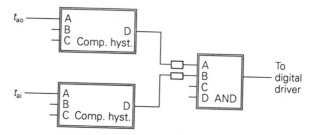

.21 Internal and external control conditions.

**Fig. 5.21**   Internal and external control conditions.

Only two of the AND module's four inputs are used here. The operation of the AND module is described by the **truth table** in Table 5.3.

**Table 5.3**   Truth table for AND module

|   | Inputs |   |   | Output |
| A | B | C | D | D |
|---|---|---|---|---|
| 0 | 0 | 1 | 1 | 0 |
| 0 | 1 | 1 | 1 | 0 |
| 1 | 0 | 1 | 1 | 0 |
| 1 | 1 | 1 | 1 | 1 |

The two redundant inputs, C and D here, would have to be set at default values of 1 for the above truth table to work.

The truth table is so called as it evolved from **boolean algebra**, or boolean logic, where 1 is associated with a statement being true and 0 represents a false statement. In boolean algebra the AND function is represented by • and so the truth table (Table 5.3) as a boolean algebraic equation would be:

$$D = A \bullet B \qquad (5.35)$$

Another way of considering the truth table for an AND function is of switches in series; if one is open, 0, then no current can pass. A current only passes when all switches are shut.

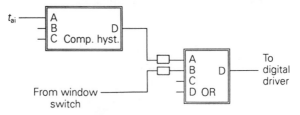

Internal temperature and window switch combined.

**Fig. 5.22**   Internal temperature and window switch combined.

It could happen with our heating control for the boiler that the room temperature is low, although $t_{ao}$ is above 15°C because the window is open. A trip switch could be fitted to the window to send a binary signal to the BEMS outstation. This could be combined with the $t_{ai}$ hysteresis comparator digital signal in an **OR** logic module.

**Table 5.4**  Truth table for OR module

|   | Inputs | Output |
|---|---|---|
| A | B | D |
| 0 | 0 | 0 |
| 0 | 1 | 1 |
| 1 | 0 | 1 |
| 1 | 1 | 1 |

In boolean algebra the OR function is represented by + and so the truth table (Table 5.4) as a boolean algebraic equation would be:

$$D = A + B \tag{5.36}$$

As with the AND function, above, another way of considering the truth table for an OR function is of switches in parallel; if either is closed, i.e. 1, then a current can pass.

Other boolean logic function modules also exist in most BEMS outstations, such as NOT, NOT AND, (NAND) and NOR, but they are not generally as useful for controlling plant as the two we have described.

These logic functions are powerful control elements and for industrial switching there are **programmable logic controllers** (PLCs) which are a lower form of BEMS outstation. In fact PLCs have been used to control some building services plant, but they have limited capabilities, even compared to the smaller BEMS outstation which are of similar cost.

## References

[1]  CIBSE (1986) CIBSE Guide, Volume A, Section A1, Environmental Criteria For Design, Chartered Institution of Building Services Engineers, London.

[2]  CIBSE (1986) CIBSE Guide, Volume A, Section A2, Weather and solar data, Chartered Institution of Building Services Engineers, London.

[3]  CIBSE (1986) CIBSE Guide, Volume A, Section A9, Estimation of plant capacity, Chartered Institution of Building Services Engineers, London.

[4]  CIBSE (1986) CIBSE Guide, Volume A, Section A7, Internal heat gains, Chartered Institution of Building Services Engineers, London.

[5]  Adams, S. and Holmes, M. (1977) *Determining Time Constants for Heating and Cooling Coils*, BSRIA Technical Note TN6/77, Building Services Research and Information Association, Bracknell.

[6]   Marshall, S. A. (1984) *Introduction to Control Theory*, Macmillan, London.

[7]   Nagrath, I. J. and Gopal, M. (1985) *Control Systems Engineering*, Wiley Eastern, New Delhi; new edition.

[8]   Gille, Pelegrin and Decaulne (1959) *Feedback Control Systems*, McGraw-Hill, New York.

[9]   CIBSE (1986) CIBSE Guide, Volume B, Section B4, Water service systems, Chartered Institution of Building Services Engineers, London.

[10]  *Minimising the Risk of Legionnaires' Disease*, CIBSE Technical Memorandum 13, Chartered Institution of Building Services Engineers, London, 1987.

[11]  Stoecker, W. F. and Stoecker, P. A. (1989) *Microcomputer Control of Thermal and Mechanical Systems*, Van Nostrand Reinhold, New York.

[12]  DiStefano, J. J., Stubberud, A. R. and Williams, J. J. (1987) *Theory and Problems of Feedback and Control Systems*, Schaum's Outline series, McGraw-Hill, New York.

[13]  Houpis, C. H. and Lamont, G. B. (1985) *Digital Control Systems Theory, Hardware, Software*, McGraw-Hill, New York.

[14]  Ogata, K. (1987) *Discrete-time Control Systems*, Prentice-Hall, Englewood Cliffs, NJ.

[15]  Iserman, R. (1981) *Digital Control Systems*. Springer-Verlag, Berlin.

[16]  Åstrom, K. J. and Witenmark, B. (1989) *Adaptive Control*. Addison-Wesley, Reading, Mass.

# 6

# PID three-term direct digital control

In Chapter 5 it was seen that on/off control either had the plant fully on or fully off, which could result in the controlled temperature overshooting the differential, due to the system and controller responses, especially at low loads. In Fig. 6.1 this is shown for room temperature control with a thermostat, demonstrating that the mean room temperature varies about the thermostat set point according to the load.

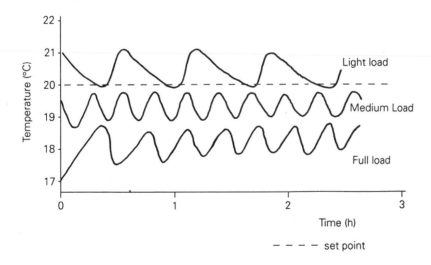

**Fig. 6.1**  Room temperature control with a thermostat.

A better form of control is to vary or modulate the plant output, so that as the temperature approaches the required value the output can be reduced to stop any overshoot. This of course can be done only if the plant can be modulated, for instance, by using a modulating control valve or, in the case of a boiler, by having a modulating burner. All of this adds to the expense of the plant but produces better control.

The control used in BEMS that can provide this modulating, or varying, action is **proportional plus integral plus differential** (PID) control. As there are three distinct parts to PID control, it is also referred to as **three-term control**. Each term will now be examined.

## 6.1 Proportional control

A crude and simple example of proportional control is the ballcock valve in a cistern. As the water rises in the cistern, so the ball is raised and gradually closes the valve. When the cistern is empty, the valve is fully open and when the cistern is full, the valve is shut.

The water cylinder analogy we have used before can also illustrate proportional control. The two-port valve in Fig. 6.2 is a modulating valve. When the water level is at $h_u$, then the valve is fully shut, and when it is at $h_l$, it is fully open. The thermal analogy to the height of water is the temperature. In Fig. 6.3 the flow of water into the cylinder is proportional to the height of the water as measured by the sensor, hence proportional control.

The difference between the upper- and lower-level limits, $h_u$ and $h_l$, is the **proportional band** (PB), or **throttling range**. It is similar to the differential

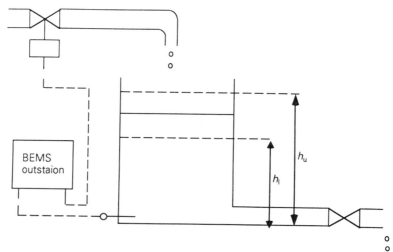

**Fig. 6.2**  Water analogy

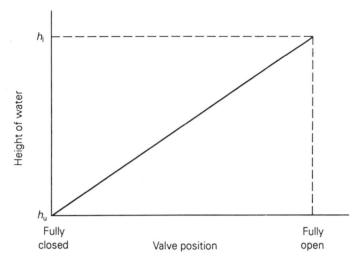

**Fig. 6.3** Proportional valve control.

for on/off control, and similar considerations have to be given to its setting. Too narrow and the control tends towards on/off control and oscillation. Too wide and there is little control as the temperature offset can be large. These effects are shown in Fig. 6.4 for a heating valve when subjected to a step change increase in the heating load. The heating valve is a mixing valve, as will be explained in Chapter 8 on compensator control, with a water temperature sensor in the pipe shortly downstream from the valve.

To set up a proportional controller, either in BEMS software, or as a stand-alone, old-fashioned proportional controller, the proportional band and the **set**

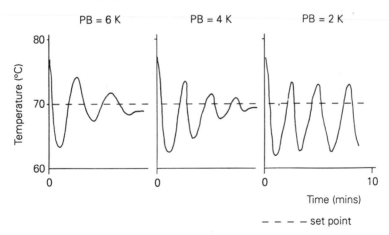

**Fig. 6.4** Responses of a proportional controller.

**point** are adjusted to the required settings. Traditionally the set point is the temperature (or in our analogy the height), in the middle of the proportional band (PB).

*Example*

A proportional controller, set to 20°C, $t_{set}$, controls a room heater which can be modulated and at full output is rated at 4 kW. When the outside temperature, $t_{ao}$, is $-2$°C, then the heater is at full output and the room temperature, $t_{ai}$, is 18°C. If the set point is in the middle of the proportional band, what is $t_{ai}$ when $t_{ao}$ is 4°C? Ignore thermal storage in the room structure.

*Solution*

The relationship between $t_{ai}$ and $t_{ao}$ is shown in Fig. 6.5. It is based on the two points given in the problem. One is where $t_{ao}$ is $-2$°C and $t_{ai}$ is 18°C, and the other is derived from the fact that $t_{set}$ is in the middle of the PB, so that:

$$PB = 2(t_{set} - t_1)$$
$$= 2(20 - 18)$$
$$= 4\text{K}$$

where $t_1$ the lower control temperature of the PB (°C).

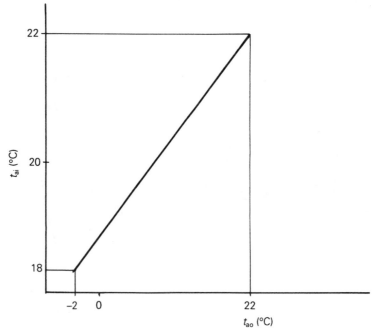

**Fig. 6.5**   The relationship between $t_{ai}$ and $t_{ao}$.

This means that the upper control temperature, $t_u$, is 22°C. So the second point of the graph is at $t_{ai}$ with a value of 22°C when there is no heating, and no need for it, so $t_{ao}$ must be 22°C as well. The equation for this line is:

$$t_{ai} = \frac{1}{6} t_{ao} + 18.33 \qquad (6.1)$$

When $t_{ao} = 4°C$:

$$t_{ai} = \frac{1}{6} 4 + 18.33$$

$$t_{ai} = 19°C$$

In this example, $t_{ai}$ is below the set point of 20°C. In fact there is only one value of outside temperature at which the set point is achieved, and this is when $t_{ao} = 10°C$. The analogy with the water cylinder is that the valve on the outflow represents the heat loss to the outside. This valve can be identical to the modulating valve on the inflow, and the flow of water into the cylinder exactly matches the outflow. The water level will come to equilibrium, but for only one valve setting will the set point level be achieved.

The difference between the set point and the measured value (either room temperature or water level in our examples) is the **error** or **offset** as we have already mentioned in Chapter 5 on on/off control. The proportional control block diagram, as shown in Fig. 6.6, is very similar to that for the on/off control. It is often assumed that the sensor introduces negligible error, so that there is unity feedback of the measured value.

### 6.1.1 Proportional gain

The output signal, $u(T)$, from the proportional control block is simply a proportional relationship with $e(T)$:

$$u(T) = \frac{1}{PB} e(T) \qquad (6.2)$$

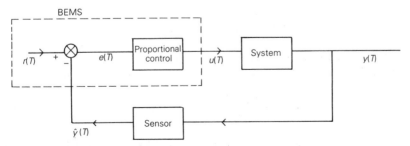

**Fig. 6.6** Proportional control with a BEMS.

When a BEMS loop module is set up, or configured, the **proportional gain**, $K_p$, is sometimes used [11] instead of the proportional band, PB, or the **proportional control action** [10]. The relationship which is often used between $K_p$ and PB is:

$$K_p = \frac{100\%}{PB} = \frac{1}{PB} \quad (K^{-1}) \qquad (6.3)$$

The 100% represents the full range of the output of the controlled device, e.g. a valve going from fully closed (0%) to fully open (100%).

Note that $K_p$ has the dimension of inverse temperature, so that the output, $u(T)$, is dimensionless. The proportional control equation in equation (6.2), now becomes:

$$u(T) = K_p \, e(T) \qquad (6.4)$$

Where $u(T)$ is the signal from the loop to the driver, 0% to 100%. The driver then converts this signal to an electrical signal for the valve.

The above example considers the proportional control from the steady state, time-independent situation. But the dynamic, time-dependent approach, although mathematically more complicated, is more revealing of the control action.

*Example*
Consider the dynamics of the 4 kW heater in the previous example, assuming that the room has a first-order response and the sensor introduces no delays or errors.

*Solution*
If $t_{set}$ is the set point temperature and $t_{ai}$ is the inside air temperature, then the error is:

$$e = t_{set} - t_{ai}$$

and the heater output is:

$$Q_{max} \frac{u(T)}{100} = Q_{max} \frac{K_p \, e(T)}{100} \quad kW$$

where $Q_{max}$ = maximum heater output, 4 kW.

The differential equation describing the first-order room system and control is:

$$\tau \frac{dt_{ai}}{dT} = \frac{Q_{max} K_p}{100 \, H} (t_{set} - t_{ai}) - (t_{ai} - t_{ao}) \qquad (6.5)$$

where $H$ = overall heat loss from the room (0.2 kW $K^{-1}$), and $\tau$ = room time constant (s).

First-order equations such as that in equation (6.5) are discussed in greater detail in Chapter 9 on optimiser control, and the solution of equation (6.5) is:

$$\left[ \frac{K_p \, \Gamma t_{set} + t_{ao} - (1 + \Gamma K_p)t_{ai}(T)}{K_p \, \Gamma t_{set} + t_{ao} - (1 + \Gamma K_p)t_{ai}(0)} \right] = \exp \left[ \frac{-T(1 + \Gamma K_p)}{\tau} \right] \tag{6.6}$$

where $\Gamma = \dfrac{Q_{max}}{100H} = 0.2 \, K$;

$t_{ai}(0) = $ inside temperature at time $T = 0$;

$t_{ai}(T) = $ inside temperature at time $T$.

The steady state inside temperature is reached as $T$ tends to infinity and the right-hand side of equation (6.6) tends to zero. This condition is fulfilled when:

$$t_{ai} = \frac{K_p \, \Gamma t_{set} + t_{ao}}{1 + \Gamma K_p}$$

When $t_{ao} = 4°C$, as in the previous example, then with $PB = 4 \, K$ ($K_p = 25\% \, K^{-1}$):

$$t_{ai} = \frac{25 \times 0.2 \times 22 + 4}{1 + 0.2 \times 25}$$

$$= 19°C$$

in agreement with the previous example. Here the set point is 22°C, due to the definition of $u(T)$ and the error. The steady state offset is given by:

$$\text{offset} = t_{set} - t_{ai}$$

$$= t_{set} - \frac{K_p \, \Gamma t_{set} + t_{ao}}{1 + \Gamma K_p} \tag{6.7}$$

It is easier to examine equation (6.7) if $t_{ao}$ is set to zero. As the gain is increased, so:

$$\frac{K_p \Gamma}{1 + \Gamma K_p}$$

tends to unity, and the offset disappears. But notice that if the gain were to go above 100% $K^{-1}$, the heater output cannot go above $Q_{max}$ or 4 kW, so the output signal is effectively limited at a maximum at larger errors.

Another factor influencing the selection of the proportional gain is the effective change in $\tau$, as shown in equation (6.6) where it is reduced by the factor:

$$\frac{1}{(1 + \Gamma K_p)}$$

A shorter value of $\tau$ speeds up the response but also increases the oscillation of the controlled element of plant, as is shown in Fig. 6.4 for a heating valve with a sensor close to it.

### 6.1.2  Loop modules and drivers

For a BEMS, the software to implement proportional control action is with a **loop controller**, or **loop module**, and a driver as shown in Fig. 6.7. The loop module is so-called because this is where the feedback loop returns and where the majority of the control of the loop is carried out.

The sensor sends the signal, $y(T)$, to the analogue input address – or **node** – of the loop module, P (process variable). Two set point analogue address points are shown; O, for the set point temperature during the building's occupancy period and U for the set point temperature during the building's unoccupied period. For frost protection, U could be set to, say, 10°C, while O is set to say 20°C. The module changes between O and U by the digital address, SS (**set point selection**), being changed to 1 or 0 from a **timing module**, which defines the occupancy times, or from a **logic module**, discussed in Chapter 10. Equation (6.2) is then used to derive the output from the loop module to the driver's analogue address. This is between 0% and 100% – 100% corresponding to the bottom of the PB and 0% corresponding to the top, when the required temperature has been reached. Here the set point is at the top of the PB, so that the error is positive when control is required, which simplifies calculation.

For testing the control of a system, for instance, during commissioning, then the **manual selection** (MS), digital node bit is set to 1 and the analogue value

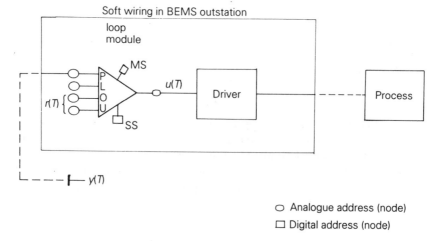

**Fig. 6.7**  BEMS loop module and driver.

written in the analogue node, L, is sent to the loop output, regardless of the set points (O and U), the sensor input (P) or the control parameters.

The driver converts the 0% to 100% signal from the loop module to a voltage or current to drive the plant, for example, a modulating valve. Two types of driver are used with loop modules for the proportional control of modulating valves: an **analogue output driver** and a **raise/lower driver**, as shown in Fig. 6.8. These are similar to the **binary driver** in Chapter 5, except for the outputs.

The analogue driver converts the 0% to 100% signal into a continuous, analogue, signal to drive the valve. A hardware link in the example outstation in Chapter 2 can simply be changed to give either a voltage or current signal depending on the plant being driven. The 0% signal is for the valve fully closed, and the 100% signal is for the valve fully open. If the valve actuator or motor requires a different range of signal, then **offset** and **range** constants can be set in the driver's software. This is done in the configuration mode from the central station or a local, portable PC, as we have discussed in Chapter 2.

The raise/lower driver can be used to drive a valve with a **split-phase** motor. The raise digital output signal, when the raise bit is 1 and the lower bit is 0, drives the motor in a direction to open the valve, and the lower signal, when the lower bit is 1 and the raise bit is 0, drives the motor in the reverse direction to close the valve. When both output bits are low, then the valve stays stationary. To position the valve the **full drive time** of the valve (the time for the valve to go from fully open to fully closed) must be known, so that the driver drives the valve for the correct time to move the valve to the required position.

With valve wear and slippage, the full drive time may change with age. In this case, a **position indicator potentiometer** can be used to provide feedback to the driver of the valve's position. An alternative is **boundless control**. With

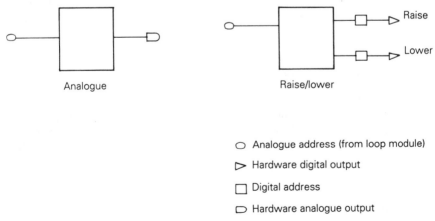

Analogue                          Raise/lower

○ Analogue address (from loop module)

▷ Hardware digital output

☐ Digital address

▭ Hardware analogue output

**Fig. 6.8** Drivers.

this method, the 0% and 100% limits are reset when the valve reaches its fully closed and fully open positions and can move no further.

A **loop reschedule time** can be used to suppress the normal schedule service time, so that valves, actuators and relays are not constantly moved and worn each service time. This suppression takes the form of increasing the service time to the relevant output.

If sensors feeding loops malfunction, then there are **loop deviation alarms** and **loop failure reactions** to ensure the sensor malfunction does not result in control malfunction. A deviation alarm is raised when the loop error goes outside limits (set by the user at the control configuration stage). Once the relevant sensor feeding the loop develops a fault, then the loop 'ignores' its reading and defaults to a loop failure action. A default can take a number of modes. The first mode is for the loop to use the last within limits sensor reading. Taking a present input value for the loop and disregarding any faulty inputs such that the loop puts out a constant output signal is a second mode. The third mode is a variation on the second, in that the loop does not return to normal control until the operator has changed the loop to manual selection (MS) and back to automatic control. This is a form of manual reset safety button (as found on boiler thermostats) and is used to draw the operator's attention to an important fault that has occurred.

With such default reactions, heating can be ensured, even when there is a fault with the BEMS. In one incident, recounted by a local authority energy manager, a BEMS outstation had been wrongly programmed to switch the heating off at the weekend. Unfortunately, the heating was for a block of flats. The BEMS operator at the civic centre had dialled up the block instead of a school. Emergency maintenance men were called during the weekend by a councillor who lived in the now cold block of flats, and although they knew nothing of the BEMS system, the councillor demanded action. So the men proceeded to take a crowbar to the outstation to open it. In so doing they managed to put the outstation into failure mode, which then started the heating. All in the plant room were amazed!

## 6.2  Time proportional control

When we first discussed proportional control, it was stated that the controlled plant had to be capable of modulation – e.g. a boiler with a modulating burner or a modulating valve. However, on/off devices can be switched on for a certain time proportional to the error signal. This is **time proportional control**, implemented with a loop module connected to a time proportional driver. A time proportional driver is shown in Fig. 6.9

The time proportional (TP) driver keeps the plant on for a defined fraction of a period of time. The period of time, $\tau$, is set by the operator when the TP driver is configured. The loop module output, denoted here as $x\%$, then keeps

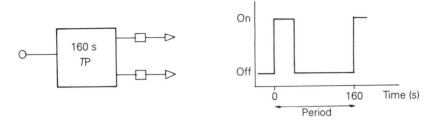

**Fig. 6.9**   A time proportional driver.

the plant on for a time:

$$\frac{x}{100} \tau$$

In Fig. 6.9 the output from the loop module is 25%, and the time period is 160 s, so the plant is on for 40 s every 160 s.

## 6.3   Proportional plus integral (PI) control

As we have already seen in the above example, there is always a persistent error, or offset, with proportional only control, except at one point where the plant output provides the heat to maintain the set point temperature. This is when the heater, in the previous example, would be half on. With a BEMS loop, where the set point is at the top of the PB, then the point of zero error would be when the set point temperature was achieved and the plant was off.

The persistent error of proportional control can be greatly reduced by increasing the control signal, $u(T)$, as the error persists with time. This is achieved by adding an integral term to the proportional term:

$$u(T) = K_p \{ e(T) + \frac{1}{T_i} \int_0^T e(T) \, dT \} \tag{6.8}$$

where $T_i$ = integral action time (s). The integral term may be considered as the 'memory' of the controller, looking at past errors. Sometimes integral action is defined in terms of $K_p/T_i$, the integral control action constant [10], or **integral gain**, $K_i$, or even **reset rate** [11]. Another term for PI control is proportional with **automatic reset**.

The BEMS loop module can be configured to PI control by setting $T_i$. Typical settings for BEMS will be about 200 s. As $T_i$ increases, so the integral action reduces, and large values of $T_i$ reduce the PI action to only P. There is no point in making $T_i$ less than the service schedule time, the time taken by the outstation microprocessor to service the other inputs and outputs before it gets back to the loop concerned. A typical value for this service time is 5 s.

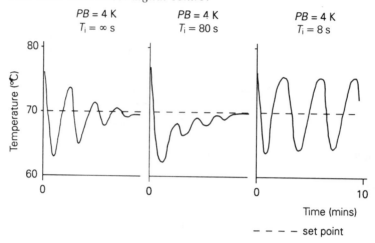

Fig. 6.10   Responses of a PI controller.

The responses of a heating valve to changes in $T_i$, for a PI controller with $K_p$ being kept constant, is shown in Fig. 6.10. $T_i$ does indeed reduce the offset inherent with P only control; but as $T_i$ is reduced, so the integral action becomes more dominant and the oscillations increase. Too much oscillation will reduce the life of the valve and actuator, so a compromise setting has to be used (as will be discussed shortly).

With two control parameters in PI control, both interact with each other. A setting of one parameter cannot be assumed to produce stable operation unless the other parameter is also carefully set. This adds to the complexity of setting up a two-term, PI control loop.

*Example*
Consider the use of a BEMS with PI control for (a) the previous example's room with the 4 kW heater, assuming that the room has a time constant of 20 min and there is a distance velocity lag of 10 min from the heater to the sensor; (b) a hot-water heating valve with a response of less than a minute and the sensor close to it; and (c) a boiler with a non-modulating burner.

*Solution*
(a) From the previous example the differential equation describing the room and the heater's proportional control was:

$$\tau \frac{dt_{ai}}{dT} = \frac{Q_{max} K_p}{100H}(t_{set} - t_{ai}) - (t_{ai} - t_{ao}) \tag{6.5}$$

where H = overall heat loss from the room ($0.2\,\text{kW K}^{-1}$), and $\tau$ = room time constant (s).

Now, however, there is integral control as well, so the heater output is:

$$Q_{max} \frac{u(T)}{100} = \frac{Q_{max}}{100} K_p \left\{ e(T) + \frac{1}{T_i} \int e(T) dT \right\} \tag{6.9}$$

where $Q_{max}$ = maximum heater output, 4 kW.

With the P only control, equation (6.5) could be solved analytically; but equation (6.9) is more difficult. One solution would be to solve equation (6.5) analytically for small time steps during which $Q_{max}$ was regarded as constant, it being varied after each time step using equation (6.9). Another method would be to transpose equation (6.5) into a difference equation (as mentioned in Chapter 5 and Section 6.5) and to solve it numerically. (See reference [12] for further details of numerical methods).

For now equations (6.5) and (6.9) will not be solved, but the problem is examined from a basic standpoint. Consider a step change either in the control or the load (the heat loss from the room). A step change shows the response of a system as was done for the heating valve example illustrated in Fig. 6.10.

Taking a step change in the control set point from the 22°C, in the previous example, to 20°C, then the error drops from 3 K to 1 K. Then, if the control were P only, the heating output would initially be reduced to 1 kW, after the 10 min distance–velocity lag, and the temperature would fall to its new steady state value. This can be determined from the steady state proportional control equation, as calculated in the first example in this chapter. With the new set point of 20°C, the steady state equation is determined from the two points $t_{ai} = 20°C$, $t_{ao} = 20°C$, and $t_{ai} = 16°C$, $t_{ao} = -4°C$:

$$t_{ao} = 6 t_{ai} - 100$$

With the first example's outside temperature of 4°C, then:

$$t_{ai} = 17.3°C$$

(In the first example with the set point at 22°C, $t_{ai} = 19°C$.)

With $K_p = 25$, and $\Gamma = 0.2$, as before, then equation (6.6)

$$\left[ \frac{K_p \Gamma t_{set} + t_{ao} - (1 + \Gamma K_p) t_{ai}(T)}{K_p \Gamma t_{set} + t_{ao} - (1 + \Gamma K_p) t_{ai}(0)} \right] = \exp \left[ \frac{-T(1 + \Gamma K_p)}{\tau} \right] \tag{6.6}$$

shows that the time to reach its steady state temperature is ∞, but to reach a temperature near to this, say, 18°C, using the log form of equation (6.6) it is:

$$\ln \left[ \frac{25 \times 0.2 \times 20 + 4 - (1 + 25 \times 0.2)18}{25 \times 0.2 \times 20 + 4 - (1 + 25 \times 0.2)19} \right] = \frac{-T(1 + 25 \times 0.2)}{20}$$

$$T = 3 \text{ min}$$

With the distance–velocity lag of 10 min, this makes 13 min. If a larger control signal were used, so that the loop output signal was large such that the heater's output were reduced to zero, then the time for the temperature to fall to 17.3°C would be given by equation (6.5) with $Q_{max}$ set to zero and the differential equation solved to give:

$$\ln\left[\frac{t_{ai}(T) - t_{ao}}{t_{ao}(0) - t_{ao}}\right] = \frac{-T}{\tau}$$

(This solution is derived in detail in Chapter 9 on optimiser control.) From this the time to reach 17.3°C, from the end of the distance–velocity lag is 2.4 min, still quite some time.

The introduction of an integral term would reduce the offset, but it would introduce a large signal during the distance–velocity lag if $T_i$ were not fairly large, effectively reducing the integral action. Even without the distance–velocity lag, the response of the system is still rather slow necessitating the use of a large $T_i$. Also to determine the responses to various settings of $K_p$ and $T_i$ would take the operator some time, and this is necessary in order to set up the PI controller, as is seen in Section 6.7. In practice, the distance–velocity lag of 10 min accounts only for the direct heat transfer from the heater to the sensor. But as will be seen in Chapter 9, there is also heat in the fabric of the building which takes some hours to respond to the heater's output, which would make the integral term even more difficult to set up. Thus P only control would be applicable in this case with the PB lowered to, say, 2 K to reduce the offset.

(b) For a hot-water heating valve with a response of less than a minute, and the sensor close to it, the response of the hot water in the pipe from the valve is going to be much faster. Here PI control is appropriate and easier to set up than in (a). Although there will be a distance–velocity lag between the valve and the sensor, this should be small as both are close together. The graphs in Figs 6.4–6.10 used to demonstrate the various settings of $K_p$ and $T_i$ are from such a heating valve.

(c) Although the boiler is either on or off, it does not have a modulating burner, the implementation of on/off control in Chapter 5 used a PID loop as an error detector in its P only mode. But if the I term were also implemented, then at large loads the integral term would be quite substantial as the temperature takes a long time to rise through the differential. The boiler is switched off when $u(T)$ is zero, or low, but with an integral term it is often non-zero when the error has become zero itself, as is shown in Fig. 6.11.

From calculus the integral operation in the integral term determines the area between the actual sensed temperature and the set point line. In Fig. 6.11 this is the area of the triangle formed by the sensed temperature and the upper

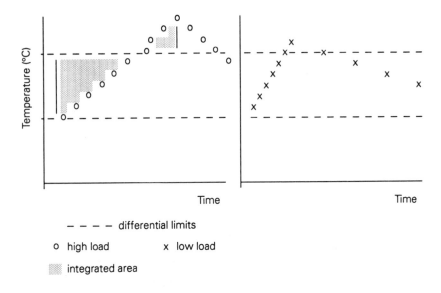

- - - - differential limits

o high load          x low load

░ integrated area

**Fig. 6.11**  PI loop for on/off device.

differential temperature, which in this case is also the set point. The error at the set point is zero, but the sensed temperature rises above the set point by an amount to make the upper triangle of an area $K_p/T_i$ times that of the lower triangle. Due to the sampling process of the BEMS, the triangles will actually be stepped.

When the load is low, though, the boiler flow water temperature rises faster through the differential, so that the integral term is not so large, and the overlap of the differential is not so high. This is counter to the normal tendency for on/off overlap to be high at low loads, as in Fig. 6.1, and smaller at higher loads. With suitable selection of a set point, $K_p$ and $T_i$, more accurate on/off control is possible.

With some BEMS, the PID loop output cannot go negative, so the integrated error when the temperature is above the set point is zero.

An ideal way of examining the control of a system before a BEMS is configured is to simulate the system on a computer, solving the differential equations of the various plant components. Hysteresis of the actuators should also be modelled. (Reference [13] constructs a mathematical model of a heater battery and its controller and examines various $K_p$ and $T_i$ settings.)

## 6.4  PID control

Full three-term, PID control has a differential term added to the PI equation (equation (6.5)), to give:

$$u(T) = K_p \left\{ e(T) + \frac{1}{T_i} \int_0^T e(T)\, dT + T_d \frac{de(T)}{dT} \right\} \qquad (6.10)$$

where $T_d$ = integral action time (s).

Whereas the integral term was the control's 'memory', the differential, or derivative, term 'looks' to the future, by examining the slope, or rate of change, of the error. It is the 'accelerator' and 'brake'. But this adds another parameter to be set up by the user, and as will be shown later, it can add to the potential for instability. As a result, when most BEMS outstations are configured the differential term is invariably left out by leaving $T_d$ at a default value of 0.

## 6.5 Discrete-time PID algorithms

So far in this discussion of the PID, three-term controller, the control equation (6.10) has been in the continuous, analogue form, whereas as has already been mentioned, BEMS CPUs operate with digital signals. The sensor signal is sampled and converted at the A/D to provide a suitable signal for the CPU. As was seen in Chapter 5 on basic control, difference equations are more appropriate [6]. In difference terms, the PID algorithm becomes:

$$u((k+1)T) = K_p \left\{ e((k+1)T) + \frac{T_{sample}}{T_i} \sum_{j=1}^{k} e(jT) \right.$$

$$\left. + \frac{T_d \left[ e((k+1)T) - e(kT) \right]}{T_{sample}} \right\} \qquad (6.11)$$

where $T_{sample}$ = sample time, which is the same as $T$ but the subscript has been used to distinguish it more clearly from the integral and derivative times.

Equation (6.11) is often referred to as the **position** form of the PID, as opposed to the **velocity** form which will be discussed shortly. The summation in equation (6.11) is the backward difference form of discrete integration, taking the integral during the last sample interval from $k$ to $(k+1)$, as a rectangle of height $e(kT)$ and width $T_{sample}$. The backward form increases the stability at long sampling intervals such as those used in BEMS ([7], [8]). Other forms of discrete integration, such as forward rectangular and trapezoidal summation [9] can give (equation (6.11)), different forms.

A simpler form of equation (6.11) comes from the $z$-transform regarding $z^{-1}$ as the backward shift operator:

$$z^{-1} f(kT) = f((k-1)T)$$

Using rectangular integration over the sampling interval, $T_{sample}$, the integral of the function, $f(kT)$, termed $I(kT)$, can be approximated to:

$$I(kT) = I((k-1)T) + T_{\text{sample}} f(kT)$$

or in terms of the $z^{-1}$ operator:

$$(1 - z^{-1}) I(kT) = T_{\text{sample}} f(kT)$$

Using this relationship and the $z^{-1}$ operator for other difference relationships, equation (6.11) can be written as:

$$U(z^{-1}) = K_{\text{p}} \left[ 1 + T_{\text{sample}} \frac{1}{T_{\text{i}}(1 - z^{-1})} + \frac{T_{\text{d}}}{T_{\text{sample}}} (1 - z^{-1}) \right] E(z^{-1})$$

where  $U(z^{-1}) = z$-transform of $u(kT)$:
        $E(z^{-1}) = z$-transform of $e(kT)$:
Rearranging this becomes:

$$(1 - z^{-1}) U(z^{-1}) = \{ a_0 + a_1 z^{-1} + a_2 z^{-2} \} E(z^{-1})$$

where $a_0 = K_{\text{p}} \left( 1 + \dfrac{T_{\text{sample}}}{T_{\text{i}}} + \dfrac{T_{\text{d}}}{T_{\text{sample}}} \right)$

$a_1 = - K_{\text{p}} \left( 1 + 2 \dfrac{T_{\text{d}}}{T_{\text{sample}}} \right)$

$a_2 = \dfrac{K_{\text{p}} T_{\text{d}}}{T_{\text{sample}}}$

Changing this back to the difference equation form, then:

$$u(kT) = u((k-1)T) + a_0 e(kT) + a_1 e((k-1)T) + a_2 e((k-2)T)$$

which is a much simpler equation than equation (6.11).
(Reference [14] discusses this equation in detail and is a good general paper on PID algorithms.)

## 6.5.1 Noise, interference and derivative kick

Noise and interference can cause sudden changes in the sensor signal, which result in sudden error changes in the PID output. This is especially true in the derivative part of the PID control, where there are two sampled values, $e((k+1)T)$ and $e(kT)$. If there is interference or noise to affect either of these values, especially if it causes a spike in $e$, then the rate of change, or slope, which the derivative term is measuring changes suddenly and dramatically. This immediately produces a large change in the control signal, $u$, due to the **derivative kick**. The following sampled value, unaffected by interference, would then go down again and a correspondingly large negative derivative control signal would result. A change in set point would also produce derivative kick and, to a lesser extent, **proportional kick** from the proportional term.

Avoidance of derivative kick from a set point change can be obtained by taking the derivative of the sensed variable, often the sensed temperature, instead of the error – i.e. the derivative term becomes:

$$T_d \frac{y((k+1)T) - y(kT)}{T_{sample}}$$

where $y(kT)$ = system output sensed by the BEMS sensor. Proportional kick can similarly be avoided by this change, with only the integral term using the error.

But the noise and interference are still present, which especially disturb the derivative terms, and, to a lesser extent, the other two terms as well. To overcome this an averaging technique can be used to smooth out noisy signals. An average of four sensor signals is taken and for an unchanged set point the resulting average error is:

$$e_{av}(k) = \frac{e(k) + e(k-1) + e(k-2) + e(k-3)}{4} \tag{6.12}$$

where $e_{av}(k)$ = average error at time $kT$;
$e(k)$ = latest error value at time $kT$;
$e(k-3)$ = earliest error considered, at time $(k-3)T$.
The resulting derivative is:

$$\frac{de_{av}}{dT} = \frac{e_{av}(k) - e_{av}(k-1)}{T_{sample}}$$

where $e_{av}(k-1)$ = average error value at time $(k-1)T$.

Williams [16] recommends a four-point difference technique for the derivative term:

$$y^* = \frac{y(k) + y(k-1) + y(k-2) + y(k-3)}{4}$$

which is the same as equation (6.12) if the set point is not altered. But the derivative is calculated from:

$$\frac{dy}{dT} = \left[ \frac{y(k) - y^*}{1.5\,T_{sample}} + \frac{y(k-1) - y^*}{0.5\,T_{sample}} + \frac{y^* - y(k-2)}{0.5\,T_{sample}} + \frac{y^* - y(k-3)}{1.5\,T_{sample}} \right]$$

$$= \frac{1}{6T_{sample}} [y(k) - y(k-3) + 3y(k-1) - 3y(k-2)]$$

Filtering and 'spike', or **logical filters** [14], can also reduce problems with the digitized input signals for derivative control.

An **error deadband** around the set point stops small oscillations in the loop output, and small oscillations in the controlled plant, due to noise, when the controller has settled the system close to the set point. This is done by only changing the error value when it has significantly changed from the set point. This produces an **effective error**, $e^*$ [15]:

$$e^* = 0 \text{ if } e \leqslant \text{deadband}$$

$$e^* = e - \text{deadband if } e > \text{deadband}$$

This applies if the set point is at the top of the proportional band, but if the BEMS has a set point in the proportional band with negative errors, then:

$$e^* = 0 \text{ if } |e| \leqslant \text{deadband}$$

$$e^* = e - \text{deadband if } e < \text{deadband}$$

$$e^* = e + \text{deadband if } e > \text{deadband}$$

where $|e|$ = modulus of the error.

In practice, most derivative control on BEMS is not implemented because of the above problems and additionally the consequent increased setting-up time with the third parameter, $T_d$, and the increased probability of unstable control.

## 6.5.2 Integral wind-up

It can be possible for a heating valve to be fully open and the controlled temperature still to be some way from the set point. Such an occurrence is during heat-up in the morning. The error will persist for some time and the integral term becomes enormously large, and is known as **integral wind-up**. This will cause overshoot when the set point is finally achieved, (as happened with the on/off boiler control in the previous example). Integral wind-up is prevented by typically limiting the integral term to a **saturation value**; that value which will produce a 100% output from the loop.

## 6.5.3 Velocity, or incremental, algorithm

In equation (6.11) the difference equation form of the PID control, the actuator and valve position can be exactly related to the output signal, $u((k + 1)T)$. When $u$ is zero, then the valve is shut, and when it is 100%, then the valve is fully open. If this is not precisely the case (i.e. the valve is fully open at 80%), then a position offset constant can simply be added to equation (6.11). Equation (6.11) is therefore called the **position algorithm** and it is transmitted to the valve actuator via a D/A converter as an analogue signal.

An alternative PID algorithm is the **velocity** or **incremental algorithm** which is derived from the difference between successive values of the position algorithm in equation (6.11). Here it is derived without the derivative term:

$$D^*(k+1) = u((k+1)T) - u(kT)$$

$$= K_p \left\{ e((k+1)T) - e(kT) + \frac{T_{\text{sample}}}{T_i} e(kT) \right\} \quad (6.13)$$

With this algorithm the change or increment in the control signal is used to control a device directly. Equation (6.13) can also be used with valves controlled by **stepper motors**, where a pulse moves the shaft through a certain rotation or step [17]. Similar actuator devices not requiring feedback of their position can also make use of this algorithm.

If the algorithm is used for proportional only control, then there could be drifting as there is no reference to a set point in equation (6.13), except in the last integral term. The set point disappears in the proportional term:

$$e((k+1)T - e(kT)$$

$$= t_{\text{set}} - t((k+1)T - t_{\text{set}} - t(kT)$$

$$= t((k+1)T - t(kT)$$

where $t(kT)$ = sensed temperature at time $kT$, and $t_{\text{set}}$ = set point temperature.

Advantages of the velocity algorithm are that integral wind-up is avoided since there is no integral summation term, the velocity integral term is limited to the single error term. Also if the set point is suddenly changed, there is no 'bump' in the controller as there is with the position algorithm.

### 6.5.4  Supervisory jacket software

The software to ensure as far as possible that the PID loop control in the BEMS is protected from noisy signals, and that integral wind-up and derivative kick are reduced as much as possible, is called the **supervisory jacket**. Also within the supervisory jacket are default values for $T_i$ and $T_d$ if the user does not set them during the configuration. This software additionally contains the relevant configuration user interface for setting up a loop control. So a BEMS program for PID loop control is more extensive due to the supervisory jacket than simply a program for the PID equation. This applies to other BEMS control programs as well, and it partly accounts for the fact that the cost of development of a complete BEMS's software can run to over a million pounds.

## 6.6  Stability

Generalizing the feedback control system of Fig. 6.6, with the proportional control and system having the transfer function, $G(s)$, and the sensor feedback loop having the transfer function $H(s)$, then the relationship between the error, $e(T)$, and the set point, $r(T)$, in Laplace transform terms is:

$$E(s) = R(s) - G(s)\,H(s)\,Y(s)$$

$$Y(s) = \frac{G(s)\,R(s)}{1 + H(s)\,G(s)}$$

The expression

$$\frac{G(s)}{1 + H(s)\,G(s)}$$

is the **closed-loop transfer function**, and $H(s)G(s)$ is the **open-loop transfer function**.

If the feedback through the sensor is accurate, the sensor has little thermal mass and the lags are short, then there is **unity feedback** and the closed-loop transfer function becomes:

$$\frac{G(s)}{1 + G(s)}$$

To cover many different types of transfer function this can be written as a general equation:

$$\frac{b_0 + b_1 s + b_2 s^2 + \ldots + b_m s^m}{a_0 + a_1 s + a_2 s^2 + \ldots + a_n s^n}$$

where the $b$s and $a$s are constants. This can be simplified to;

$$\frac{C_1}{s - r_1} + \frac{C_2}{s - r_2} + \frac{C_3}{s - r_3} + \ldots + \frac{C_n}{s - r_n}$$

where the $C$s are constants and the $r$s are the roots of the **characteristic equation**:

$$a_0 + a_1 s + a_2 s^2 + \ldots + a_n s^n = 0$$

From our knowledge of Laplace transforms we know that the transform of $C_1/(s - r_1)$ is:

$$C_1\, e^{r_1}\, T$$

These roots of the characteristic equation determine the transient response of the system and its control. If a root, say, $r_1$, is negative, then $e^{r_1}T$ decreases with time and the transient response reaches a steady, stable value, as is shown in Fig. 6.12. If the root is positive, then the transient response increases and the system cannot achieve a stable state. In practice, the system's response will not increase indefinitely, but will oscillate, or **hunt**.

If the root is complex:

$$r_1 = \sigma + j\mu$$

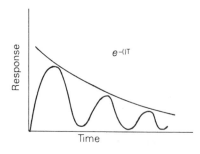
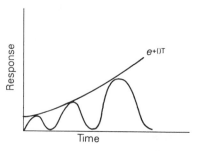

**Fig. 6.12** Stable and unstable response.

then the transform yields $e^{\sigma T} e^{j\mu T}$, and:

$$e^{j\mu T} = \cos \mu T + j \sin \mu T$$

which is a steadily oscillating function.

These observations lead to the Nyquist criterion [1] that the system and its control is unstable if the denominator of the transfer function has any roots that are positive. (For more details on this refer to references [2] and [3]; reference [4] is a useful general introduction.)

## 6.7 Configuring a PID loop for stability

For simple plant, one can derive a straightforward differential equation to determine whether the system will be stable for various settings. But for most practical heating plant, the differential equations and transfer functions will be complex. One can get an idea of the response of a system by looking at a BEMS graph of the system when it is turned on, or the set point is changed; the response to a step function. There are also various software programs for analysing the response of systems and determining the transfer functions.

In commissioning a plant for a building limitless time cannot be spent in attempting to determine the transfer functions of all of the plant. There are empirical rules determined by Zeigler and Nichols [5] for two commissioning procedures, the closed-loop ultimate cycling method and the open-loop process reaction curve method.

### 6.7.1 The closed-loop ultimate cycling method

In this method, which is the most common for BEMS configuration of loop modules, the loop is set for proportional control only. $T_i$ is set to $\infty$, or a very large value, and $T_d$ is set to 0. The proportional gain, $K_p$, is initially set to a small value and progressively increased until the system starts to oscillate or hunt. $K_p^*$ is the value of gain at which this commences. It is also necessary to measure the period of oscillation, $\tau_p$. The empirical settings that are recommended are given in Table 6.1.

**Table 6.1** Closed-loop ultimate cycling method settings

| | | |
|---|---|---|
| P control | $K_p = 0.5\,K_p^*$ | |
| PI control | $K_p = 0.45\,K_p^*$ | $T_i = 0.8\,\tau_p$ |
| PID control | $K_p = 0.6\,K_p^*$ | $T_i = 0.5\,\tau_p$    $T_d = 0.125\,\tau_p$ |

## 6.7.2 The open-loop process reaction curve method

This is a less useful method for configuring a loop as it entails disconnecting the loop module from the control element (e.g. the valve), as shown in Fig. 6.13.

Hence it is an open-loop method. A step input signal is then applied to the control element and the response of the system measured by the BEMS. Generally the response is of the form of an $n$th-order system, as shown in Fig. 6.14.

Such an $n$th order system is approximately described mathematically by the transfer function:

$$\frac{y(T)}{i(T)} = \frac{K\,e^{-sT}\,(T_1)}{1 + sT_2}$$

where  $T_1$ = dead time (s);
        $T_2$ = effective time constant (s);
    $y(T)$ = output (°C);
    $i(T)$ = input (°C);
       $K$ = gain.

As can be seen from Fig. 6.14, the dominant slope of the curve is $y_\infty/T_2$, where $y_\infty$ is the output that the system tends to as $T$ tends to infinity. Table 6.2 shows the empirical settings for stable control of the system.

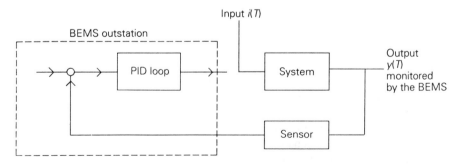

**Fig. 6.13**  Opened loop.

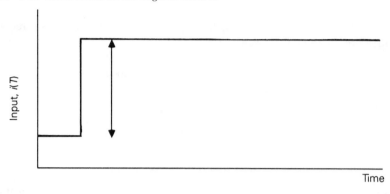

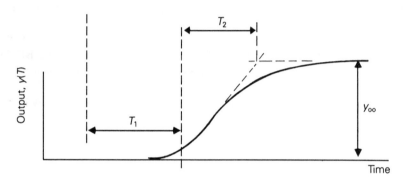

**Fig. 6.14**   Open-loop response.

**Table 6.2**   Open-loop process reaction curve settings

| | | | |
|---|---|---|---|
| P control | $K_p = \dfrac{iT_2}{y_\infty T_1}$ | | |
| PI control | $K_p = 0.9 \dfrac{iT_2}{y_\infty T_1}$ | $T_i = 3.3 T_1$ | |
| PID control | $K_p = 1.2 \dfrac{iT_2}{y_\infty T_1}$ | $T_i = 2 T_1$ | $T_d = 0.5 T_1$ |

## References

[1]   Nyquist, H. (1932) Regeneration theory. *Bell Systems Technical Journal*, January.

[2]   DiStefano, J. J. Stubberud, A. R. and Williams, I. J. (1987) *Feedback and Control Systems*, Schaum's Outline series, McGraw-Hill, New York.

[3]   Healy, M. (1975) *Principles of Automatic Control*, Hodder and Stoughton, London.

[4]  Morris, N. M. (1983) *Control Engineering*, 3rd edn, McGraw-Hill, London.

[5]  Zeigler, J. G. and Nichols, N. B. (1942) Optimum settings for automatic controllers. *Transactions of ASME*, **64**.

[6]  Spiegel, M. R. (1971) *Calculus of Finite Differences and Difference Equations*, Schaum's Outline series, McGraw-Hill, New York.

[7]  Bristol, E. H. (1977) Designing and programming control algorithms for DDC systems. *Control Engineering*, January.

[8]  Stoecker, W. F. and Stoecker, P. A. (1989) *Microcomputer Control of Thermal and Mechanical Systems*, Van Nostrand Reinhold, New York.

[9]  Ogata, K. (1987) *Discrete-time Control Systems*, Prentice-Hall, New York.

[10] CIBSE (1985) Automatic Controls and their implications for systems design, *Applications Manual*, CIBSE, London.

[11] ASHRAE Handbook, Heating, ventilating, and air-conditioning applications. American Society of Heating, Refrigerating and Air-Conditioning Engineers, Atlanta, 1991.

[12] Chapra, S. C. and Canale, R. P. (1987) *Numerical Methods for Engineers with personal computer applications*, McGraw-Hill, New York.

[13] Shavit, G. and Brandt, S. G. (1982) The dynamic performance of a discharge air-temperature system with a P-I controller. *ASHRAE Transactions*, **88**, pt 2.

[14] Clarke, D. W. (1984) PID algorithms and their computer implementation, *Transactions of the Institute of Measurement and Control*, **6**, 6.

[15] Nesler, C. G. and Stoecker, W. F. (1984) Selecting the proportional and integral constants in the direct digital control of a discharge air temperature. *ASHRAE Transactions*, **90**, pt 2.

[16] Williams, T. J. (1984) *The Use of Digital Computers in Process Control*, Instrument Society of America, North Carolina.

[17] Chesmond, C. J. (1986) *Control System Technology*, Edward Arnold, London.

# 7

# Building heat loss and heating

Having dealt with the basic elements of control, on/off and PID, it is necessary to appreciate the heating system and its sizing to further our development of its control. The main element of designing a heating system is to determine the heat loss from the building when the inside is maintained at a comfortable temperature. As was briefly mentioned in Chapter 4 on sensors and their responses, an index of comfort is not the inside air temperature, $t_{ai}$, but the **dry resultant temperature**, or resultant temperature, $t_{res}$:

$$t_{res} = \frac{t_r + t_{ai} \sqrt{(10v)}}{1\sqrt{(10v)}} \tag{7.1}$$

where $t_{ai}$ = inside air temperature (°C);
$\quad\quad t_r$ = mean radiant temperature (°C);
$\quad\quad v$ = inside air speed ms$^{-1}$.
In typical interiors $v$ is low, of the order of 0.1 ms$^{-1}$, so:

$$t_{res} = \tfrac{1}{2}t_r + \tfrac{1}{2}t_{ai} \tag{7.2}$$

Typically most design centres on a $t_{res}$ of about 20°C. The CIBSE Guide [1] gives the recommended design values for $t_{res}$, and Table 7.1 shows some of the recommendations.

People's assessment of comfort is also influenced by outside temperatures, and the temperature change experienced upon entering a building [2]. (Further details of comfort can be found in references [3] and [4].)

Many designers still refer to, and use in calculation, air temperature, $t_{ai}$, as it simplifies calculations. The error introduced by using $t_{ai}$ instead of $t_{res}$ is often

**Table 7.1** Recommended dry resultant temperatures

| Type of building | $t_{res}$ |
|---|---|
| Bank | 20 |
| Canteen | 20 |
| Church | 18 |
| Factory | |
|     sedentary work | 18 |
|     light work | 16 |
|     heavy work | 13 |
| Residence | |
|     living-room | 21 |
|     bedroom | 18 |
| Offices | 20 |
| Schools | 18 |
| Shops | 18 |

not large because when a building is in equilibrium, $t_r$ is reasonably close to $t_{ai}$, the exact difference depending on the type of heating system. This is considered in a later example.

## 7.1  Heat loss

The heat loss from a building is made up of losses through the building fabric and by infiltration and ventilation. The losses occur due to the processes of **heat transfer**. Consider the heat transfer in a room heated by a radiator, as shown in Fig. 7.1. The single panel, or single column, radiator transfers heat to the room air by **convection**, and to the room surfaces by **radiation**. For a single panel radiator, the split between radiation and convection is equal [5].

The air in the room is warmed by the radiator and then transfers some of its heat to the room surfaces. The internal room surfaces are warmer than the external wall and window, so there is transfer of heat from the warm surfaces to the colder external surfaces by radiation. Heat is then transferred by **conduction** through the external wall and window to their outside surfaces. At the outside surface of the wall and window heat is transferred and lost to the air and surroundings by convection and radiation.

### 7.1.1  Conduction

Conduction is the process of heat transfer through a substance such as a wall. It is described by Fourier's equation [6]:

$$\rho C_p \frac{dt}{dT} = k \left[ \frac{\partial^2 t}{\partial x^2} + \frac{\partial^2 t}{\partial y^2} + \frac{\partial^2 t}{\partial z^2} \right] \tag{7.3}$$

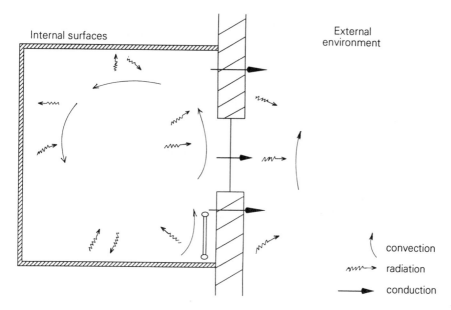

Internal surfaces

External environment

convection

radiation

conduction

**Fig. 7.1**   Heat transfer in a room.

where $T$ = time (s);

$t$ = temperature (°C);

$k$ = thermal conductivity (W m$^{-1}$ K$^{-1}$);

$\rho$ = density (kg m$^{-3}$);

$C_p$ = specific heat capacity (kJ kg$^{-1}$ K$^{-1}$);

$x, y, z$ = coordinates in space or dimensions (m).

The above equation is a highly complex one, indeed there is a large book solely devoted to solutions of it [7]. For the fabric of buildings, the equation can be reduced to one dimension, $x$, ignoring the small errors that would arise at the building corners and other points where the heat flow is not uniformly perpendicular to the surfaces.

For traditional building heat loss calculations the time element is surprisingly ignored, which reduces Fourier's equation to a **steady state equation** – i.e. the temperature does not vary with time:

$$0 = k \left[ \frac{d^2 t}{dx^2} \right] \tag{7.4}$$

By integration and application of boundary conditions this leads to:

$$Q = -kA \frac{dt}{dx} \tag{7.5}$$

where $Q$ = the rate of heat flow (W), and $A$ = the cross sectional area (m$^{-2}$).

The minus sign in the above equation is due to the convention that $Q$ is positive as $x$ increases but $t$ decreases along the $x$-axis. This can be written as:

$$Q = kA \frac{(t_{hot} - t_{cold})}{l} \qquad (7.6)$$

where $t_{hot}$ = temperature at the hot end (°C);

$t_{cold}$ = temperature at the cold end (°C);

$l$ = the length of the conductor (m).

Some textbooks refer to heat flux, $q$, and this is:

$$q = Q/A \quad (\text{W m}^{-2})$$

Typical conductivities of materials are given in Table 7.2. More conductivities are contained in the CIBSE Guide [8].

**Table 7.2**   Conductivities of materials

| Material | Conductivity (W m$^{-1}$ K$^{-1}$) |
|----------|-----------------------------------|
| Copper | 388 |
| Aluminium | 202 |
| Mild steel | 45 |
| Concrete | 1.4 |
| Water | 0.6 |
| Air | 0.026 |

We can compare the flow of heat to the flow of electricity through a resistance, as was considered earlier in the water/electrical/thermal analogies of Chapter 4 on sensors and their responses. Ohm's law for electricity flow gives:

$$V = IR \qquad (7.7)$$

where $V$ = potential difference (or voltage) (V);

$I$ = current (A);

$R$ = resistance ($\Omega$).

Comparing this with equation (7.6), the heat flow, $Q$, being analogous to $I$ and temperature difference being analogous to $V$, then the thermal resistance is:

$$R_{th} = \frac{l}{kA} \qquad (7.8)$$

This makes equation (7.6):

$$(t_{hot} - t_{cold}) = QR_{th} \qquad (7.9)$$

where $R_{th}$ = thermal resistance K W$^{-1}$.

The North Americans use thermal resistance as defined above [9], but it is worth noting that the thermal resistance referred to in the CIBSE Guide [8], is:

CIBSE:
$$R_{th}^* = \frac{1}{k}$$
(7.10)

where $R_{th}^*$ = the resistance (m$^2$ K W$^{-1}$).

Equation (7.10) substituted into equation (7.6) gives:

$$\frac{QR_{th}}{A} = q\,R_{th} = t_{hot} - t_{cold}$$

## 7.1.2  Convection

Heat transfer by convection takes place in fluids where the heated or cooled fluid particles move, taking their heat or 'coolth' with them. There are two types of convection: **natural** and **forced**.

Natural convection takes place when the fluid flow is due only to fluid temperature differences, consequently changes in fluid density. It therefore primarily takes place in the vertical plane around hot and cold bodies such as radiators and room surfaces.

Forced convection occurs when the fluid flow is enhanced by mechanical means such as a pump or fan. With both natural and forced convection, there is a stationary laminar film of fluid close to the solid surface, as shown in Fig. 7.2.

The heat transfer is initially through this layer by conduction (the film does not move), the genuine convection taking place in the bulk of the fluid. The thickness of the film and hence the resistance to heat transfer is dependent on the fluid velocity. Hence with forced convection there is more heat transfer than natural convection, consequently the heat transfer coefficient for forced convection is larger than that for natural convection. Both processes are described by the following general equation, often referred to as Newton's law of cooling:

$$Q = h_c\,A\,(t_{surf} - t_{fluid})$$
(7.11)

where $h_c$ = heat transfer coefficient (W m$^{-2}$ K$^{-2}$);

 $A$ = heat transfer area (m$^2$);

 $t_{surf}$ = surface temperature (°C);

 $t_{fluid}$ = bulk fluid temperature (°C).

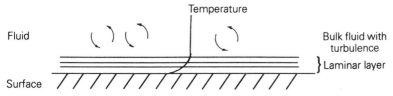

**Fig. 7.2**  The convection process.

Equation (7.11) is deceptively simple as $h_c$ is very complex. It is usually obtained from empirical data where it is often quoted in the dimensionless **Nusselt number**, Nu:

$$Nu = \frac{h_c\,l}{k} \tag{7.12}$$

where $l$ = a characteristic linear dimension (m).

As the heat transfer equations are often complex and long, they are simplified by using the dimensionless **Reynolds number**, Re; **Prandtl number**, Pr; and the **Grashof number**, Gr. These dimensionless numbers are defined in reference [6], and values are given in [9] and [10].

The general form of the heat transfer equation for natural convection is :

$$Nu = Cf\{Gr^x\,Pr^y\} \tag{7.13}$$

where $f$ signifies a function of $x, y$ = indices, and $C$ = a constant.

The general form of the heat transfer equation for forced convection is:

$$Nu = Kf\{Re^v\,Pr^w\} \tag{7.14}$$

where $f$ signifies a function of $v, w$ = indices, and $K$ = a constant.

Table A3.4 of the CIBSE Guide [8] gives values of $h_c$ for still air conditions (defined as the air speed at the surface being less than 0.1 ms$^{-1}$). These are shown below in Table 7.3.

**Table 7.3**   CIBSE convective heat transfer coefficients

| *Direction of heat flow* | $h_c$ (W m$^{-2}$ K$^{-1}$) |
| --- | --- |
| Horizontal | 3.0 |
| Upward | 4.3 |
| Downward | 1.5 |
| Average | 3.0 |

The values in Table 7.3 are for specific conditions of air speed and also only valid over a small range of room temperatures (see reference [11]). This then reduces the complex convection equation to a linearized form like the conduction equation and Ohm's law:

$$Q = h_c\,A\,(t_{surf} - t_{ai}) \tag{7.15}$$

### 7.1.3   Radiation

Radiation is the transfer of heat through space by electromagnetic waves which are similar to light, except that light waves have a higher frequency and shorter wavelength. The thermal radiation from a black body is given by the Stefan–Boltzman law:

$$Q = \sigma A \, T^{*4} \tag{7.16}$$

where $\sigma$ = Stefan–Boltzman constant ($5.67 \times 10^{-8}$ W m$^{-2}$ K$^{-4}$);

$\quad A$ = heat transfer area (m$^2$);

$\quad T^*$ = absolute temperature (K).

For an actual material, the radiation will be more like that from a grey body:

$$Q = \sigma \varepsilon A \, T^{*4} \tag{7.17}$$

where $\varepsilon$ = emissivity of the surface, which for most building materials is 0.9.

The radiation exchanged between two surfaces, 1 and 2 is:

$$Q_{12} = A_1 \sigma \, F_a \, F_e \, (T_1^{*4} - T_2^{*4}) \tag{7.18}$$

where $\quad F_a$ = a form factor determined by the relative geometries of the two surfaces;

$\quad\quad F_e$ = a factor taking into account the emissivities and absorptivities of the surfaces;

$\quad\quad A_1$ = surface area of surface 1 (m$^2$) (see Table 7.4).

**Table 7.4** Radiation factors

|  | Area | $F_e \, F_a$ |
|---|---|---|
| Large parallel surfaces of area $A_1$ and $A_2$ | $A_1$ or $A_2$ | $\dfrac{\varepsilon_1 \, \varepsilon_2}{\varepsilon_1 + \varepsilon_2 - \varepsilon_1 \, \varepsilon_2}$ |
| Small area, $A_1$, within an enclosed area | $A_1$ | $\varepsilon_1$ |
| Small surfaces well separated, so that amount of radiation re-radiated back to emitter is small | $A_1$ | $\varepsilon_1 \, \varepsilon_2 \, F_a$ |

For further details on these factors see the CIBSE Guide [10]. For normal rooms, $F_a \, F_e$ can be taken as 0.87 giving an accuracy of within 10% to equations (7.18) and (7.12).

It is convenient to linearize the radiation heat transfer equation to:

$$Q = A \varepsilon h_r \, (t_1 - t_2) \tag{7.19}$$

and it can be shown (equation (7.10)) that by rearranging equation (7.18) into:

$$Q_{12} = A_1 \sigma \, F_a \, F_e \, (T_1^* - T_2^*) \, (T_1^* + T_2^*) \, (T_1^{*2} - T_2^{*2}) \tag{7.18}$$

then at normal ambient temperatures $(T_1^* - T_2^*)$ dominates, and the radiation heat transfer coefficient, $h_r$, is given by:

$$h_r = \sigma (T_1^* + T_2^*)(T_1^{*2} + T_2^{*2}) \tag{7.20}$$

Another approximation that reinforces this is [18]:

$$(T_1^* + T_2^*)(T_1^{*2} + T_2^{*2}) \approx 4 T_{av}^{*2}$$

where $T_{av}^*$ is the average temperature of the building surfaces radiating heat.

**Table 7.5**   Values of $h_r$ from CIBSE Guide, Section A3

| Surface temperature (°C) | $h_r$ (W m$^{-2}$ K$^{-1}$) |
|---|---|
| − 10 | 4.1 |
| 0 | 4.6 |
| 10 | 5.1 |
| 20 | 5.7 |

Table 7.5 gives values of $h_r$ quoted in the CIBSE Guide, Section A3 [8]. Although not stated there, one infers that the temperatures of the transmitting and receiving surfaces are similar, so that the $h_r$ values are only valid for surfaces up to 10°C different. In Volume C, Section C3, of the Guide more details for values of $h_r$ are given. Table 7.6 gives some of the values when one of the surfaces is kept at 20°C.

**Table 7.6**   Values of $h_r$ from of CIBSE Guide, Section C3. [10]

| $t_1 = 20$°C, when $t_2$ is: | $h_r$ (W m$^{-2}$ K$^{-1}$) |
|---|---|
| − 10°C | 4.9 |
| 0 | 5.2 |
| 10 | 5.4 |
| 20 | 5.7 |
| 25 | 5.9 |
| 30 | 6.0 |

*Example*
How much heat transfer in a warm room is made up of radiation and convection? The room is cubic and of 3 m height. One wall is external facing, the other surfaces are internal. The emissivities of the surfaces are 0.9.

*Solution*
If we consider a room with one external wall whose inside surface temperature is 10°C (280 K), with the inside air at 20°C and the other surfaces at 18°C (288 K), the heat transfer will be primarily from the warm walls and warm air to the cold external wall.

The radiation that the external wall receives from the other warmer walls can be derived by first calculating $h_r$:

$$h_r = \sigma (T_1^* + T_2^*)(T_1^{*2} + T_2^{*2}) \tag{7.20}$$

$$= 5.67 \times 10^{-8}(280 + 288)(280^2 + 288^2)$$

$$= 5.2 \text{ W m}^{-2}\text{ K}^{-1}$$

Assuming that the cold wall is a small area surrounded by the warmer walls, so that $F_a F_e = \varepsilon$, and that $\varepsilon = 0.9$, then the heat received from the warmer surfaces is:

$$Q_{rad} = 5.2 \times 0.9 \times 9 \times (288 - 280)$$

$$= 337 \text{ W}$$

For convective heat transfer from the warm air to the cold wall, taking the horizontal heat transfer coefficient from Table 7.3, of $3.0 \text{ W m}^{-2} \text{ K}^{-1}$:

$$Q_{conv} = 3.0 \times 9 \times (20 - 10)$$

$$= 270 \text{ W}$$

Radiation is the larger heat transfer process. It is interesting to calculate the dry resultant temperature of the room. The mean radiant temperature is approximately the mean surface temperature:

$$t_r \approx \frac{(5 \times 18) + (1 \times 10)}{6}$$

$$\approx 16.7°\text{C}$$

So:

$$t_{res} = \tfrac{1}{2} t_{ai} + \tfrac{1}{2} t_r,$$

$$= 18.4°\text{C}$$

As was mentioned in an earlier chapter, the BEMS sensor will be primarily monitoring the air temperature.

### 7.1.4  Surface resistance

The linearized radiation and convection heat transfer processes may be combined into a single heat transfer process for building surfaces. This gives rise to a combined resistance to heat flow at the surface, the **surface resistance**, $R_s$. In the CIBSE Guide [8] $R_s$ is defined as:

$$R_s = \frac{1}{Eh_r + h_c} \quad \text{m}^2 \text{ K W}^{-1} \tag{7.21}$$

where  $E$ = emissivity factor $\Theta \varepsilon_1 \varepsilon_2$;
$\Theta$ = CIBSE A3 notation for form or shape factor, $F_a$;
$\varepsilon_1, \varepsilon_2$ = emissivities of surfaces;
$h_r$ = radiative heat transfer coefficient ($\text{W m}^{-2} \text{ K}^{-1}$);
$h_c$ = convective heat transfer coefficient ($\text{W m}^{-2} \text{ K}^{-1}$).

For outside surfaces, the outside surface resistance, $R_{so}$, is evaluated with the form factor, $F_a$ or $\Theta$, as unity. The CIBSE Guide [8] quotes values of $R_{so}$ for sheltered, normal and severe exposures of the surfaces. These are necessary due to the influence of wind speed on the convection component of the heat loss. Normal exposure corresponds to a wind speed at roof level of $3 \text{ ms}^{-1}$. Table 7.7 gives some of the values for $R_{so}$ for a wall.

**Table 7.7**   Values of $R_{so}$ (m$^2$ K W$^{-1}$)

|                                    | *Sheltered* | *Normal* | *Severe* |
|------------------------------------|-------------|----------|----------|
| High emissivity ($\varepsilon = 0.9$) | 0.08        | 0.06     | 0.03     |
| Low emissivity ($\varepsilon = 0.05$) | 0.11        | 0.07     | 0.03     |

Most building materials have high emissivities and correspond to the $\varepsilon = 0.9$ values, above, but polished metal surfaces as in some wall claddings have low emissivities. Table 7.8 gives some values for the inside surface resistance, $R_{si}$.

**Table 7.8**   Values of $R_{si}$ (m$^2$ K W$^{-1}$)

| *Element*               | *Heat Flow* | *High emissivity surface* |
|-------------------------|-------------|---------------------------|
| Wall                    | Horizontal  | 0.12                      |
| Ceiling, floor or roof  | Upward      | 0.10                      |
| Ceiling and floor       | Downward    | 0.14                      |

The derivation of $R_{si}$ is related to the inside environmental temperature, $t_{ei}$. This temperature was introduced by CIBSE to account for the fact that room surface temperatures are different to (often lower than) the room air temperature. Therefore the environmental temperature is employed to combine the mean room surface temperature and the air temperature:

$$t_{ei} = 1/3\ t_{ai} + 2/3\ t_m \qquad (7.22)$$

where $t_{ai}$ = room air temperature (°C), and $t_m$ = mean temperature of the room surfaces and:

$$t_m = \frac{\Sigma\,(At_s)}{\Sigma\,(A)}$$

where $A$ = surface area (m$^2$), and $t_s$ = surface temperature (°C).

The derivation of $t_{ei}$ is given in Section A5 of the CIBSE Guide [13]. So the heat exchange at an inside room surface and the rest of the room and air is:

$$Q = A_s\,\frac{(6Eh_r + h_c)}{5}\,[t_{ei} - t_{si}] \qquad (7.23)$$

where  $Q$ = heat flow (W);
$\quad A_s$ = area of room surface considered (m$^2$);
$\quad t_{si}$ = surface temperature (°C).
This gives:

$$R_{si} = \left[ \frac{6\,Eh_r + h_c}{5} \right]^{-1}$$

which is slightly different to the resistance defined in equation (7.21). This is due to the use of $t_{ei}$ in equation (7.22) [8].

It is often convenient to generalize heat flow equations for heat transfer from emitters and within rooms. The CIBSE Guide [10] gives a generalized heat transfer equation which will be the basis of emitter heat transfer equations used later:

$$Q = C\,(T_s^* - T_a^*)^n \qquad (7.24)$$

where  $C$ = a constant, $0.64 \leqslant C \leqslant 1.4$;
   $T_s^*$ = absolute temperature of the surface (K);
   $T_a^*$ = absolute temperature of the air (K);
   $n$ = an index, either 1.33 or 1.25.

## 7.2  Temperature relationships

A number of temperatures such as $t_{ei}$, $t_{ai}$ and $t_m$ were mentioned in Section 7.1 and $t_{res}$, $t_r$ were introduced in the discussion on comfort at the beginning of the chapter. These temperatures can be related to each other and it is necessary to relate them in heat loss and comfort calculations.

At the centre of a cubical room, and also approximately for most other rooms, $t_m$, the mean temperature of the room surfaces effectively equals the mean radiant temperature, $t_r$, referred to earlier in equation (7.2) for the dry resultant temperature:

$$t_m \approx t_r$$

This was the assumption made in the previous example in working out $t_{res}$.

CIBSE also refer to $t_{res}$, the dry resultant temperature, as $t_c$ at the centre of the room and it is often $t_c$ that is referred to as the design criterion:

$$t_c = \tfrac{1}{2} t_{ai} + \tfrac{1}{2} t_m$$

CIBSE uses factors $F_1$ and $F_2$ to relate the various design temperatures:

$$F_1 = \frac{t_{ei} - t_{ao}}{t_c - t_{ao}}$$

$$F_2 = \frac{t_{ai} - t_{ao}}{t_c - t_{ao}}$$

Tables of $F_1$ and $F_2$ are given in Section A9 of the Guide [14] for various types of emitter and their variations in radiant and convective heat output. For example, a single panel radiator, with 50% radiant and 50% convective output has higher values of $F_1$ but lower values of $F_2$ than a fan convection heater with 100% convective heat output. This means that $t_{ei}$ is higher for the radiator, and $t_{ai}$ is higher for the convector.

In well-insulated buildings with convective heating:

$$t_{ei} \approx t_{ai}$$

Because $t_{ei}$ and $t_{ai}$ can be close in some cases, it leads many designers to be lazy and to simply use $t_{ai}$ as a design criterion for comfort. In fact in other countries, such as the USA, $t_{ai}$ is used still, and it is only recently that the CIBSE in the UK has adopted $t_{ei}$.

## 7.3  Heat loss resistance network

Now that the internal and external surface resistances have been derived to complement the conduction resistance, the overall resistance network of a wall can be derived. Consider the example room at the beginning of this chapter. The resistance network for the external wall is shown in Fig. 7.3.

In Fig. 7.3 the resistances are:

$R_{sic}$ = inside surface convection resistance (m² K W⁻¹);
$R_{sir}$ = inside surface radiation resistance (m² K W⁻¹);
$R_{soc}$ = outside surface convection resistance (m² K W⁻¹);
$R_{sor}$ = outside surface radiation resistance (m² K W⁻¹);
$R_{c}$ = conduction resistance of wall = $1/k$ (m² K W⁻¹);
$t_{si}$ = inside surface temperature (°C);
$t_{so}$ = outside surface temperature (°C).

As the radiation and convection resistances are in parallel, just as in electrical resistance calculations:

$$\frac{1}{R_{si}} = \frac{1}{R_{sic}} + \frac{1}{R_{sir}} \tag{7.25}$$

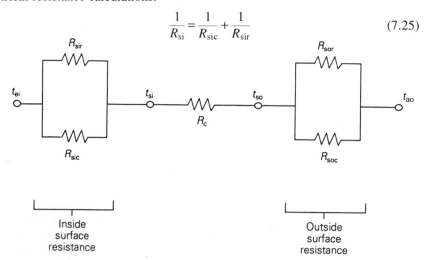

**Fig. 7.3**   The resistance network of a wall.

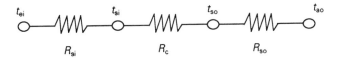

**Fig. 7.4**   The simplified resistance network.

or:

$$R_{si} = \frac{R_{sir} R_{sic}}{R_{sic} + R_{sir}}$$

where $R_{si}$ = inside surface resistance (m² K W$^{-1}$).

Comparing equation (7.25) with the inverse of the CIBSE surface resistance derived from equation (7.24):

$$R_{si}^{-1} = \frac{6\,Eh_r + h_c}{5}$$

it can be calculated that:

$$R_{sir} = \frac{5}{6Eh_r} \quad \text{and} \quad R_{sic} = \frac{1}{h_c}$$

With the surface resistances combined, the network is as shown in Fig. 7.4.

The overall, equivalent resistance of the whole wall, $R_{eq}$, is:

$$R_{eq} = R_{si} + R_c + R_{so}$$

## 7.4   *U*-value or overall thermal transmittance

Buildings have a number of walls and windows as well as ceilings and floors, and each of these elements has its own equivalent resistance. To calculate the equivalent resistance of this network of resistors it is necessary to sum six or more resistors in parallel. The network for the four external walls of a simple one-room building is shown in Fig. 7.5.

The equivalent resistance of this simple room is:

$$\frac{1}{R_1} + \frac{1}{R_2} + \frac{1}{R_3} + \frac{1}{R_4} \tag{7.26}$$

This is rather tedious so the reciprocal of the resistances, the transmittances, (or *U*-values), are used in heat loss calculations. The CIBSE Guide [8] quotes *U*-values for common building elements. Many walls and building elements consist of a composite of layers and the derivation of the *U*-value for such a composite is:

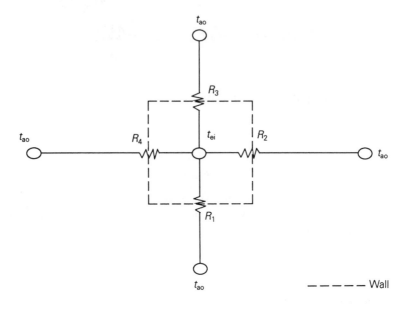

**Fig. 7.5**   The network for four walls.

$$U = \frac{1}{R_{si} + R_1 + R_2 + \ldots + R_a + R_{so}} \qquad (7.27)$$

where  $U$ = overall thermal transmittance (W m$^{-2}$ K$^{-1}$);
$R_{si}$ = inside surface resistance (m$^2$ K W$^{-1}$);
$R_1$ = conduction resistance of element 1 of fabric (m$^2$ K W$^{-1}$);
$R_2$ = conduction resistance of element 2 of fabric (m$^2$ K W$^{-1}$);
$R_a$ = airspace resistance, typically 0.18 m$^2$ K W$^{-1}$;
$R_{so}$ = outside surface resistance.
The airspace is included for cavity walls.
   Using $U$-values, equation (7.26) is simplified to:

$$U_1 + U_2 + U_3 + U_4$$

The heat loss through the fabric of a building, $Q_{fab}$, is therefore given by:

$$Q_{fab} = \sum_i (U_i A_i)\{t_{ei} - t_{ao}\} \qquad (7.28)$$

## 7.5  Infiltration and ventilation loss

Heat is not only lost through the building fabric, but also through warm air leaking out of the building and cold air leaking in, or infiltrating. Deliberate leakage, by window opening for natural ventilation or mechanical ventilation with a fan system, also results in a heat loss. The infiltration and ventilation loss, $Q_v$, is given by:

$$Q_v = \rho C_p G (t_{ai} - t_{ao}) \tag{7.29}$$

where  $\rho$ = density of air $(\mathrm{kg m^{-3}})$;
    $C_p$ = specific heat capacity of air $(\mathrm{kJ\,kg^{-1}\,K^{-1}})$;
    $G$ = infiltration and ventilation of air $(\mathrm{m^3 s^{-1}})$.
  Putting in standard values for density of 1.2 $\mathrm{kg m^{-3}}$, and for $C_p$ of 1.02 $\mathrm{kJ\,kg^{-1}\,K^{-1}}$ and putting in the room volume, $V$, gives:

$$Q_v = \frac{1}{3} NV (t_{ai} - t_{ao}) \tag{7.30}$$

where $V$ = volume of the building $(\mathrm{m^3})$, and $N$ = number of air changes per hour $(\mathrm{h^{-1}})$.
  Determination of $N$ is difficult, although techniques are being developed and much research is being conducted in this area ([15], [16]). In heating system design, empirical values of $N$ are taken from the CIBSE Guide [16]. Typically most values of $N$ are centred around 1.0.
  The $1/3 \, NV$ term can be considered as an infiltration heat resistance, $R_v$:

$$R_v = \frac{3}{NV} \tag{7.31}$$

## 7.6  Total building heat loss

The total heat loss from a building due to both fabric and infiltration and ventilation heat losses is:

$$Q = Q_{fab} + Q_v$$

$$= \Sigma \, (UA)(t_{ei} - t_{ao}) + (1/3)NV(t_{ai} - t_{ao}) \tag{7.32}$$

Using the factors $F_1$ and $F_2$, a common temperature difference may be used for both loss terms:

$$Q = \{F_1 \, \Sigma \, (UA) + (1/3)F_2 \, NV\}(t_c - t_{ao}) \tag{7.33}$$

  It is worth noting that traditionally there is no consideration of internal heat gains, such as the heat from the lights, equipment, the occupants and solar radiation (equation (7.17)), in heat loss calculations. If these gains were included, they would offset the heat losses and the heating system would be smaller. As these gains mostly occur during occupancy, the smaller heating system might not be able to bring the building up to temperature prior to the occupancy period during colder weather. So ignoring the internal heat gains acts as a safety factor on the design.

It may, however, be necessary to consider the influence of internal gains on the temperature of the building, and Section A5 of the CIBSE Guide [13] details the equations for this. Solar radiation is an interesting case. Under steady state conditions any solar radiation entering a room is not stored in the fabric, but absorbed and then partly transmitted through the room surface and partly retransmitted back into the room to the environmental point (where $t_{ei}$ is measured). The steady state surface factor, $\bar{F}_s$, determines the heat retransmitted to the environmental point:

$$\bar{F}_s = \frac{1/U - R_{si}}{1/U}$$

$$= 1 - UR_{si} \qquad (7.34)$$

If the room surface receiving the radiation is internal and separates two rooms at equal temperatures, then $\bar{F}_s$ is unity.

Many heat emitters are either fixed to walls or embedded in room surfaces. Not all of the heat is emitted into the room but some is lost directly to the surface. This is termed **back loss**, $Q_{bl}$, and for a wall-mounted radiator is:

$$Q_{bl} = A_R U(t_R - t_{ei}) \qquad (7.35)$$

where $A_R$ = area of radiator (m$^2$);
   $U$ = $U$-value of surface that radiator is on (W m$^{-2}$ K$^{-1}$);
   $t_R$ = mean radiator temperature (°C).

For a radiator heating system, $Q_{bl}$ must be added to the building heat loss to size the system.

For embedded heating systems, such as ceiling panels or underfloor heating, a steady state **back loss factor**, $\bar{F}_{bl}$, is used and is given by:

$$\bar{F}_{bl} = 1 - UR_s \qquad (7.36)$$

where $R_s$ = resistance between the surface and the environmental point (°C).

The conductance (inverse resistance) network linking all the temperatures in a room, $t_{ei}$, $t_{ai}$, $t_c$ and $t_{ao}$ is shown in Fig. 7.6.

A in Fig. 7.6 is the **inside air point**; E the **environmental point**; C the **dry resultant point**; and O the **outside air point**. The conductances, $h_{ac}\, \Sigma\, A$, and $h_{ec}\, \Sigma\, A$ are derived in the CIBSE Guide in the appendix of Section A5 [13], where it is calculated that:

$$h_{ac} = 6 \text{ W m}^{-2} \text{ K}^{-1}$$
$$h_{ec} = 18 \text{ W m}^{-2} \text{ K}^{-1}$$

So the heat flow from the dry resultant point to the inside air point is, $Q_{ae}$:

$$Q_{ae} = h_{ac}\, \Sigma\, (A)\, (t_c - t_{ai})$$

and likewise from the environmental point to the outside air point, $Q_{fab}$:

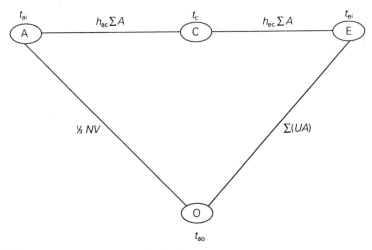

**Fig. 7.6**  Conductance network relating temperatures.

$$Q_{fab} = \Sigma (UA) (t_{ei} - t_{ao})$$

*Example*
Compare the heat loss from a factory heated by radiant heaters (90% radiant, 10% convective) to the heat loss when heated by fan convective heaters (100% convective). The total inside surface area of the factory is 450 m$^2$ and $\Sigma(UA) = 470$ W K$^{-1}$ (1/3)$NV = 280$W K$^{-1}$. Primarily sedentary work is done in the factory, so the design $t_c = 19°C$ and the design $t_{ao} = -1°C$. Section A9 of the CIBSE Guide [14] gives tables of $F_1$ and $F_2$ for different heating systems and values of $\Sigma(UA)/\Sigma(A)$ and $NV/3 \Sigma (A)$. For the fan convective heaters in this factory, the tables give $F_1 = 0.95$ and $F_2 = 1.17$. For the radiant heaters, $F_1 = 1.06$ and $F_2 = 0.83$.

*Solution*
It was mentioned earlier that sometimes $t_{ai}$ is wrongly used as the design criterion, and also in fabric heat loss calculations instead of $t_{ei}$. This example shows the error of this.
The heat loss is given by equation (7.33):

$$Q = \{F_1 \Sigma(UA) + (1/3)F_2 NV\} (t_c - t_{ao}) \qquad (7.33)$$

For the radiant heating, this is:

$$Q = \{(1.06 \times 470) + (280 \times 0.83)\} (19 - [-1]) \text{ W}$$

$$= \{498.2 + 232.4\} (20) \text{ W}$$

$$= 14.6 \text{ kW}$$

The air temperature, $t_{ai}$, is calculated from:

$$F_2 = \frac{t_{ai} - t_{ao}}{t_{ai} - t_{ao}}$$

so:

$$0.83 = \frac{t_{ai} - [-1]}{19 - [-1]}$$

$$t_{ai} = (0.83 \times 20) - 1$$

$$= 15.6°C$$

For the fan convective heaters, the heat loss is:

$$Q = \{(0.95 \times 470) + (280 \times 1.17)\} \, (19 - [-1] \text{ W}$$

$$= \{446.5 + 327.6\} \, (20) \text{ W}$$

$$= 15.5 \text{ kW}$$

The air temperature, $t_{ai}$, is given by:

$$F_2 = \frac{t_{ai} - t_{ao}}{t_c - t_{ao}}$$

so:

$$1.17 = \frac{t_{ai} - [-1]}{19 - [-1]}$$

$$t_{ai} = (1.17 \times 20) - 1$$

$$= 22.4°C$$

For the radiant heaters, the heat loss (14.6 kW) is less than for the fan convectors (15.5 kW), but the radiant heaters produce a lower air temperature (15.6°C) compared to the fan convectors' $t_{ai}$ (22.4°C).

If the heat loss had been calculated wrongly on a design $t_{ai}$ of 19°C, then the heat loss would have been:

$$Q = \{\Sigma(UA) + (1/3)NV\} \, (t_{ai} - t_{ao})$$

$$= \{470 + 280\} \, (19 - [-1])$$

$$= 15 \text{ kW}$$

Care is needed in selecting sensors for the control of radiant heating systems as most sensors, as mentioned in Chapter 4, respond primarily to air temperature, which (as shown here) can be significantly different to comfort temperature, $t_c$.

## 7.7  Heating system design

Having determined the steady state heat loss from the building, the heating system is sized to match it but, in practice, often surpasses it by about 25%. This excess acts as a safety factor.

The heat output from the boiler system to match the building heat loss is given by:

$$\dot{m}C_p(t_f - t_r) \qquad (7.37)$$

where $\dot{m}$ = mass flow rate of water (kg s$^{-1}$);

$\qquad C_p$ = specific heat capacity of water (kJ kg$^{-1}$ K$^{-1}$);

$\qquad t_f$ = flow water temperature from the boiler system (°C);

$\qquad t_r$ = return water temperature to the boiler system (°C).

The boiler system then delivers hot water to the heat emitters. These then heat the building and their output is given by:

$$B(t_m - t_{ai})^n \qquad (7.38)$$

where $t_m$ = the emitter mean water temperature (°C)

$\qquad = (t_f + t_r)/2$;

$\qquad B$ = a constant relating to heat transmission from the emitter and the emitter size;

$\qquad n$ = an index

$\qquad = 1.3$ for radiators

$\qquad = 1.5$ for natural convectors

$\qquad = 1.0$ for fan convectors.

It is worth noting that equation (7.38) is a form of equation (7.24), for heat transfer involving both radiation and convection. A single panel radiator, for instance, gives out its heat in the form of 50% radiation and 50% convection.

Equations (7.37) and (7.38) can be equated to the building heat loss to form the **heat balance equation** (which can be derived from the conservation of energy):

$$p_1 \dot{m}C_p(t_f - t_r) = p_2 B(t_m - t_{ai})^n$$

$$= \{F_1 \Sigma (UA) + (1/3)F_2 NV\}(t_c - t_{ao}) \qquad (7.39)$$

or:

$$p_1 \dot{m}C_p(t_f - t_r) = p_2 B(t_m - t_{ai})^n$$

$$= \frac{1}{F_2} \{F_1 \Sigma (UA) + (1/3)F_2 NV\}(t_{ai} - t_{ao}) \qquad (7.40)$$

where $p_1$ = boiler system plant size ratio related to the initial design condition heat loss:

$$\{F_1 \Sigma (UA) + (1/3)F_2 NV\} (t_c - t_{ao})_{des} \tag{7.41}$$

where $(t_c - t_{ac})_{des} =$ design condition temperature difference.

$t_{ai}$ in equation (7.40) and $t_c$ in equation (7.39) will differ from the design values when $p_1$ is non-zero.

Similarly, $p_2 =$ emitter plant size ratio again related to the initial design condition heat loss

$n = 1.5$ for natural convectors

$= 1.3$ for radiators

$= 1.0$ for fan convectors.

In the design process one would aim to make $p_1 = p_2$ but the available sizes of boilers and emitters from manufacturers will undoubtedly make $p_1$ and $p_2$ slightly different.

Having sized the emitters and the boiler system, the final design task is to size the pipework and the pump to ensure that an adequate flow of hot water gets to all the emitters.

## 7.8  Intermittent heating

So far, the heat loss from a building has been considered as a steady state process – i.e. there is no time element and temperatures do not change with time. This is a reasonable assumption for the design process, especially if the heating system were to be run 24 hours a day. But this is a rarity now and heating systems are switched off outside the occupancy period to save energy. However, if the heating is switched off for, say, 8 hours a day, the saving in energy is not $8/24 = 33\%$, but much less. This is due to the building fabric storing energy and acting as a storage heater. The building has thermal capacitance, to store heat energy, as well as thermal resistance.

### 7.8.1  Admittance

When the temperatures change with time, the electrical analogy of heat flow used earlier to describe heat conduction can be used again, but with an alternating voltage source. Also the thermal capacitance of the fabric of the building has to be included as a capacitor(s). So the electrical analogy for the steady state resistor analogy in Fig. 7.4 becomes an alternating resistor capacitor network for varying temperatures, as shown in Fig. 7.7.

The $n$-capacitors represent the fabric capacity, and the conduction resistance, $R_c$, has been split into $(n + 1)$ resistances, where

$$R_{c1} = R_{c2} = \ldots = R_{c(n + 1)} = \frac{R_c}{n + 1} \tag{7.42}$$

for a homogeneous wall. The number of resistors, $n + 1$, and capacitors, $n$, depends on the accuracy required and the number of elements, if it is a

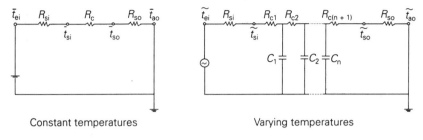

Constant temperatures                    Varying temperatures

**Fig. 7.7**  Constant and varying temperature networks.

multi-component wall. For the latter, the resistors and capacitances will not necessarily be equal. One model of a building, based on a resistor capacitor network, uses one capacitor for the fabric with reasonable accuracy [19].

The varying temperatures are denoted in the CIBSE Guide as $\tilde{t}$, and the constant temperatures as $\overline{t}$. The period of the alternating temperature (analogous to the alternating voltage) is 24 hours. So $\overline{t}$ is the mean temperature over 24 hours, and $\tilde{t}$ is the variation about this mean. CIBSE refer to $\tilde{t}$ as the 'cyclic variation' in $t$ [13], where it is the amplitude of the temperature variation about the mean [21]:

$$t_{ei}(T) = \overline{t}_{ei} + \tilde{t}_{ei} \tag{7.43}$$

Although the outside temperature is shown as $\tilde{t}_{ao}$, in fact it is 'earthed' and does not vary from the mean value, $\overline{t}_{ao}$.

As with alternating electrical circuits, the waveform of the temperatures and heat flows is assumed to be a sine wave:

$$Q = \tilde{Q} \sin(\omega T) \tag{7.44}$$

$$t = \tilde{t} \sin(\omega T - \Phi) \tag{7.45}$$

where $\tilde{Q}$ = amplitude of the heat flow (W);
    $\tilde{t}$ = amplitude of the temperature (°C);
    $T$ = time (s)
    $\omega$ = frequency (radians s$^{-1}$);
    = $2\pi/T_{period}$
    = $2\pi/(24 \times 3600)$ for 24 h;
    $T_{period}$ = time period of the cycle (s)
    = $24 \times 3600$ for 24 h;
    $\Phi$ = temperature phase lag behind the heat flow (radians).

This assumption of a sine wave allows Fourier's equation, equation (7.3), to be solved exactly, although the actual daily variations in reality may not be exact sine waves at all [20].

For an interior source of alternating heat flow, the fabric has an impedance of its 'RC circuit', relating the interior temperature to the interior heat flow, $\tilde{Q}_i$:

$$Z_{ii} = \tilde{t}_{ei} / \tilde{Q}_i \qquad (7.46)$$

and another impedance, $Z_{io}$, relating the exterior temperature to the inside heat flow:

$$Z_{io} = \tilde{t}_{ao} / \tilde{Q}_i \qquad (7.47)$$

If the alternating heat source is placed on the exterior side of the wall, with the interior environmental point earthed, then there are two more impedances:

$$Z_{oo} = \tilde{t}_{ao} / \tilde{Q}_{oo} \qquad \text{and} \qquad Z_{oi} = \tilde{t}_{ei} / \tilde{Q}_{oo}$$

$Z_{oo}$ differs from $Z_{ii}$ because the alternating heat source has $R_{so}$ facing it when it is outside. $R_{si}$ faces an internal heat source. The surface resistance is important in determining the impedance. A carpet on a concrete floor increases the impedance by about twice that of the bare concrete floor [22] (Table 7.9).

**Table 7.9**   Overall resistances and impedances

| Element | Overall resistance (m² K W⁻¹) | Modulus of impedance Y $|Z_{ii}|$ (m² K W⁻¹) |
|---|---|---|
| Cast concrete floor with carpet or wood-block finish | 2.5 | 0.3 |
| Cast concrete floor with PVC tiles or bare screed | 2.5 | 0.17 |
| Single glazing | 1.8 | 1.8 |

In the table the impedance of the glazing is the same as its resistance due to its having negligible thermal capacitance.

As with steady state resistances of building fabric, it is easier to manipulate the reciprocal impedances, **admittances**. The admittance value referred to in the CIBSE Guide refers to the admittance derived from $Z_{ii}$, which here is given the symbol $Y_{ii}$. It is worth noting that $Z_{ii}$ is a complex number, as is electrical impedance:

$$Z_{ii} = R + \frac{1}{j\omega C} \qquad (7.48)$$

$$Y_{ii} = \frac{1}{Z_{ii}}$$

where   $R$ = resistance of the wall and surface resistance (m² K W⁻¹);
        $C$ = thermal capacitance of the wall (J m⁻² K⁻¹);
        $j = \sqrt{(-1)}$.
Similarly, $Y_{ii}$ is also a complex number, but to simplify matters CIBSE quote values of the modulus of $Y_{ii}$, which is denoted as $Y$:

$$Y = |Y_{ii}|$$

$$= \left| \frac{j\omega C}{1 + j\omega CR} \right|$$

$$= \left| \frac{j\omega C + \omega^2 C^2 R}{1 + \omega^2 C^2 R^2} \right|$$

$$= \left[ \frac{\omega^2 C^2 + \omega^4 C^4 R^2}{(1 + \omega^2 C^2 R^2)^2} \right]^{0.5}$$

$$= \left[ \frac{\omega^2 C^2}{(1 + \omega^2 C^2 R^2)} \right]^{0.5} \tag{7.49}$$

Bassett and Pritchard [11] show that the equation for deriving $Z_{ii}$ is:

$$Z_{ii} = \frac{R_{so} \cosh \sqrt{(j\omega RC)} + \sqrt{(R/j\omega C)} \sinh \sqrt{(j\omega RC)}}{\cosh \sqrt{(j\omega RC)} + R_{so} \sqrt{(j\omega C/R)} \sinh \sqrt{(j\omega RC)}} + R_{si} \tag{7.50}$$

where  $R$ = total wall conduction resistance (m$^2$ K W$^{-1}$), and
$C$ = thermal capacitance of the wall (J m$^{-2}$ K$^{-1}$).

Sinh and cosh can be put in terms of exponential values and sines and cosines [8], or in terms of a series [11] to enable calculation in a computer program without the facility of imaginary numbers.

Notice the potential influence of the inside surface resistance, $R_{si}$. If insulation is put on to the inside of the wall, then the insulation resistance, $R_{ins}$, will be added to $R_{si}$ (as would be the resistance of the carpet on the floor in Table 7.9). Both the carpet and insulation have high resistances but very small thermal capacities, so they are considered as resistances alone. This will increase the overall resistance of the fabric element, so increasing its imped-

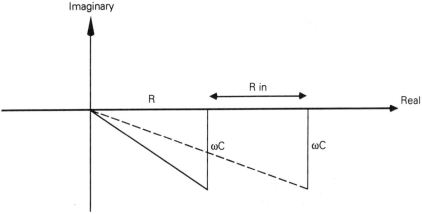

**Fig. 7.8**   Influence of insulation.

ance (decreasing its admittance) and also increasing its time constant, as Fig. 7.8 shows. $Z_{ii}$ is the equivalent impedance of the resistor and capacitor of the fabric element. The time constant of the fabric element, $\tau$, is RC, as was mentioned in Chapter 4 on sensors and their responses. This means that the element will be slower at soaking up heat and will have a lower admittance and capacity to store heat.

The CIBSE Guide's Section A3 [8] uses matrix notation to relate internal temperatures and heat flows to their external equivalents. For a homogeneous fabric element the matrix equation (with the $\sim$ missed out over the temperatures and heat flows for clarity):

$$\begin{bmatrix} t_i \\ q_i \end{bmatrix} = \begin{bmatrix} M_1 & M_2 \\ M_3 & M_1 \end{bmatrix} \begin{bmatrix} t_o \\ q_o \end{bmatrix} \quad (7.51)$$

$$= \begin{bmatrix} \{(M_1 \times t_o) + (M_2 \times q_o)\} \\ \{(M_3 \times t_o) + (M_1 \times q_o)\} \end{bmatrix}$$

where $t_i$ = internal temperature;
$t_o$ = outside temperature;
$q_i$ = internal heat flux (W m$^{-2}$);
$q_o$ = external heat flux (W m$^{-2}$);
$M$ = a matrix element.

Included in the matrix elements are the internal and external resistances, the latter for an external wall. Internal walls contribute to the heat storage of the building, so they are included in the total building admittance, unlike the steady state $\Sigma U$ value which is for external fabric primarily:

$$\begin{bmatrix} M_1 & M_2 \\ M_3 & M_1 \end{bmatrix} = \begin{bmatrix} 1 & R_{so} \\ 0 & 1 \end{bmatrix} \begin{bmatrix} m_1 & m_2 \\ m_3 & m_1 \end{bmatrix} \begin{bmatrix} 1 & R_{si} \\ 0 & 1 \end{bmatrix}$$

where $m_1 = \cosh(p + jp)$

$$m_2 = \frac{1 \sinh(p + jp)}{k(p + jp)}$$

$$m_3 = \frac{k(p + jp) \sinh(p + jp)}{1}$$

$$p = \left[ \frac{\omega l^2 \rho C_p}{2k} \right]^{0.5}$$

and where $l$ = thickness of the element (m);
$\rho$ = density of element (kg m$^{-3}$);
$\omega$ = frequency (radians s$^{-1}$);
$k$ = conductivity (W m$^{-1}$ K$^{-1}$).

From this the admittance is given by:

$$Y_{ii} = \frac{M_1}{M_2} \qquad (7.52)$$

This can be derived from the matrix in equation (7.51) with $t_0$ at zero:

$$t_i = M_1 t_0 + M_2 q_0$$

$$= M_2 q_0$$

$$q_i = M_3 t_0 + M_1 q_0$$

$$= M_1 q_0$$

from which:

$$q_i = \frac{M_1}{M_2} t_i$$

$$= Y_{ii} t_i$$

*Example*
Calculate the admittance for a 220 mm brick wall with the following data:

| | |
|---|---|
| Density | $\rho = 1700 \text{ kg m}^{-3}$ |
| Conductivity | $k = 0.84 \text{ W m}^{-1} \text{ K}^{-1}$ |
| Specific heat capacity | $C_p = 800 \text{ J kg}^{-1} \text{ K}^{-1}$ |
| Inside surface resistance | $R_{si} = 0.12 \text{ m}^2 \text{ K W}^{-1}$ |
| Outside surface resistance | $R_{so} = 0.06 \text{ m}^2 \text{ K W}^{-1}$ |

*Solution*
This example comes from the CIBSE Guide [8], but instead of solving it by the matrix method initially, equation (7.50) will be used:

$$Z_{ii} = \frac{R_{so} \cosh \sqrt{(j\omega RC)} + \sqrt{(R/j\omega C)} \sinh \sqrt{(j\omega RC)}}{\cosh \sqrt{(j\omega RC)} + R_{so} \sqrt{(j\omega C/R)} \sinh \sqrt{(j\omega RC)}} + R_{si} \qquad (7.50)$$

where $R$ = total wall conduction resistance ($\text{m}^2 \text{ K W}^{-1}$), and $C$ = thermal capacitance of the wall ($\text{J m}^{-2} \text{ K}^{-1}$).

Putting $j\omega C = S$, the susceptance:

$$S = 21.8j$$

and:

$$R = \frac{0.22}{0.84} = 0.26 \text{ m}^2 \text{ K W}^{-1}$$

Using the expansions:

$$\cosh \sqrt{(RS)} = 1 + \frac{RS}{2} + \frac{RS^2}{24} + \frac{RS^3}{720}$$

$$\sqrt{(R/S)}\,\sinh\sqrt{(RS)} = R\left\{1+\frac{RS}{6}+\frac{RS^{2}}{120}+\frac{RS^{3}}{5040}\right\}$$

$$\sqrt{(j\omega C/R)}\,\sinh\sqrt{(j\omega RC)} = S\left\{1+\frac{RS}{6}+\frac{RS^{2}}{120}+\frac{RS^{3}}{5040}\right\}$$

Hence:

$$Z_{\mathrm{ii}} = \frac{0.06\,(-0.34+2.59\,j)+(0.19+0.24\,j)}{(-0.34+2.59\,j)+0.06\,(-19.8+16\,j)}$$

$$= 0.077 - 0.08\,j$$

The total impedance, adding on the internal resistance is:

$$Z_{\mathrm{ii}} + R_{\mathrm{si}}$$

$$= 0.197 - 0.08\,j$$

Inverting this yields:

$$Y_{\mathrm{ii}} = \frac{0.197+0.08\,j}{(0.197-0.08\,j)\,(0.197+0.08\,j)}$$

$$= 4.34 + 1.76\,j$$

CIBSE admittance is:

$$|Y_{\mathrm{ii}}| = \sqrt{(4.34^{2}+1.76^{2})}$$

$$= 4.68\ \mathrm{W\ m^{-2}\,K^{-1}}$$

In comparison, the CIBSE matrix method gives:

$$p = 1.688$$

and using the expressions:

$$\cosh\,(p+jp) = \tfrac{1}{2}\,\{(e^{p}+e^{-p})\cos p + j(e^{p}-e^{-p})\sin p\}$$

$$\sinh\,(p+jp) = \tfrac{1}{2}\,\{(e^{p}+e^{-p})\cos p + j(e^{p}-e^{-p})\sin p\}$$

which gives:

$$\begin{bmatrix} M_{1} & M_{2} \\ M_{3} & M_{1} \end{bmatrix} = \begin{bmatrix} 1 & 0.12 \\ 0 & 1 \end{bmatrix}\begin{bmatrix} m_{1} & m_{2} \\ m_{3} & m_{1} \end{bmatrix}\begin{bmatrix} 1 & 0.06 \\ 0 & 1 \end{bmatrix}$$

where $m_{1} = -0.33 + 2.59\,j$
$\quad\quad m_{2} = 0.19 + 0.24\,j$
$\quad\quad m_{3} = -0.19 + 15.9\,j$
so that the overall matrix is:

$$\begin{bmatrix} M_1 & M_2 \\ M_3 & M_1 \end{bmatrix} = \begin{bmatrix} (-2.72+4.5j) & (-0.013+0.821j) \\ (-19.9+15.9j) & (-1.52+3.54j) \end{bmatrix}$$

from which:

$$Y_{ii} = \frac{(-1.52+3.54j)}{-0.013+0.821j)}$$

$$= 4.35 + 1.78j$$

which is very similar to the non-matrix method, above.

Thankfully there are tables of admittances given in the CIBSE Guide [8], and these tedious calculations do not have to be regularly done to derive values.

The admittance calculated here relates to the swing in internal temperature due to internal swings in the internal heat flux, most likely due to the heating or gains. The influence of outside swings in temperature and heat flux is related to $Y_{oi}$ or, in CIBSE terms, a **decrement factor** and **phase lag** [8], relating the amplitude and phase of the internal sine wave compared to the external sine wave producing it.

### 7.8.2 CIBSE response factor

In Chapter 5, on basic control, the need for control was considered and the design conditions for a heavyweight and lightweight building were quoted. But heavyweight and lightweight were not defined in detail. By heavyweight and lightweight is meant the thermal capacity of the building. CIBSE [22] uses the **response factor**, $f_r$, to define the thermal weight of a building:

$$f_r = \frac{\Sigma (YA) + (1/3)NV}{\Sigma (UA) + (1/3)NV} \tag{7.53}$$

where $\Sigma (YA)$ = sum of the internal and external elements' products of admittances and areas (W K$^{-1}$);
$\Sigma (UA)$ = sum of the external elements' products of $U$-values and areas (W K$^{-1}$);
$N$ = air change rate, number of air changes per hour;
$V$ = volume of building (m$^3$).

The denominator approximates to the steady state heat loss as in equation (7.33):

$$Q = \{F_1 \, \Sigma(UA) + (1/3)F_2 NV\} \, (t_c - t_{ao}) \tag{7.33}$$

but without $F_1$ and $F_2$.

Correspondingly, the numerator of equation (7.53) gives the swing in the heat gain about the mean value:

$$\tilde{Q} = (\Sigma \ (YA) + \frac{1}{3} \, NV) \ \tilde{t}_{ei}$$

The greater the thermal capacity, the greater the numerator of equation (7.53), and so the larger the value of $f_r$. CIBSE defines [23] the weight of a building as in Table 7.10.

**Table 7.10**   Thermal weight in terms of the response factor

| Nominal building | Response factor |
|---|---|
| Classification | $f_r$ |
| Heavyweight | $\geqslant 6$ |
| Lightweight | $\leqslant 4$ |

From the response factor the rate of energy supply for an intermittently heated building is [22]:

$$Q = \frac{\{\Sigma(UA) + 1/3 \ NV\} \ (t_{im} - t_{om})}{\eta_H} \qquad (7.54)$$

where  $Q$ = rate of energy supply (W);

$t_{im}$ = mean inside temperature over heating season (°C);

$t_{om}$ = mean outside temperature over heating season (°C);

$\eta_H$ = heating system efficiency

and:

$$(t_{im} - t_{om}) = \frac{Hf_r(t_r - t_{om})}{Hf_r + (24 - H)} \qquad (7.55)$$

where $H$ = average daily heating period, including the pre-heating period (h), and $t_r$ = required internal temperature (°C).

As the building weight increases, so $f_r$ increases, and equation (7.55) shows that $(t_{im} - t_{om})$ increases, and from equation (7.54) the rate of energy supply must also increase. Hence lightweight buildings should be more efficient than heavyweight ones. An alternative determination of energy supply is dealt with in Chapter 10 on monitoring and targeting, and the influence of thermal weight is considered in Chapter 9 on optimiser control.

The CIBSE response factor should not be confused with the ASHRAE response factors which are the transfer functions (Z-transfer functions), of building elements [9].

### 7.8.3   Sizing of intermittent heating system

For intermittent heating, CIBSE determine that the heating system size should be:

$$F_3Q$$

where $F_3 = 1.2 \dfrac{(24 - n)\,(f_r - 1)}{24 + n\,(f_r - 1)} + 1$

$n =$ daily plant operation time (h)

and:

$$Q = \{F_1\,\Sigma(UA) + (1/3)F_2 NV\}\,(t_c - t_{ao}) \qquad (7.33)$$

This yields, for an eight hour plant operation period:

$$F_3 = 1.8$$

which seems rather large. An alternative expression is used in Section A5 of the CIBSE Guide [13], which is rather complex. Really this is a difficult problem for the admittance method as it is dealing with heat input from a heating system, which is more like a step function than a diurnal sine wave. A simpler and more appropriate method, considering the system as a first-order system, is used in Chapter 9 to examine heating system size.

## References

[1]   CIBSE (1988) CIBSE Guide, Volume A, Section A1, Environmental criteria for design, Chartered Institution of Building Services Engineers, London.
[2]   Humphreys, M. A. (1978) Outdoor temperatures and comfort indoors. *Building Research and Practice*, March–April.
[3]   Fanger, P. O. (1972) *Thermal Comfort*, McGraw-Hill, New York.
[4]   Humphreys, M. A. (1976) Field studies of thermal comfort. *Building Services Engineer*, 44, April.
[5]   CIBSE (1988) CIBSE Guide, Volume A, Section A9, Estimation of plant capacity, Chartered Institution of Building Services Engineers, London.
[6]   Holman, J. P. (1990) *Heat Transfer*, McGraw-Hill. New York.
[7]   Carslaw, H. S. and Jaeger, J. C. (1959) Conduction of heat in solids 1959 Oxford University Press (Oxford).
[8]   CIBSE (1988) CIBSE Guide, Volume A, Section A3, Thermal properties of building structures, Chartered Institution of Building Services Engineers, London.
[9]   ASHRAE Handbook Fundamentals, American Society of Heating, Refrigerating and Air Conditioning Engineers, Atlanta, 1989.
[10]  CIBSE (1988) CIBSE Guide, Volume C, Reference Data Section C3, Heat transfer, Chartered Institution of Building Services Engineers, London.
[11]  Bassett, C. R. and Pritchard, M. D. W. (1968) *Environmental Physics Heating*, Longman, Harlow.
[12]  Shaw, E. W. (1970) *Heating and Hot Water Services*, Crosby Lockwood, London.

[13] CIBSE (1988) CIBSE Guide, Volume A, Section A5, Thermal response, Chartered Institution of Building Services Engineers, London.

[14] CIBSE (1988) CIBSE Guide, Volume A, Section A9, Estimation of plant capacity, Chartered Institution of Building Services Engineers, London.

[15] Liddament, M. W. (1986) *Air Infiltration Calculation Techniques – an Applications Guide*, Air Infiltration and Ventilation Centre, Warwick.

[16] CIBSE (1986) CIBSE Guide, Volume A, Section A4, Air infiltration, Chartered Institution of Building Services Engineers, London.

[17] CIBSE (1986) CIBSE Guide, Volume A, Section A7, Internal heat gains, Chartered Institution of Building Services Engineers, London.

[18] O'Callaghan, P. W. (1978) *Building for Energy Conservation*, Pergamon, Oxford.

[19] Crabb, J. A. Murdoch, N. and Penman, J. M. (1987) *A Simplified Thermal Response Model*, Building Services Engineering Research and Technology 8, Chartered Institution of Building Services Engineers, London.

[20] Levermore, G. J. (1989) Which program? *Chartered Institution of Building Services Engineers Journal* (London), **11**, 3.

[21] Fisk, D. J. (1981) *Thermal Control of Buildings*, Applied Science Publishers, London.

[22] CIBSE Building Energy Code, Pt 2, Calculation of energy demands and targets for the design of new buildings and services: Section A, Heated and naturally ventilated buildings, Chartered Institution of Building Services Engineers, London, 1981.

[23] CIBSE (1988) CIBSE Guide, Volume A, Section A8, Summertime temperatures, Chartered Institution of Building Services Engineers, London.

# 8
# Compensation

---

Although PID loop control has been discussed in Chapter 4, a modified version is used in most BEMS to control the heating. This modified PID control is a **compensator loop controller**. It enables the heating system output to be varied in relation to the outside temperature. A whole building's heating, or its zones, can be controlled by compensator loops, without the need for a myriad of room thermostats, wiring and valves. Also if windows are opened, the heating output is not increased and wasted. Hence compensation control is widely used but there are complications in its use that this chapter will explore.

## 8.1  Fundamentals

Before we consider in detail the compensator loop controller, it is worth considering a simple heating system, of a boiler pump and emitter, as shown in Fig. 8.1.

The boiler and pump are switched on and off by a BEMS outstation receiving signals from a room temperature sensor. This would be the type of system for a domestic installation. To determine the average steady state temperatures in the system the balance equation, from Chapter 7, is used:

$$p_1 \dot{m} C_p(t_f - t_r) = p_2 B(t_m - t_{ai})^n$$

$$= \frac{1}{F_2} \{F_1 \Sigma (UA) + (1/3) F_2 NV\} (t_{ai} - t_{ao}) \quad (7.40)$$

Assuming $p_1 = 1.0$, $p_2 = 1.0$, and:

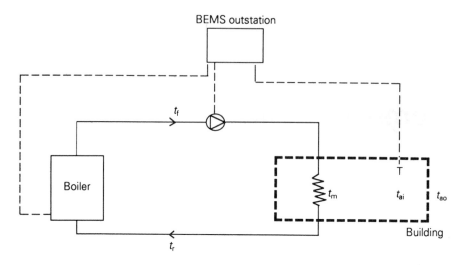

**Fig. 8.1**   A simple heating system.

$$A = \frac{1}{F_2}\{F_1 \, \Sigma \, (UA') + (1/3)F_2 NV\}$$

then where $A'$ = fabric area (m²) and:

$$\dot{m}C_p(t_f - t_r) = B(t_m - t_{ai})^n = A(t_{ai} - t_{ao})$$

Putting in the design conditions, simplified for easy calculation, of:

$$t_f = 80°C, \ \ t_r = 70°C, \ \ t_{ai} = 20°C$$

$$t_{ao} = 0°C, \ \ \ n = 1.3 \text{ for a radiator system}$$

and the building heat loss is 100 kW gives:

$$\dot{m}C_p = 10 \text{ kW K}^{-1}$$

$$A = 5 \text{ kW K}^{-1}$$

$$B = 0.546$$

It is interesting to consider how the system temperatures change as the heat load changes. Consider when $t_{ao} = 10°C$.
Assuming that the heating system can be controlled to maintain the room at 20°C, the heat load has now changed to 50 kW:

$$5(20 - 10) = 50 \text{ kW}$$

Also the boiler output would need to match this, so:

$$10(80 - 75) = 50 \text{ kW}$$

However, the radiator is now:

$$0.546(77.5 - 20)^{1.3} = 106 \text{ kW}$$

The dynamics of the heating system have not been considered here, but obviously $t_m$, the mean water temperature in the radiator, is too high and has to be reduced to get the correct 50 kW for the emitter. Consequently, $t_f$ has to be reduced. The required value of $t_m$ can be found by solving the heat balance equation:

$$0.546(t_m - 20)^{1.3} = 5(20 - 10)$$

giving:

$$t_m = 52.3°C$$

and so:

$$t_f = 54.8°C \quad \text{and} \quad t_r = 49.8°C$$

These values from the balance equation are the average, steady state values. If the boiler cycles, then the values are the average values during the cycle periods.

So far, the control of the heating system has not been considered. A simple control would be that the outstation controls the pump only, as is the control in most domestic heating systems. When the pump turns off, the boiler will heat the water in itself and the surrounding pipework, until it is switched off by its own thermostat at 80°C. So $t_f$ will remain near to 80°C, especially during the pump off time. In order to obtain $t_m$ at 52°C, $t_f$, the return water temperature would have to have a value well below 52°C, near to 24°C if $t_f$ was around

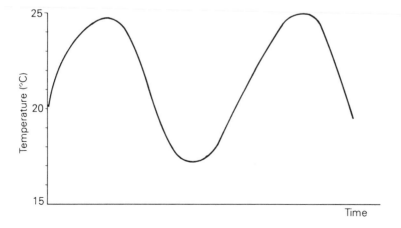

**Fig. 8.2** The effect of simple heating control.

80°C. This would mean large amplitude cycling, and with the delays and dead times in the system, it would lead to poor control. If $t_m$ could not be kept near to 52°C, then the room temperature, $t_{ai}$, would rise. This is a strong possibility due to the cycling of the system and the potential power of the heating as shown in Fig. 8.2

The load will affect the overshoot, as discussed in Chapter 4. If the boiler is controlled by the BEMS, as well as the pump, then there is a better chance of keeping the boiler flow temperature down.

## 8.2  The compensator circuit

The best way of achieving a lower flow water temperature is by using a 3-port mixing valve, as shown in Fig. 8.3. Here the 3-port valve reduces $t_f$, the flow water temperature, to the appropriate level according to the heating load, by reducing the water flow from the boiler while increasing the flow of return water to be mixed.

The value of $t_f$ is set in proportion to the outside temperature, $t_{ao}$, sensed by the temperature sensor sited on an external, north-facing wall.

A typical schedule for a BEMS compensator loop is shown in Fig. 8.4. The equation for this schedule is:

$$t_f = 80 - 2\, t_{ao} \tag{8.1}$$

The signal from the $t_{ao}$ sensor is used to determine $t_f$, which is monitored by a water temperature sensor just after the valve. The valve is controlled by the

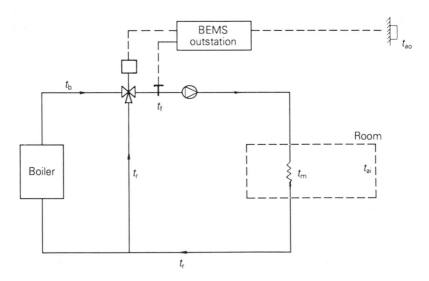

**Fig. 8.3**  A compensator circuit.

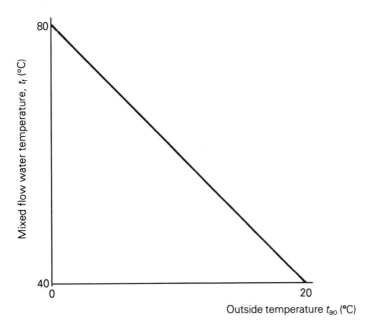

**Fig. 8.4**   Typical compensator loop schedule.

signal from the $t_f$ sensor. Hence the $t_f$ sensor and the valve are referred to as the sub-master control, receiving its control set point from the master $t_{ao}$ sensor. North Americans refer to this as a 'reset controller'. Control of the valve is by a PI control loop whose set point is determined, or reset, by the $t_{ao}$ signal.

Compensator control enables the heating system to be adjusted in relation to the coldness of the weather. It obviates the need for many thermostats and valves to be installed, at considerable expense in medium and large buildings.

This is compensator control, and most BEMS outstations contain compensator loops to perform this control.

## 8.3   BEMS compensator loop

The configuration for a compensator is shown in Fig. 8.5. Sensor S1, a type-1 sensor or flow water sensor, sends back a signal of $t_f$ to loop 1, input $P$. Sensor S2, a type-3 sensor, sends a signal of $t_{ao}$ to the function module, $F1$, input $G$. This function module calculates the schedule of $t_f$ against $t_{ao}$, from the values set for $E$, $H$ and $F$. The output from $F1$, $D$ is given by the function equation:

$$D = (E \times G) + (F \times H)$$

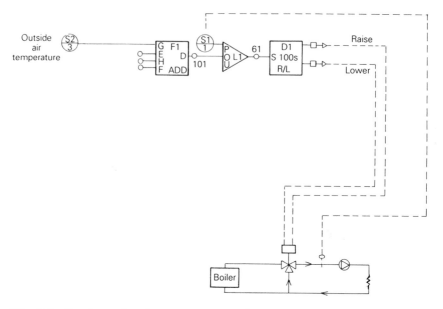

**Fig. 8.5** Configuration for a compensator loop.

For a straight-line schedule with the equation:

$$t_f = -2t_{ao} + 80$$

then the function module is configured to give:

$$D = (-2 \times G) + (1 \times 80)$$

where $D$ = output to PID loop, L1;
$\quad G$ = input from S2 ($t_{ao}$);
$\quad F = 80$;
$\quad H = 1$.

The output from the function module, $D$, is then the input, via an analogue node, 101, to the PID loop, L1. This input from $F1$ is the occupation set point, O, for loop L1 and is the required value for $t_f$. Loop L1 then sends a control signal, via analogue node 61, to the raise/lower driver, D1. In turn, D1 sends a digital signal to a raise relay or to a lower relay, which moves the valve actuator or motor to respectively open and close the valve.

This motor may well be a split-phase motor which moves in one direction when receiving an in-phase or raise signal from the raise relay, and moves in the other direction when receiving an anti-phase, or lower, signal. This will move the valve either forward for more recirculation or back for less. The 100 s inside the raise/lower box refers to the time to drive the valve from fully open to fully shut.

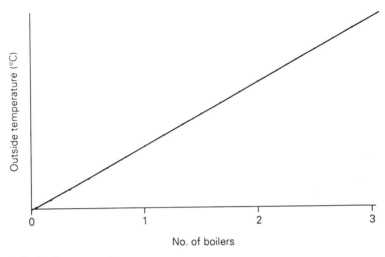

**Fig. 8.6**   Boiler control.

## 8.4  Alternative compensator loop control

Compensation can be carried out without the need for a 3-port mixing valve, by operating straight on to the boiler control. For a single boiler it can either switch off the boiler at a flow water temperature related to the outside temperature, or it can control the boiler by a time proportional signal, again related to $t_{ao}$. Neither of these methods is as satisfactory as using a 3-port valve as boiler cycling can interfere with the control.

For multiple boilers, compensator control can be used to sequence the number of boilers required. The control signal for this is simply a proportional control, as shown in Fig. 8.6.

## 8.5  Inside air temperature variation

The compensator loop commonly used in most BEMSs simply regulates the heating system in relation to the outside temperature, $t_{ao}$. There is no feedback of room temperature, $t_{ai}$. Hence $t_{ai}$ can vary slightly, according to the compensator schedule used.

*Example*
Consider a heating system, with radiators, with the following design conditions:

$t_{ao} = 0°C$, $t_{ai} = 20°C$, design heat loss $= 100$ kW

$t_f = 80°C$, $t_r = 70°C$, and the compensator loop schedule is:

$t_f = 80 - 2\, t_{ao}$

What is $t_{ai}$ when $t_{ao} = 10°C$?

*Solution*

From the design conditions, the constants in the heat balance equation (7.40) are:

$$\dot{m}C_p = 10, \quad B = 0.546, \quad A = 5$$

So at $t_{ao} = 10°C$, $t_f = 60°C$

$$10(60 - t_r) = 0.546(t_m - t_{ai})^{1.3} = 5(t_{ai} - 10)$$

Putting this in terms of $t_m$ and $t_{ai}$ only:

$$20(60 - t_m) = 0.546(t_m - t_{ai})^{1.3} = 5(t_{ai} - 10)$$

From the boiler output and the heat loss parts of this equation $t_{ai}$ may be found in terms of $t_m$:

$$20(60 - t_m) = 5(t_{ai} - 10)$$

we get:

$$250 - 4t_m = t_{ai} \tag{8.2}$$

substituting into the balance equation:

$$0.546(t_m - 250 + 4t_m)^{1.3} = 5(250 - 4t_m - 10)$$

$$0.546(5t_m - 250)^{1.3} = 5(240 - 4t_m) \tag{8.3}$$

There are basically two ways of solving this. The first is by guessing and adjusting until both sides are equal. There are limits to guide such guesses; however, the left-hand side, the emitter output, cannot be negative, so:

$$5t_m - 250 \geqslant 0$$

$$t_m \geqslant 50°C$$

Similarly, on the right-hand side:

$$240 - 4t_m \geqslant 0$$

$$t_m \leqslant 60°C$$

So a suitable guess would be $t_m = 55°C$:

left-hand side = 35.9 kW          right-hand side = 100 kW

So $t_m$ needs to be increased. Eventually $t_m$ will be determined.

A quicker but more complicated way is by Newton's method of approximation. Using this method the roots of a function of $x$, $f(x) = 0$, are found where $f(x) = 0$ is a generalized function of $x$. In our case:

$$f(x) \equiv f(t_m) = 0.546(5t_m - 250)^{1.3} - 5(240 - 4t_m)$$

This method is readily applicable to a computer program. To understand the principle of the method it can be explained geometrically, as shown in Fig. 8.7.

Newton's method starts by making an educated guess as to the root of the function, $t_{m0}$. The true, unknown root is shown as $t_{mr}$. A tangent at $t_{m0}$ cuts the $t_m$ axis nearer to $t_{mr}$, at $t_{m1}$. Repeating the process gets closer to the true root, $t_{mr}$. From the construction of the tangent it can be seen that:

$$\frac{df(t_{m0})}{dt_m} = \frac{f(t_{m0})}{t_{m0} - t_m}$$

Rearranging gives:

$$t_{m1} = t_{m0} - \frac{f(t_{m0})}{f'(t_{m0})}$$

where $f'(t_{m0}) = \dfrac{df(t_{m0})}{dt_m}$

Instead of differentiating $f(t_m)$, a difference approximation can be made, as shown in Fig. 8.8.

$$f'(t_{m0}) = \frac{f(t_{m0} + k) - f(t_{m0})}{k}$$

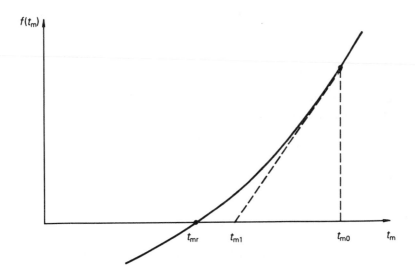

**Fig. 8.7** Newton's method of finding the roots of $f(t_m) = 0$.

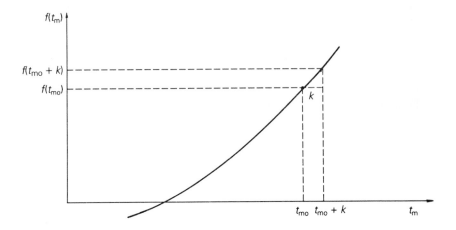

**Fig. 8.8**   Newton's method by small increment.

where $k$ is a small increment in $t_m$; this yields:

$$t_{m1} = t_{m0} - \frac{kf(t_{m0})}{f(t_{m0} + k) - f(t_{m0})}$$

In our example, let us take the same value of $t_m$ as in our guess method, $t_{m0} = 55°C$, with $k = 1°C$. This yields:

$$t_{m1} = 55 - \frac{1 \times \{0.546[5 \times 55 - 250]^{1.3} - 5(240 - 4 \times 55)\}}{\{0.546(5 \times 56 - 250)^{1.3} - 5(240 - 4 \times 56)\} - f(t_{m0})}$$

where $f(t_m)$ in the denominator is the same as the numerator, only there is not room to put it easily in the equation. Further calculation gives:

$$t_{m1} = 55 - \frac{\{0.546[65.66] - 100\}}{\{0.546(83.23) - 80\} - \{0.546[65.66] - 100\}}$$

which works out to:

$$t_{m1} = 57.168°C$$

This can be checked by putting 57.2°C into equation (8.3):

left-hand side = 57.26 kW      right-hand side = 56.64 kW

These results are close together, but if greater accuracy were required, then $t_{m1}$ could be used in Newton's method as the guessed value to produce $t_{m2}$.

$t_{ai}$ can be found by substituting $t_{m1}$ above into equation (8.4):

$$t_{ai} = 250 - 4t_m$$
$$= 21.3°C$$

The room temperature has risen above its design value by 1.3°C.

With straight-line schedules such as in the above example, compensator loops invariably allow the room temperature to vary slightly as the outside temperature varies. If the schedule is dropped to, say, $t_f = 80 - 3t_{ao}$, to stop the room temperature rising, it then falls below the design temperature of 20°C, as is shown in Fig. 8.9.

## 8.6 Variation of heating system output

It is interesting to note that the heating system under compensator loop control will be putting out heat until the room temperature, $t_{ai}$, equals the emitter mean water temperature, $t_m$. In other words, until the heat emitter output is zero:

$$B(t_m - t_{ai})^{1.3} = 0$$

The other terms in the balance equation, the boiler output and the building heat loss, will also have to be zero for there to be no heat output. This zero output occurs when:

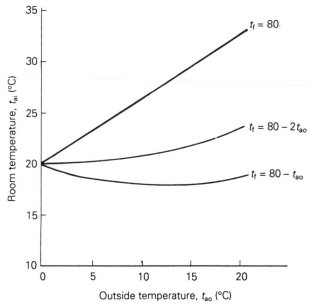

**Fig. 8.9** Variation in $t_{ai}$ with schedule.

$$t_f = t_r = t_m = t_{ao} = t_{ai}$$

So for the schedule $t_f = 80 - 2t_{ao}$, the zero output temperature is when:

$$t_f = 80 - 2t_f$$

$$t_f = 26.67°C$$

Changing the schedule to $t_f = 80 - 3t_{ao}$ produces a zero output temperature of:

$$t_f = 20°C$$

The heating system output can be derived from the heat balance equation. If the heating system output is defined in terms of the heat load factor, $\Phi$, where:

$$\Phi = \frac{\text{heat output}}{\text{maximum heat output}}$$

then for the boiler output:

$$\Phi = \frac{t_f - t_m}{t_{f\,des} - t_{m\,des}}$$

$$\Phi = \frac{0.5\,\delta t_b}{0.5\delta t_{b\,des}} = \frac{\delta t_b}{\delta t_{b\,des}} \tag{8.4}$$

where $t_{f\,des}$ = design mixed flow water temperature (°C);
$t_{m\,des}$ = design return water temperature (°C);
$\delta t_b = t_f - t_r$
$\delta t_{b\,des} = t_{f\,des} - t_{r\,des}$

$t_m$ is used in the upper equation to maintain consistency with the emitter output term in the balance equation. Similarly, for the heat emitter and the building heat loss the outputs are respectively:

$$\Phi^{1/1.3} = \Phi^{0.769} = \frac{\delta t_e}{\delta t_{e\,des}} \tag{8.5}$$

and;

$$\Phi = \frac{\delta t_a}{\delta t_{a\,des}} \tag{8.6}$$

where $\delta t_e = t_m - t_{ai}$
$\delta t_{e\,des} = t_{m\,des} - t_{ai\,des}$
$\delta t_a = t_{ai} - t_{ao}$
$\delta t_{a\,des} = t_{ai\,des} - t_{ao\,des}$

Adding equations (8.4)–(8.6) together yields:

$$\delta t_a + \delta t_e + 0.5\,\delta t_b = \Phi\delta t_{a\,des} + \Phi^{0.769}\delta t_{e\,des} + 0.5\,\Phi\delta t_{b\,des}$$

$$t_f - t_{ao} = \Phi \delta t_{a\ des} + \Phi^{0.769} \delta t_{e\ des} + 0.5\ \Phi \delta t_{b\ des} \tag{8.7}$$

Substituting the compensator loop schedule equation into this gives the relationship between $\Phi$ and $t_{ao}$. Using the schedule and the design values in the previous example:

$$80 - 3t_{ao} = 25\Phi - 55\Phi^{0.769} \tag{8.8}$$

A graph of this equation, which has a shallow curve, is shown in Fig. 8.10.

Equation (8.8) can be used to check the solution to the previous example. There $t_{ao} = 10°C$ and the load was 57.26 kW (from the left-hand side of the equation), or 56.64 kW (from the right-hand side of the equation). Taking 56.64 kW gives:

$$\Phi = 0.566$$

Putting this value into equation (8.8) gives:

$$t_{ao} = 10.1°C$$

close to the given value of $t_{ao}$.

To ensure that the BEMS, with its compensator loop, does not allow the heating system to continue heating in mild weather, a function module can be used to stop the heating beyond certain values of $t_{ao}$. As we have already seen, with a schedule of $t_f = 80 - 2t_{ao}$, the zero output temperature is $t_{ao} = 26.67°C$. Unless the heating is manually switched off, then there will be heating during the summer. The addition of a **comparator function module** and a **gate**

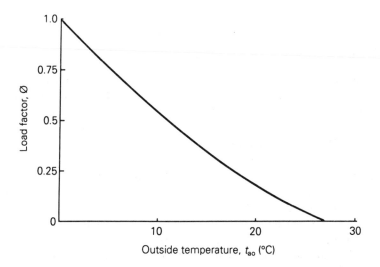

**Fig. 8.10** Variation of load factor with $t_{ao}$.

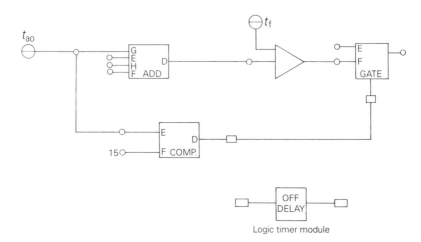

**Fig. 8.11**   Configuration to stop compensated heating in mild weather.

**function module**, as shown in Fig. 8.11, closes the 3-port valve to the boiler when $t_{ao} \geqslant 15°C$.

The comparator's function is given by:

$$D = 1 \quad \text{when } E < F$$

$$D = 0 \quad \text{when } E > F$$

So with $F$ set at, for instance, 15°C, then $D = 0$ when $E$, the $t_{ao}$ value, is above 15°C. The gate module's function is:

$$D = F \quad \text{when } B = 1$$

$$D = E \quad \text{when } B = 0$$

The value of $E$ can be set to 0, so that the signal to the driver closes the 3-port valve to the boiler as if there was no error signal from the mixed flow temperature sensor and loop.

To ensure that there is no rapid switching of the valve when $t_{ao}$ hovers around 15°C, a **logic timer module**, as shown in Fig. 8.11, can be inserted between the comparator and the gate. This timer module introduces a delay, (which can be up to 9 h) of, say, 15 min before the 0, or OFF, signal is transmitted to the gate. If at the end of the 15 min delay $t_{ao}$ has dropped below 15°C, then the output signal to the gate remains 1, or ON.

If this heating shut-down were required from an older stand-alone compensator controller, then a separate external thermostat would have to be wired up to switch off the heating. With the BEMS, it is simply a reconfiguration, using the existing outside temperature sensor, so no wiring and separate thermostat are required.

## 8.7 The ideal schedule

The ideal schedule to ensure that $t_{ai}$ stays constant as the outside temperature varies is given by solving the balance equation, equation (7.40), for constant $t_{ai}$:

$$2\dot{m}C_p(t_f - t_m) = B(t_m - t_{ai})^n = A(t_{ai} - t_{ao})$$

where $n$ is the index for emitter output (for radiators $n = 1.3$). From this equation the schedule can be derived:

$$t_f = \frac{A}{2\dot{m}C_p}(t_{ai} - t_{ao}) + t_m$$

$t_m$ can be equated to terms in $t_{ao}$ and $t_{ai}$ from the balance equation:

$$t_m = [(A/B)(t_{ai} - t_{ao})]^{1/n} + t_{ai}$$

hence:

$$t_f = \frac{A}{2\dot{m}C_p}(t_{ai} - t_{ao}) + \left[\frac{A}{B}(t_{ai} - t_{ao})\right]^{1/n} + t_{ai} \qquad (8.9)$$

This schedule is shown in Fig. 8.12, and it can be seen that it is curved, especially at the higher values of $t_{ao}$.

This schedule requires knowledge of the constants in the balance equation: $\dot{m}C_p$, $B$, $A$ and $t_{ai}$. The constants may not be readily available, and $t_{ai}$ needs to be measured, entailing the use of an inside sensor. But a number of compensator loops are curved to reflect the non-linear output of heat emitters.

When occupants feel cold in a building, then they often touch the heat emitters to determine whether the heating is working. Unless the radiator is

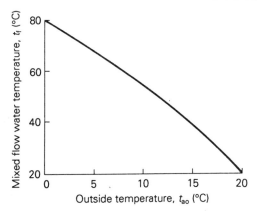

**Fig. 8.12** Ideal compensator loop schedule.

very hot, they sometimes incorrectly conclude that the heating system is not working. This could apply in spring and autumn periods when a BEMS compensator loop will maintain the emitter mean temperature at a reduced level due to its schedule. If the schedule reduces the mean temperature too steeply with respect to $t_{ao}$, then there is a greater risk of the occupants feeling warm rather than hot radiators and complaining of the heating not working. Also, with steep schedules, the room temperature will be reduced, as Fig. 8.9 shows. This is why many compensator loop schedules have a value of $t_f$ around 40°C when $t_{ao}$ is near 20°C.

## 8.8  Plant size implications

In the examination of compensator loops we have considered the heat balance equation with the various elements equally sized, i.e. $p_1 = 1.0$ and $p_2 = 1.0$. But the balance equation can also be used to examine the variations in $t_{ai}$ due to differing plant sizes.

*Example*
Consider a radiator heating system controlled by a BEMS compensator loop with a 3-port mixing valve. The design conditions are the same as in the last example. How does $t_{ai}$ vary when $t_{ao} = 10$°C, if:

(a) the boiler is 100% oversized;
(b) the emitters are 10% oversized?

The schedule is now $t_f = 80 - 3t_{ao}$, whereas it was $t_f = 80 - 2t_{ao}$ in the previous example.

*Solution*
Before the main question is answered, it will be of use in later comparison to determine what $t_{ai}$ would be if everything was equally sized. The compensator schedule makes $t_f = 50$°C and calculation reveals that:

$$t_m = 47.85°C \quad \text{and} \quad t_{ai} = 18.6°C$$

As a check, the emitter output is:

$$0.546(47.85 - 18.6)^{1.3}$$

$$= 43.5\,\text{kW}$$

and the heat loss is:

$$5(18.6 - 10)$$

$$= 43\,\text{kW}$$

To return to part (a) of the question, the boiler is 100% oversized, so $p_1 = 2.0$, while $p_2$ remains 1.0. The oversizing assumes that the water flow rate has been increased to allow a 10 K drop across the boiler if it were on full load. The balance equation becomes:

$$2 \times 2 \dot{m} C_p(t_f - t_m) = B(t_m - t_{ai})^{1.3} = A(t_{ai} - t_{ao})$$

so:

$$40(t_f - t_m) = 0.546(t_m - t_{ai})^{1.3} = 5(t_{ai} - t_{ao})$$

$$40(50 - t_m) = 0.546(t_m - t_{ai})^{1.3} = 5(t_{ai} - 10)$$

Following through Newton's method with $t_{mo} = 47$, and $k = 2$ yields:

$$t_m = 48.9°C$$

and:

$$t_{ai} = 19.0°C$$

This is above $t_{ai}$ with an equal sized plant ($p_1 = 1.0$), where it was shown above that $t_{ai} = 18.6°C$ (lower than the design value of 20°C).

(b) Now the emitters are 10% oversized, hence $p_2 = 1.1$ and $p_1 = 1.0$. The balance equation becomes:

$$20(t_f - t_m) = 1.1 \times 0.546(t_m - t_{ai})^{1.3} = 5(t_{ai} - t_{ao})$$

So:

$$20(50 - tm) = 0.6552(t_m - t_{ai})^{1.3} = 5(t_{ai} - 10)$$

Analysis yields:

$$t_m = 47.68°C \quad t_{ai} = 19.3°C$$

Comparing this with (a) and the previous example, it can be seen that a 10% increase in emitter size produces a greater increase in room temperature than 100% increase in boiler size! The emitter size has a considerable influence on the room temperature, more so than the boiler size. An increase in room temperature would result in a corresponding increase in energy consumption, $A\delta t_{ai}$, where $\delta t_{ai}$ is the increase in room temperature.

These influences of boiler and emitter size can be examined in more detail by partial differentiation of equation (8.9), where $t_f$ is kept constant and the plant size ratios are included:

$$t_f = \frac{A}{2\dot{m}p_1 C_p}(t_{ai} - t_{ao}) + \left[\frac{A}{p_2 B}(t_{ai} - t_{ao})\right]^{1/n} + t_{ai} \tag{8.9}$$

Considering the earlier example with $A = 5$, $\dot{m}C_p = 10$, $B = 0.546$, $n = 1.3$ for radiators, but to see the influence of boiler size, $p_1$ is left as a variable:

$$t_f = \frac{(t_{ai} - t_{ao})}{4p_1} + \left[\frac{9.16}{p_2}(t_{ai} - t_{ao})\right]^{0.769} + t_{ai}$$

For assessing boiler size, $p_2 = 1.0$ and differentiating (partially) with constant $t_f$:

$$0 = -\frac{(t_{ai} - t_{ao})}{4p_1^2}\,\partial p_1 + \frac{\partial t_{ai}}{4p_1} + 0.769 \times 9.16\,\partial t_{ai}\,[9.16(t_{ai} - t_{ao})]^{-0.231} + \partial t_{ai}$$

$$\frac{(t_{ai} - t_{ao})}{4p_1^2}\,\partial p_1 = \partial t_{ai}\left[\frac{1}{4p_1} + 7.05\,[9.16(t_{ai} - t_{ao})]^{-0.231} + 1\right] \qquad (8.10)$$

For our example, above, with $t_{ai}$ varying around 18.6°C, and $t_{ao}$ at 10°C:

$$8.6\frac{\partial p_1}{4p_1^2} = \partial t_{ai}\left[\frac{1}{4p_1} + 7.05\,[79.1]^{-0.231} + 1\right]$$

$$= \partial t_{ai}\left[\frac{1}{4p_1} + 3.57\right]$$

For a boiler 100% oversized (which is stretching the calculus rather), $p_1 = 1.0$, $\partial p_1 = 1.0$, then:

$$\partial t_{ai} = 0.57°C$$

So the new temperature with the oversized boiler will be 19.2°C, reasonably close to the example answer of 19°C. But this is not much of an increase, considering the increase in boiler size. Equation (8.10) can be used to show that over the various values of $t_{ao}$ the increase in temperature will be small and that the increase in power:

$$A\partial t_{ai}$$

will also be small [1].

For the emitter size, the same exercise can be conducted, with $p_1$ set to unity:

$$t_f = \frac{(t_{ai} - t_{ao})}{4} + \left[\frac{9.16}{p_2}(t_{ai} - t_{ao})\right]^{0.769} + t_{ai}$$

Rearranging this prior to differentiation:

$$p_2\{t_f - 1.25\,t_{ai} + 0.25\,t_{ao}\}^{1.3} = 9.16(t_{ai} - t_{ao})$$

Differentiating this yields:

$$1.3p_2\{\}^{0.3} + \partial p_2\{\}^{1.3} = 9.16\,\partial t_{ai}$$

where $\{\} = \{t_f - 1.25\,t_{ai} + 0.25\,t_{ao}\}$

For our example above with $t_{ai}$ varying around 18.6°C and $t_{ao}$ at 10°C, and with the emitters 10% oversized, i.e. $\partial p_2 = 0.1$ and $p_2 = 1.0$, then:

$$\partial t_{ai} = 0.6°C$$

making $t_{ai} = 19.2°C$, close to the numerical value earlier of 19.3°C. This is a much larger increase than that for the boiler rise, even though the emitters are only 10% oversized.

## 8.9  Internal gains

So far, we have not considered the gains in the building due to occupants, or solar radiation through windows and heat gain due to equipment. If these gains are sufficient to raise the temperature of the room by $t_g$ then there is a heat gain term, $At_g$, to subtract from the heat loss from the building term in the heat balance equation. So the heat balance equation becomes:

$$\dot{m}C_p(t_f - t_r) = B(t_m - t_{ai})^n = A(t_{ai} - t_{ao}) - At_g$$

The best way to examine this is by way of an example.

*Example*
Consider a BEMS compensator loop with a schedule:

$$t_f = 80 - 2t_{ao}$$

The heating system has radiators, and there are heat gains giving $t_g = 2°C$. What is the room temperature when $t_{ao} = 10°C$?

*Solution*
This is similar to a previous example, without the gains. There $t_{ai} = 21.3°C$ and $t_m = 57.2°C$. In the present example, $t_g$ will raise the room temperature which, in turn, reduces the radiator heat output. The balance equation is therefore:

$$2 \times 10(60 - t_m) = 0.546(t_m - t_{ai})^{1.3} = 5(t_{ai} - 12)$$

hence:

$$4(60 - t_m) = t_{ai} - 12$$

or:

$$t_{ai} = 252 - 4t_m$$

Substituting into the emitter part of the balance equation yields:

$$0.546(t_m - 252 + 4t_m)^{1.3} = 5(252 - 4t_m - 12)$$

or:

$$0.546(t_m - 252)^{1.3} = 5(240 - 4t_m)$$

Solving this by Newton's method produces:

$$t_m = 57.3°C$$

so:

$$t_{ai} = 22.8°C$$

Without any heat gains, i.e. $t_g = 0$ °C, then $t_{ai}$ would be 21.3°C, as shown in the first example in this chapter. It is interesting that $t_{ai}$ has not simply risen by $t_g = 2$°C to 23.3°C. The radiator system under BEMS compensator loop control has actually utilized some of the gains. This is due to the inherent feedback of the radiator, reacting to the gains and raising its return water temperature, $t_r$, as a consequence.

It has been shown [1] that by differentiating equation (8.9), modified to account for $t_g$, in a similar way to analysing the influence of boiler size and emitter size, that a radiator system will utilize 30% of the heat gains. If $t_g = 2$°C, then the room temperature rise will be 1.4°C, close to the numerical results above. Table 8.1 shows the utilization of gains both for fan convector and natural convector emitters as well as radiators.

**Table 8.1**   Utilization of internal heat gains

| Emitter | Index, p | Heat gain utilized (%) |
|---------|----------|------------------------|
| Radiator | 1.3 | 30 |
| Natural convector | 1.5 | 32 |
| Fan convector | 1.0 | 25 |

## 8.10  Inside temperature and cascade control

Although between 25% and 32% of the heat gains are utilized by the emitters, the remaining 75% and 68% of the heat gains are still wasted, besides which the compensator loop still allows heating in mild weather. To overcome these deficiencies the loop can be controlled on internal temperature, $t_{ai}$, rather than external temperature, $t_{ao}$. The example below illustrates such an application.

*Example*
The control of a radiator heating system with a BEMS compensator loop is changed from outdoor control to indoor control, using an internal sensor. The outdoor schedule was $t_f = 80 - 2t_{ao}$. The indoor schedule maintains $t_f$ at 80°C, when $t_{ai}$ is 19°C and when $t_{ai}$ is 21°C $t_f$ is kept at 40°C. What is $t_{ai}$ when $t_{ao}$ is 10°C? Assume the same design conditions as in previous examples.

*Solution*
The equation for the new schedule is:

$$t_f = 460 - 20\, t_{ai}$$

and the balance equation is:

$$20(t_f - t_m) = 0.546(t_m - t_{ai})^{1.3} = 5(t_{ai} - 10)$$

Substituting $t_f$ in the schedule into the balance equation yields:

$$20(460 - 20\,t_{ai} - t_m) = 0.546(t_m - t_{ai})^{1.3} = 5(t_{ai} - 10)$$

Equating the boiler output and building heat loss part of this equation gives:

$$462.5 - 20.25\,t_{ai} = t_m$$

Substituting for $t_m$ in the emitter part of the balance equation and equating it to the heat loss makes the following equation:

$$0.546(462.5 - 21.25\,t_{ai})^{1.3} = 5(t_{ai} - 10)$$

Solving this numerically, by Newton's method gives:

$$t_{ai} = 20.24°C$$

The outside controlled loop, as shown in the first example in this chapter, would have allowed the temperature, $t_{ai}$, to rise to 21.3°C. So the internally controlled compensator loop can maintain a closer control of room temperature.

The closer control can also be seen from the lower zero output temperature for inside control, derived from the schedule:

$$t_f = 460 - 20\,t_{ai}$$

the zero output temperature occurring when $t_f = t_{ai}$.

$$t_{ai} = 460 - 20\,t_{ai}$$

$$t_{ai} = 21.9°C$$

For the outside controlled loop, in comparison, the zero output temperature was $t_{ai} = 26.7°C$.

Significant savings have been reported from changing BEMSs' compensator loop control from outdoor to indoor control [2]. However, a suitable, representative position must be found for the inside sensor. This is not easy and the average temperature from a number of sensors placed around the building gives better results but costs more. Also if a window is opened near one of the sensors, then the heating is increased to compensate for the loss!

The configuration for indoor control could be similar to that for outdoor control, namely using an adding function element/module. But if the inside temperature, $t_{ai}$, was well below its set point, say, on a cold day, or if someone opened a window, then ridiculously high values of $t_f$ would be set. For instance, if with the above indoor schedule $t_{ai}$ were 15°C, then:

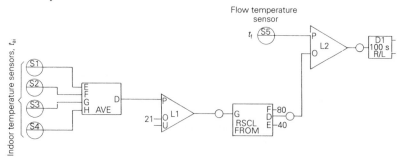

**Fig. 8.13**   Configuration for indoor compensator loop control.

$$t_f = 460 - 20 \times 15$$
$$= 160°C$$

A wider indoor schedule could be used, but a better way is to feed the average inside temperature into a PID loop whose output becomes the set point for the $t_f$ PID loop, as used in the outdoor compensator loop. Hence for the indoor temperature control there are two PID loops, one cascaded into the next, **(cascade control)**. The configuration for this control is shown in Fig. 8.13.

The 'AVE' module averages the four inside sensor signals. At the 'RSCL FROM' module the 0% to 100% output from Loop 1 is rescaled to give the indoor schedule (40°C to 80°C) as the set point for Loop 2. For the above indoor schedule the rescale values are 80 and 40. Notice that when $t_{ai}$ is low, say, 15°C, then with the set point of Loop 1 at 21°C and a gain of 50 (proportional band = 2°C), the error is 6°C. But the loop cannot put out a signal greater than 100% corresponding to the 3-port valve being fully open to the boiler.

A compromise is to use an inside sensor and an outside sensor and combine their signals. The schedule for this, using the above inside and outside schedules, is:

$$t_f = A(80 - 2t_{ao}) + (1 - A)\{460 - 20t_{ai}\}$$

where $A$ = the authority of the sensors, $A \leqslant 1$.

When $A = 0.5$, then both sensors have equal authority and contribute equally to determining the set point for $t_f$. As mentioned above, there should be limits on $t_{ai}$ and, to a lesser extent, $t_{ao}$. So in the configuration for combined inside and outside control, shown in Fig. 8.14, a PID loop (L3) has been used for the outside schedule.

Loop 3 has a gain of 5 (proportional band = 20°C), and the RSCL FROM module provides the upper and lower limits of $t_f$ on the schedule. For instance, the upper limit is 80°C when there is a 100% signal from L3 which corresponds to an error of 20°C, i.e. $t_{ao} = 0°C$.

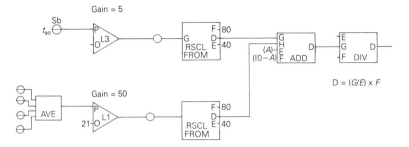

**Fig. 8.14** Configuration for internal and external compensator loop control.

The 'ADD' module combines the indoor and outdoor schedules, and here the authority can be applied:

$$D = [A \times G] + [(10 - A) \times H]$$

Here $A$ has to be an integer, and $A \leq 10$. The DIV module brings the signal back to a value between 80 and 40 for the set point of Loop 2, controlling $t_f$. The DIV module equation is:

$$D = (G/E) \times F$$
$$= (G/10) \times 1$$

The user still has to decide the authority to use for this combined control. Potentially better control means more decisions for the operator.

## 8.11 Three-port valve

An essential element of compensator control is the three-port valve. This regulates the water recirculated from the return pipe, mixing it with hot water from the boiler at temperature $t_b$, as is shown in Fig. 8.15.

A fraction of return water, $x$, is recirculated to be mixed at the valve with a fraction $(1 - x)$ of boiler water. If differences in the specific heat capacity of water, $C_p$, between $t_b$ and $t_r$ are ignored, and they are very small, then at the valve a heat balance (like the heat balance equation (7.40) in Chapter 7) gives the relationship between $x$ and the average temperatures:

$$xmC_p(t_r - t_0) + (1 - x)mC_p(t_b - t_0) = mC_p(t_r - t_0)$$

$$xt_r + (1 - x)t_b = t_f$$

where $t_0$ = a reference temperature, say, 0°C.
so:

$$x = \frac{t_b - t_f}{t_b - t_r}$$

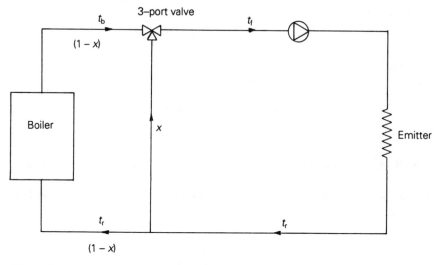

**Fig. 8.15**   Three-port valve for mixing water flows.

Consider the heating system on half-load, as in the first example in this chapter. There $t_f = 60°C$, $t_r = 54.4°C$, so:

$$x = \frac{80 - 60}{80 - 54.4}$$

$$= 0.78$$

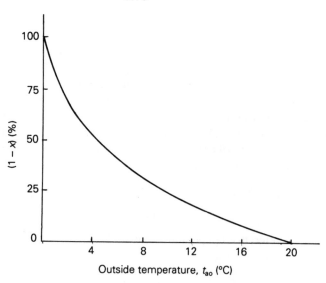

**Fig. 8.16**   Flow of water $(1 - x)$ through three-port mixing valve.

Some 78% of the return water is recirculated, and only 22% comes from the boiler. This shows that the valve action is not proportional to the load but should have a non-linear characteristic. This is due to the non-linear heat emitter. The ideal valve characteristic is shown in Fig. 8.16. Some common 2- and 3-port valve types are shown in Fig. 8.17.

To appreciate 3-port valves it is first easier to understand a 2-port valve. For a 2-port valve to control a non-linear heat emitter, an **equal percentage**, or **logarithmic**, flow characteristic is required under constant pressure conditions. The valve characteristic is shown in Fig. 8.18.

Such a valve produces an equal percentage increase in opening area for equal increments of valve movement, or **stroke**, $s$. Mathematically this is expressed as:

$$s = K \ln \left[ \frac{Q}{Q_0} \right]$$

where $s$ = valve stem position, or stroke, as a percentage of the maximum (100% at valve fully open);

$Q$ = flow as a percentage of maximum flow when the valve is full open, with flow $Q_{max}$ (m$^3$ s$^{-1}$);

$Q_0$ = flow of the valve at minimum controllable flow, as a percentage of maximum flow, $Q_{max}$;

$K$ = constant.

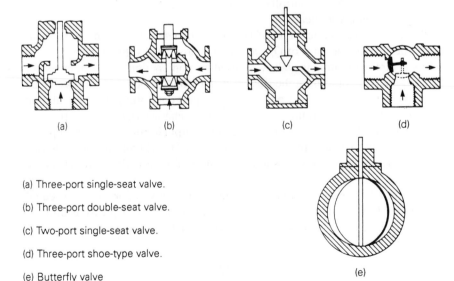

(a) Three-port single-seat valve.

(b) Three-port double-seat valve.

(c) Two-port single-seat valve.

(d) Three-port shoe-type valve.

(e) Butterfly valve

**Fig. 8.17** Different valve types.

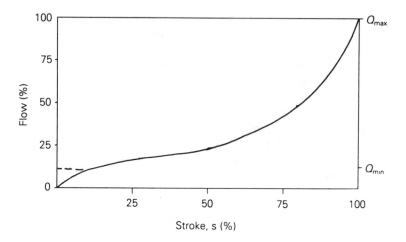

**Fig. 8.18**   Equal percentage valve characteristic.

Manufacturers sometimes refer to the relationship:

$$n = \ln \left[ \frac{Q_{max}}{Q_{min}} \right]$$

where $Q_{max}$ = maximum flow at valve full open (m³ s⁻¹);

$Q_{min}$ = minimum controllable flow (m³ s⁻¹);

$n$ = index, typically 4.

This is the logarithmic value of another parameter of a valve, its **rangeability**, defined as the ratio of $Q_{max}/Q_{min}$. For most valves this is 50.

For a three-port mixing valve, as used in conjunction with compensator control, the port controlling the flow of water from the boiler circuit is shaped similarly to the logarithmic 2-port valve. The port controlling the recirculation water on a three-port mixing valve has a linear characteristic ([6], [7]).

The most useful parameter of a valve is the **capacity index**, $C_v$, in Imperial units, $K_v$ in continental terms and $A_v$ in SI units. The SI units are the flow rate through the valve (in m³ s⁻¹) when a pressure of 1 Pa is dropped across the valve.

Manufacturers usually quote $K_v$ values, which also approximately equal $C_v$ values. The $K_v$ value is the flow rate (m³ h⁻¹) when a pressure drop of $10^2$ kPa (1 bar) exists across the valve. The equation relating $K_v$ to the flow and pressure is:

$$K_v = \frac{Q_h}{\Delta P^{0.5}}$$

where $\Delta P$ = pressure drop (Pa or kPa), and $Q_h$ = volume flow rate (m³ h⁻¹).

From D'Arcy's equation (references [3]–[5]) relating the volume flow rate through a pipe to the pressure drop across it by means of a resistance:

$$\Delta P = RQ^2$$

where $Q$ = volume flow rate (m$^3$ s$^{-1}$).

It can be seen that the resistance is related to the capacity index:

$$K_v = \frac{3600}{\sqrt{(R)}}$$

The 3600 arises from the disparity in hours and seconds between the flow rates.

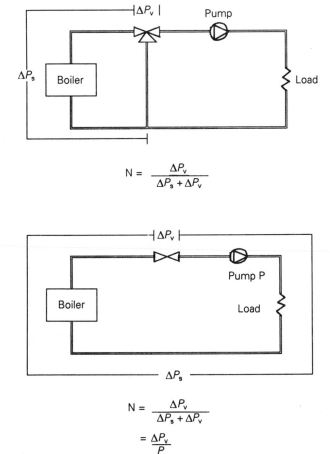

**Fig. 8.19** Valve authority.

The authority, $N$, is:

$$N = \frac{\Delta P_v}{\Delta P_v + \Delta P_s}$$

where $\Delta P_s$ = pressure drop across the whole system, apart from the valve ($Pa$), and $\Delta P_v$ = pressure drop across the valve, or relevant port of a 3-port valve ($Pa$). (Fig. 8.19).

In terms of resistance, the authority is:

$$N = \frac{R_v}{R_v + R_s}$$

where $R_s$ = resistance of the whole system, apart from the valve ($Pa\,[m^3\,s^{-1}]^{-0.5}$) and $R_v$ = resistance across the valve, or relevant port of a 3-port valve ($Pa\,[m^3\,s^{-1}]^{-0.5}$).

It is recommended that $N$ is not less than 0.3 for a mixing valve to provide good control [10], which means that the resistance across the valve is $0.3/0.7 = 43\%$ of the system it controls.

*Example*

For an equal percentage valve, it is stated that there is a 4% reduction in the initial flow for a 1% movement of the stroke, or movement of the valve stem. What is the mathematical equation and its constants if the index, $n$, is 4?

*Solution*

If the index $n$ is 4, then:

$$4 = \ln\left[\frac{100}{Q_{min}}\right]$$

where $Q_{max}$ has been put in as a percentage, giving:

$$Q_{min} = 1.83\%$$

so the valve has a rangeability of 54.6.

From the valve being fully open, the stroke is reduced by 1%:

$$99 = K\,\ln\left[\frac{96}{1.83}\right]$$

$$= 3.96\,K$$

So:                                      $$K = 25$$

Further details on valves can be found in references [6]–[10], suffice it to say that it is important that good valve selection is required for efficient compensator loop control, irrespective of how good is the BEMS itself.

# References

[1]  Levermore, G. J. (1986) A simple model of a heating system with a compensator control. *BSERT*, **7**, 2.

[2]  ETSU (1986) *Monitoring of a Microprocessor-based Energy Management System. A Demonstration Project at Various Tenanted Office Buildings*, ETSU Final Report ED/105/127 1986, Harwell.

[3]  Hansen, E. G. (1985) *Hydronic System Design and Operation: A Guide to Heating and Cooling with Water*, McGraw-Hill, New York.

[4]  CIBSE (1988) CIBSE Guide, Volume C, Section C4, Flow of fluids in pipes and ducts, Chartered Institution of Building Services Engineers, London.

[5]  ASHRAE Handbook Fundamentals, American Society of Heating, Refrigerating and Air Conditioning Engineers, Atlanta, 1989.

[6]  Wolsey, W. H. (1975) *Basic Principles of Automatic Controls with Special Reference to Heating and Air Conditioning Systems*, Hutchinson Educational, London.

[7]  Wolsey, W. H. (1971) A theory of 3-way valves with some practical conclusions. *Journal of the Institute of Heating and Ventilating Engineers*, **39**, May.

[8]  CIBSE (1986) CIBSE Guide, Volume B, Section B11, Automatic controls, Chartered Institution of Building Services Engineers, London.

[9]  CIBSE (1986) CIBSE Guide, Volume B, Section B16, Miscellaneous equipment, Chartered Institution of Building Services Engineers. London.

[10] CIBSE (1985) CIBSE Applications Manual, Automatic controls, and their implications for systems design. Chartered Institution of Building Services Engineers. London.

# 9
# Optimiser control

A standard control loop on almost all BEMSs is the **optimiser loop**. This switches on the heating plant at the latest possible time to get the building warm by the start of occupancy. It can also be used with air conditioning systems with both heating and cooling. In terms of the notation in Fig. 9.1, the optimiser determines the shortest **preheat time**, $T_3 - T_2$, to get the occupied space up to the design temperature, $t_d$. $t_p$ is the inside temperature at which the

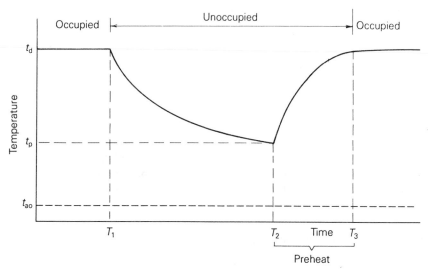

**Fig. 9.1** Inside temperature during intermittent heating.

optimiser switches on the heating and starts the preheat, which occurs at the time denoted by $T_2$. The outside temperature is $t_{ao}$.

## 9.1 Optimiser development

Initial work on optimisers, in the UK, was carried out by the Department of Environment's Property Services Agency (PSA), using early electromechanical optimisers, based on time switches. When these were installed considerable savings were reported [1]. However, the savings were assessed by comparison with a compensator control with a **night set-back setting**. Night set back is the reduction of the occupancy temperature by a few degrees, with the heating ticking over to maintain it. It is not comparable to the modern practice of intermittent heating, where the system is switched off overnight. So the considerable savings of the PSA work would be reduced if comparison was with intermittent heating.

The PSA work on electromechanical optimisers initiated the development of optimisers into microprocessor-based controllers. The modern BEMSs now incorporate these optimisers into their own outstations, using similar algorithms for their optimiser loops.

It is quite revealing to examine these electromechanical optimisers to appreciate optimum start control, even though they are now dated. One type of electromechanical optimiser has an electrical resistor placed inside a room thermostat. During the night, a voltage would be applied to the resistor which would heat the thermostat, raising its temperature by an amount $\delta t$:

$$\delta t = \frac{V^2}{R(UA)_{t/s}} \tag{9.1}$$

where $V$ = voltage applied (V);
  $R$ = resistance of resistor ($\Omega$);
  $(UA)_{t/s}$ = heat loss from the thermostat (W K$^{-1}$).

With the additional heat, the thermostat has an apparent temperature, $t_{app}$, of:

$$t_{app} = t_{ai} + \delta t \tag{9.2}$$

If, for instance, the thermostat were to be set at 20°C and $\delta t$ were 10°C, then $t_{app}$ would be 10°C above room air temperature, $t_{ai}$. The thermostat would close when $t_{app}$ dropped below the set point, $t_{set}$, fulfilling the condition:

$$t_{app} \leqslant t_{set} \tag{9.3}$$

In the present case, this would be:

$$t_{app} \leqslant 20$$

or:

$$t_{ai} \leqslant 10$$

This could be interpreted as the set point of the thermostat, $t_{set}$, being reduced to an effective set point, $t_{eff\,set}$:

$$t_{eff\,set} = t_{set} - \delta t$$

and the heating would come on when:

$$t_{ai} \leq t_{eff\,set} \qquad (9.4)$$

In the above example, this would give:

$$t_{eff\,set} = 20 - 10$$
$$= 10°C$$

so from equation (9.4) the optimiser would therefore close and bring on the heating if $t_{ai}$ fell below 10°C.

For optimum start control, a time switch would be set to engage a little potentiometer (a variable resistor) at a set time. The time switch would then turn the potentiometer and reduce the current to the room thermostat's resistor. This would happen over a number of hours before the start of occupancy. By doing this the optimiser would be reducing $\delta t$ and so raising the effective set point of the thermostat over a period of time. As Fig. 9.2 shows, the lower the room temperature, $t_{ai}$, the lower $t_{eff\,set}$ would have to be to bring on the heating, so the earlier the heating would be switched on. Figure 9.2 relates to the figures above, with the heating coming on under optimum start control at the earliest possible time of midnight. The start of occupancy is taken as 9 a.m.

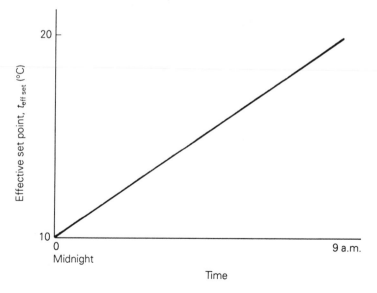

**Fig. 9.2** The change in effective set point due to optimiser.

## 9.2  Self-adapting optimisers

For the electromechanical optimiser discussed above, the preheat time varies linearly with $t_{\text{eff set}}$, as shown in Fig. 9.2. This means that the preheat time also varies with the room temperature at the start of preheat, $t_p$, which leads to the preheat curve of Fig. 9.1 being approximated to the straight line shown in Fig. 9.3.

Unfortunately, as the cooling of the building changes with the weather, so does the preheat curve, as Fig. 9.4 shows. A new straight line is needed for each preheat curve, otherwise the optimiser will be very inaccurate.

In the electromechanical optimiser discussed in Section 9.1, the preheat line cannot easily be changed, as the time period during which the potentiometer is turned by the time switch is fixed. Only the set point of the room thermostat, $t_{\text{set}}$, can be changed which simply moves the line up or down as Fig. 9.5 demonstrates.

Flexible movement of the line was achieved by the later optimisers which were based on microprocessors and employed **self-adaption**, to tune the line to the response of the building and heating system. Self-adaption is quite straightforward, provided that the building and heating system response during preheat is still regarded as linear, as shown in Fig. 9.3, rather than it actually is, as in Fig. 9.1.

If the slope of the preheat line $S$, is given by:

$$S = \frac{t_d - t_p}{T_3 - T_2} \qquad (9.5)$$

then a self-adapting algorithm is:

$$S_{i+1} = wS_e + (1 - w)S_i \qquad (9.6)$$

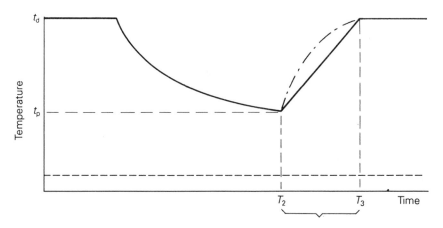

**Fig. 9.3**  Preheat response approximated to a straight line.

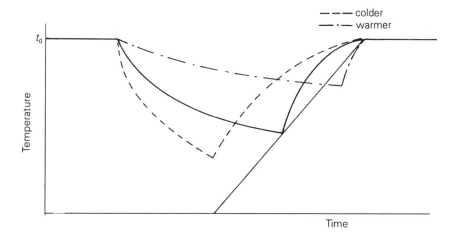

**Fig. 9.4**  Variation in preheat curves with weather.

where $S_i$ = slope used for previous day, day i (K h$^{-1}$);
$\quad\quad S_{i+1}$ = adapted slope to be used for current day's preheat, day i + 1(K h$^{-1}$);
$\quad\quad S_e$ = slope that would have produced exactly correct preheat time for previous day;
$\quad\quad w$ = weighting, or forgetting, factor $0 \leqslant w \leqslant 1.0$.

$S_e$ can be determined from the overshoot or undershoot of the temperature at the occupancy time, $T_3$, as shown in Fig. 9.6, ($\delta t_{over/under}$), and equation (9.7):

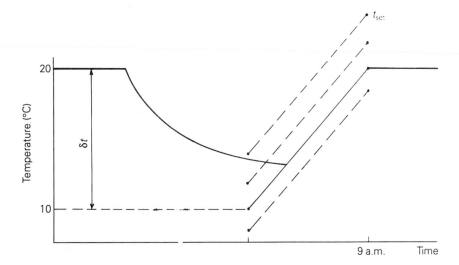

**Fig. 9.5**  Changing the line by changing $t_{set}$.

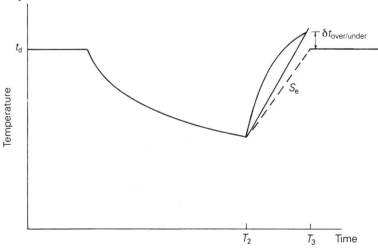

**Fig. 9.6** Determination of the best slope, $S_e$.

$$S_e = \frac{t_d + \delta t_{over/under} - t_p}{T_3 - T_2} \qquad (9.7)$$

Initially, when the optimiser has just been installed, the slope has to be guessed. Gradually equation (9.6) will correct it to a closer approximation of the true slope. The larger the value of $w$, the quicker this process will be. When $w = 1.0$, then:

$$S_{i+1} = S_e$$

However, if there is a brief disturbance to the heating system (e.g. one boiler in a multiple boiler installation failing to fire one day), then the slope will be drastically altered. If the boiler failed to fire (the burner went to **lock out**) because its burner control unit sensed a malfunction, the burner will most probably have its manual reset button pressed once its locked out burner is discovered, and it will again become operational. So the slope will have to change again dramatically. It would have been better if $w$ had been set to a lower value, say, less than 0.5.

Invariably the advice given by BEMS manufacturers is to start with $w$ high and then to reduce it once the building response has been approximated. Some adaption will always be needed with a straight-line preheat algorithm as the true preheat line is curved.

### 9.3 Non-linear algorithms

Birtles and John [2] examined a building's preheating process and derived an empirical curve of preheat time $(T_3 - T_2)$ against preheat temperature difference $(t_p - t_d)$, as shown in Fig. 9.7.

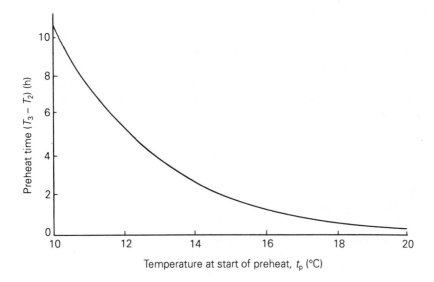

**Fig. 9.7** Birtles and John's empirical preheat curve.

The equation for this curve is:

$$\ln(T_3 - T_2) = A_{BJ}(t_p - t_d) + B_{BJ} \tag{9.8}$$

where $A_{BJ}$ = a constant associated with the thermal weight of the building, and $B_{BJ}$ = a constant associated with the time between switching on the heating and the interior starting to heat up.

Only the inside temperature is considered in equation (9.8) in determining the preheat time. This accords with other findings that inside air temperature correlates well with the preheat time, whereas there is little correlation with outside air temperature [9,3].

However, Birtles and John [2] later modified their algorithm to include outside air temperature as the initial algorithm was not as accurate when the outside air temperature was low and the plant size was on the small side. Resulting from this, equation (9.8) is modified to:

$$\ln(T_3 - T_2) = A_{BJ}(t_p - t_d) + B_{BJ} + C_{BJ}t_{ao} \tag{9.9}$$

where $C_{BJ}$ = a constant, less than $A$, so that the inside temperature is still the dominant term at most moderate temperatures.

Equation (9.9) is the basis of an optimiser algorithm called BRESTART, and its self-adaption is by recursive least squares. The least-squares method is discussed in Chapter 10 on monitoring and targeting, but the use of the method for parameter identification is dealt with in reference [4].

## 9.4  An optimiser model

Equation (9.9) has been found from observation, i.e. it is empirical. But it is useful to understand the basis of this equation, and a useful insight can be found from examination of simple theory.

Analytical derivations of preheat times for walls have been developed from Dufton's equation (see references [5], [6] or [7]). As quoted in reference [6], Dufton's equation is:

$$\Theta_{si} - \Theta_{so} = pQ \left[ \frac{5T}{4k\rho C_p} \right]^{0.5} \tag{9.10}$$

where $T$ = duration of heating, or preheat time (s);

$\Theta_{si}$ = inside surface temperature (°C);
$\Theta_{so}$ = outside surface temperature (°C);
$p$ = plant size ratio (plant size to steady state heat loss);
$Q$ = steady state heat loss (kW);
$k$ = thermal conductivity of fabric (W m$^{-1}$ K$^{-1}$);
$\rho$ = density (kg m$^{-3}$);
$C_p$ = specific heat capacity (kJ kg$^{-1}$ K$^{-1}$).

From this equation it can be seen that the preheat time, $T$, is reduced as the heating plant size is increased. McLaughlin, McLean and Bonthron [6] discuss an empirical way of determining the average value of $\rho C_p$ for a building, so that the preheat time can be estimated.

A more informative approach is to consider the heating system from the heat balance equation discussed in previous chapters. Here, though, there are additional terms for storage of heat in the fabric of the building and the inside air. These are the two terms added to the heat loss term:

$$p_1 \dot{m} C_p(t_f - t_r) = p_2 B(t_m - t_{ai})^n$$

$$= \frac{H_{des}}{F_2} (t_{ai} - t_{ao}) + (mC_p)_{fab} \frac{dt_{fab}}{dT} + (mC_p)_{air} \frac{dt_{ai}}{dT} \tag{9.11}$$

where $(mC_p)_{fab}$ = thermal capacity of the building's fabric, both internal and external (kJ K$^{-1}$);

$t_{fab}$ = mean temperature of the building's fabric, both internal and external (°C);

$(mC_p)_{air}$ = thermal capacity of the air inside the building (kJ K$^{-1}$);

$t_{ai}$ = temperature of the air inside the building (°C);

$H_{des} = \{F_1 \Sigma (UA) + \frac{1}{3} F_2 NV\}$ (kW K$^{-1}$);

$H_{des}(t_c - t_{ao})_{des}$ = design heat loss = $Q_{des}$ (kW);

$(t_c - t_{ao})_{des}$ = design temperature difference (K).

The other terms have been defined in earlier chapters. This equation is an oversimplification of a complex situation, involving radiative, convective and conductive heat transfer processes. For a more detailed exposition on dynamic thermal models the reader is referred to Clarke's book [8], and Fisk's book [9]. However, Crabb, Murdoch and Penman [10] with their Excalibur model, which uses only two time constants – a short time constant for the air and lightweight fabric, and a longer time constant for the main fabric elements – have achieved satisfactory results. Excalibur is similar to equation (9.11), except that Excalibur's steady state heat loss term more correctly relates to the fabric temperature rather than the overall steady state heat loss. So equation (9.11) is used and later simplified, to demonstrate the underlying principles of the building dynamics, rather than as a rigorous model.

Before much analysis can be carried out on equation (9.11), and indeed before it can be used for a simple optimiser algorithm, some simplifying assumptions need to be made. The first is that the boiler(s) is at maximum output during the preheat period and therefore dictates the heating system output. This is a reasonable assumption, except when $p_1$ is much larger than $p_2$ and the emitters will limit the heat output. Such a case will be considered later.

So the heat output from the heating system is:

$$pQ_{des}$$

where $\quad p = p_1$
$\qquad$ = boiler system plant size ratio;
$p_1 \dot{m} C_p (t_f - t_r) = p_1 Q_{des}$
$\qquad Q_{des} = H_{des}(t_c - t_{ao})_{des}$
$\qquad$ = design heat loss (kW)
and equation (9.11) becomes:

$$pQ_{des} = \frac{H_{des}}{F_2}(t_{ai} - t_{ao}) + (mC_p)_{fab}\frac{dt_{fab}}{dT} + (mC_p)_{air}\frac{dt_{ai}}{dT} \qquad (9.12)$$

The second assumption is that the mean temperature of the fabric, $t_{fab}$, can be related linearly to the inside air temperature, $t_{ai}$, and the outside air temperature, $t_{ao}$. This unfortunately eliminates the time delay for the heat to diffuse through the fabric, but Fig. 9.8 shows that this is not a gross distortion, although if the outside surface of the structure receives an appreciable amount of heat from the sun, as in summer, then the assumption leads to distortion, as Fig. 9.9 shows.

Using the steady state resistor network of a solid wall, as shown in Fig. 9.10,

$$t_{fab} = \frac{t_{si} + t_{so}}{2} \qquad (9.13)$$

From the resistor network it can be shown that:

$$t_{si} + t_{so} = (t_{ei} - t_{ao})\{1 - (R_{si} - R_{so})U\} + 2t_{ao} \qquad (9.14)$$

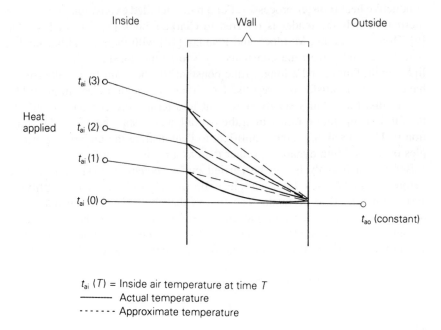

Inside                    Wall                 Outside

Heat
applied

$t_{ai}$ (3)

$t_{ai}$ (2)

$t_{ai}$ (1)

$t_{ai}$ (0)

$t_{ao}$ (constant)

$t_{ai}$ (T) = Inside air temperature at time T
———— Actual temperature
- - - - - - Approximate temperature

**Fig. 9.8**   Temperature development in wall.

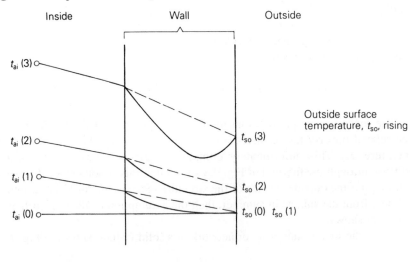

Inside                Wall               Outside

$t_{ai}$ (3)

$t_{ai}$ (2)

$t_{ai}$ (1)

$t_{ai}$ (0)

$t_{so}$ (3)

$t_{so}$ (2)

$t_{so}$ (0)  $t_{so}$ (1)

Outside surface
temperature, $t_{so}$, rising

———— Actual temperature
- - - - - - Approx. temperature

**Fig. 9.9**   Temperature development when the outside surface heats up.

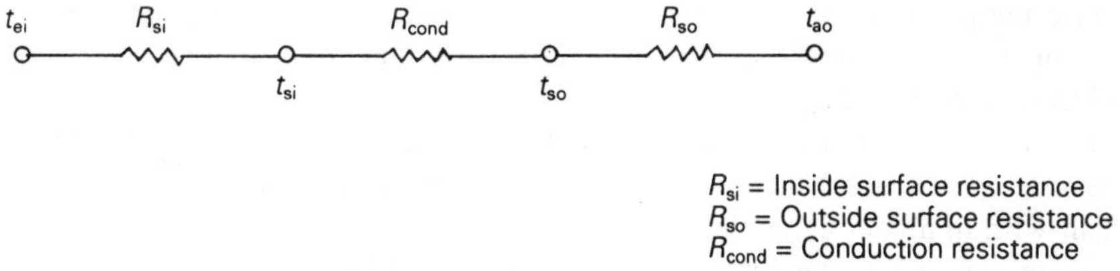
$t_{ei}$
$R_{si}$
$R_{cond}$
$R_{so}$
$t_{ao}$
$t_{si}$
$t_{so}$
$R_{si}$ = Inside surface resistance
$R_{so}$ = Outside surface resistance
$R_{cond}$ = Conduction resistance

**Fig. 9.10** Steady state resistor network for wall.

Relating $t_{ei}$ to $t_{ai}$ by the temperature ratios given in the CIBSE Guide [12];

$$F_1 = \frac{t_{ei} - t_{ao}}{t_c - t_{ao}}$$

and:

$$F_2 = \frac{t_{ai} - t_{ao}}{t_c - t_{ao}}$$

So equation (9.14) becomes:

$$t_{si} + t_{so} = \frac{F_1}{F_2}(t_{ai} - t_{ao})\{1 - (R_{si} - R_{so})U\} + 2t_{ao} \tag{9.15}$$

and the mean fabric temperature, $t_{fab}$, is:

$$t_{fab} = \frac{F_1}{2F_2}(t_{ai} - t_{ao})\{1 - (R_{si} - R_{so})U\} + t_{ao} \tag{9.16}$$

Assuming the outside temperature is constant, then equation (9.16) can be substituted into equation (9.11) to give:

$$pQ_{des} = \frac{H_{des}}{F_2}(t_{ai} - t_{ao}) + (m^*C_p)_{fab}\frac{dt_{ai}}{dT} + (mC_p)_{air}\frac{dt_{ai}}{dT} \tag{9.17}$$

where $m^*$ = effective thermal mass (kg)

$$= m\frac{F_1}{2F_2}\{1 - (R_{si} - R_{so})U\}$$

Notice that this effective thermal mass is approximately half the actual mass of the solid wall, which would consequently lead to a time constant of approximately:

$$\tau \approx \frac{mC_p}{2U}$$

which is almost half the normal time constant. This arises because the fabric is now associated with the room air temperature, which is almost twice the fabric temperature. So instead of the fabric time constant being the time to rise up to within $0.63\,t_{fab}$, it is now effectively the time to rise to within $0.315\,t_{ai}$, with $t_{ai} \approx 2\,t_{fab}$.

For a multi-layered wall, each element would have to be considered with its mean temperature to calculate the effective thermal mass of the wall. This is dealt with in a later example.

More important, the internal fabric of the building (the partition walls, intermediate floors and ceilings) will be capable of storing a considerable amount of heat. Mean temperatures of the internal fabric will be close to the internal temperature of the building, and so quite close to $t_{ai}$. In the optimiser model the effective thermal mass of the internal fabric is assumed to be equal to the actual mass, with a mean temperature of $t_{ai}$.

With the inclusion of the internal and external fabric of the building for storing heat, as well as the air, the total effective thermal mass of the building can be grouped into one summed term, $\Sigma(m^*C_p)$, so that equation (9.17) can be expressed as:

$$pQ_{des} = \frac{H_{des}}{F_2}(t_{ai} - t_{ao}) + \Sigma\,(m^*C_p)\,\frac{dt_{ai}}{dT} \qquad (9.18)$$

In comparison with the fabric, the air stores very little heat. The example below demonstrates this.

*Example*
Calculate the heat stored in the office building, shown in Fig. 9.11, under

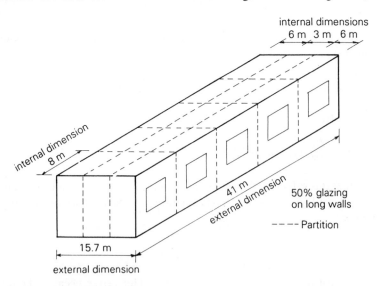

internal dimensions
6 m  3 m  6 m

internal dimension
8 m

41 m
external dimension

50% glazing
on long walls

- - - - Partition

15.7 m
external dimension

**Fig. 9.11**  Example building.

steady state design conditions of $t_{ao} = 0°C$ and $t_{ai} = 20°C$. The building is single storey, with individual offices and a central corridor running along its long axis. In Fig. 9.11 the external and internal dimensions of the building are shown, as may be ascertained from the following details:

Walls:       105 mm brick, 50 mm air gap, 100 mm concrete block;
Roof:        100 mm concrete block;
Partitions:  100 mm block;
Window:      single-glazed with 6 mm glass, each long wall
             having 50% glazing.

For the wall, $R_{si} = 0.12$ m$^2$ K W$^{-1}$    $R_{so} = 0.06$ m$^2$ K W$^{-1}$
For the roof, $R_{si} = 0.10$ m$^2$ K W$^{-1}$    $R_{so} = 0.04$ m$^2$ K W$^{-1}$
For the air gap, $R_{air} = 0.20$ m$^2$ K W$^{-1}$

|  | *brick* | *block* | *window* |
|---|---|---|---|
| Conductivity (W m$^{-1}$ K$^{-1}$) | 0.8 | 0.25 | 1 |
| Density (kg m$^{-3}$) | 1700 | 750 | 2500 |
| $C_p$ (J kg$^{-1}$ K$^{-1}$) | 800 | 800 | 910 |

*Solution*
This example building has been seen before in Section 4.8.1 in Chapter 4 on 'Monday morning blues'.

The steady state average temperatures of the external fabric elements can be calculated from the resistance network between the inside and outside temperatures. It is assumed that the partitions are at the inside temperature of 20°C. The floor slab has been ignored. Mean fabric temperatures are:

| *Element* | *Mean temperature* (°C) |
|---|---|
| Brick | 2.4 |
| Block | 13.0 |
| Window | 6.8 |
| Roof | 8.9 |
| Partitions | 20.0 |

Now the heat stored in the fabric elements, from raising them from 0°C to their mean temperatures, can be calculated from:

$$mC_p(t_{fabric} - t_{ao\ des})$$

where $t_{fabric}$ = mean fabric temperature (°C).

The heat stored in the fabric elements and the air in the rooms (not the wall air gap), is given in Table 9.1.

**Table 9.1**   Heat stored in example building

| Element | Heat stored (MJ) | Fraction of total (%) |
|---|---|---|
| Window | 13 | 1 |
| Air | 59 | 4 |
| Brick | 100 | 8 |
| Block | 229 | 17 |
| Roof | 340 | 25 |
| Partitions | 614 | 45 |
| Total | 1355 | 100 |

It is assumed in the above calculation for the air that the corridor is maintained at the same temperature as the rooms, with $t_{ai} = 20°C$.

From the above, it can be seen that the windows and the air have little heat content compared to the rest of the elements. If the differential equation for the heat stored and heat lost from a fabric element is considered, then a time constant for the element can be derived. Considering equation (9.17) for one external element of fabric alone (with the effective thermal mass and using the air temperature), the cooling of the element, without heating, is:

$$0 = \frac{H_{des}}{F_2}(t_{ai} - t_{ao}) + (m^*C_p)\frac{dt_{ai}}{dT}$$

This is a first-order differential equation with a time constant:

$$\tau = \frac{(m^*C_p)\,F_2}{H_{des}}$$

Considering the element on its own, then the surface resistances are ignored, and:

$$\tau = \frac{(mC_p)}{2UA}$$

$$= \frac{(\rho l C_p)}{2U}$$

where $\rho$ = density (kg m$^{-3}$), and $l$ = thickness of the element (m) and where the $U$-value here is without any surface resistances. For this external element, the effective thermal mass is half the actual mass. This is because the effective thermal mass relates to the warm surface temperature of the element, which has twice the temperature rise over the outside surface temperature as the mean fabric temperature.

For internal fabric elements of the building, the mean fabric temperature is taken as the mean inside temperature, so the effective thermal mass is equal to the actual mass, giving the time constant as:

$$\tau = \frac{(mC_\mathrm{p})}{UA}$$

The time constants for the building in this example are given below, calculated on the heat stored method.

| Element | Time constant $\tau$(h) |
|---|---|
| Brick | 5.8 |
| Block | 5.1 |
| Window | 0.7 |
| Roof | 4.5 |
| Partitions | 6.7 |
| Air (1 air change per hour) | 1.0 |

For the whole building, it is very tempting to simply add the time constants together, but this is only possible if the internal resistance of the elements is negligible, and the element internal temperature is essentially uniform [11]. The whole building time constant is found from equation (9.18) below, developed from equation (9.17), except that the heat stored, being much less than that in the fabric, has been omitted and all the fabric effective thermal capacities have been summated:

$$pQ_\mathrm{des} = \frac{H_\mathrm{des}}{F_2}(t_\mathrm{ai} - t_\mathrm{ao}) + \Sigma\,(m^*C_\mathrm{p})\frac{\mathrm{d}t_\mathrm{ai}}{\mathrm{d}T} \qquad (9.18)$$

giving:

$$\tau = \frac{\Sigma\,(m^*C_\mathrm{p})\,F_2}{H_\mathrm{des}}$$

$\Sigma\,(m^*C_\mathrm{p})$, the effective thermal capacity for the whole building, can be derived from the design steady state conditions. From equation (9.18) the heat stored in the building is simply the last storage term integrated from the time when all the fabric is at $t_\mathrm{ao\ des}$ until $t_\mathrm{ai\ des}$ is achieved – i.e. the heat stored is:

$$\Sigma\,(m^*C_\mathrm{p})\{t_\mathrm{ai\ des} - t_\mathrm{ao\ des}\}$$

This was earlier determined as 1355 MJ (which includes the small amount of storage in the air), so $\Sigma(m^*C_\mathrm{p}) = 67.8$ MJ K$^{-1}$. For this building, with a single-panel radiator heating system, $F_1 \approx 1$ and $F_2 \approx 1$. Hence $H_\mathrm{des} = 3.2$ kW K$^{-1}$, so:

$$\tau = \frac{67.8 \times 10^6}{3.2 \times 10^3}\ \mathrm{(s)}$$

$$= 5.9\,\mathrm{h}$$

This is a surprisingly short time, but there are two reasons for this. The first is that there is a lot of glazing which increases the heat loss without adding to the thermal storage. As shown below, over half of the losses are through the windows and air (Table 9.2).

**Table 9.2**   Heat loss in example building

| Element | Heat loss (kW) | Fraction of total (%) |
|---|---|---|
| Window | 17.7 | 27.7 |
| Air | 16.0 | 25.0 |
| Brick and block wall | 6.5 | 10.1 |
| Roof | 23.8 | 37.2 |
| Total | 64.0 | 100 |

Second, the block has a low density, reducing the storage both in the external and internal walls. If the external wall were solid brick, of 255 mm thickness, the time constant of it would be, ignoring the surface resistances:

$$\tau \approx \frac{pC_p l^2}{2k}$$

$$= \frac{1700 \times 800 \times (0.255)^2}{2 \times 0.8}$$

$$= 15.4\,h$$

a considerable increase on 5.2 h for the 105 mm brick leaf. Notice that $\tau$ increases with the thickness, $l$, squared.

These time constants have been derived from simple theory, but the BEMS user can simply log the inside temperature of a room and during the heating off period examine a plot of the cooling curve and determine the dominant long term time constant. The early rapid drop in temperature will be due to the cooling of the air, but the later cooling will be due to the more massive fabric. Normalizing the axes and making a logarithmic/linear graph will make any first-order responses into straight-lines graphs [16].

The above example demonstrates that the heat stored in the air is typically much less than that in the fabric, and to all intents and purposes it can be neglected for most buildings. However, as was mentioned in Chapter 4, the BEMS room temperature sensor will monitor the air temperature primarily and the fabric temperature will take longer to rise than the air temperature. So the dry resultant temperature will still be uncomfortable at the start of the week if there has not been sufficient preheating to warm the fabric.

In the example equation (9.18) was developed, which is a straightforward first-order equation describing the preheating:

$$pQ_{des} = \frac{H_{des}}{F_2}(t_{ai} - t_{ao}) + \Sigma\,(m^*C_p)\frac{dt_{ai}}{dT} \tag{9.18}$$

This equation also describes the cooling down process, when the heating is off and $pQ_{des} = 0$:

$$0 = \frac{H_{des}}{F_2} (t_{ai} - t_{ao}) + \Sigma (m^*C_p) \frac{dt_{ai}}{dT} \qquad (9.19)$$

This can be rearranged to give:

$$\frac{1}{\tau} \int_{T_1}^{T_2} dT = \int_{t_d}^{t_p} \frac{dt_{ai}}{(t_{ai} - t_{ao})}$$

where $\tau = \dfrac{F_2 \Sigma(m^*C_p)}{H_{des}}$

= time constant (s)

The time and temperature limits of integration are as shown in Fig. 9.1.
   Integration of the equation yields

$$\frac{T_2 - T_1}{\tau} = \ln \left[ \frac{t_d - t_{ao}}{t_p - t_{ao}} \right] \qquad (9.20)$$

Similarly, equation (9.18) may be rearranged for integration:

$$\frac{1}{\tau} \int_{T_2}^{T_3} dT = \int_{t_p}^{t_d} \frac{dt_{ai}}{p(t_{ai} - t_{ao})_{des} - (t_{ai} - t_{ao})}$$

yielding:

$$\frac{T_3 - T_2}{\tau} = - \ln \left[ \frac{p(t_{ai} - t_{ao})_{des} - (t_d - t_{ao})}{p(t_{ai} - t_{ao})_{des} - (t_p - t_{ao})} \right] \qquad (9.21)$$

This is the preheat curve with the heating on full output for the preheat duration. If the optimum start controller did not reduce the heating at the occupancy time of $T_3$ (when hopefully the temperature is $t_d$), then the inside temperature would increase to the steady state equilibrium temperature with the full heat output. This can be determined from equation (9.18). Steady state conditions prevail when the fabric has soaked up all its heat and the air temperature is constant, so:

$$\Sigma (m^*C_p) \frac{dt_{ai}}{dT} = 0$$

and:

$$pQ_{des} = \frac{H_{des}}{F_2} (t_{ai\ ss} - t_{ao})$$

where $t_{ai\ ss}$ = steady state temperature (°C)

giving:

$$t_{\text{ai ss}} = \frac{F_2 \, pQ_{\text{des}}}{H_{\text{des}}} + t_{\text{ao}}$$

$$= pF_2(t_{\text{c}} - t_{\text{ao}})_{\text{des}} + t_{\text{ao}}$$

$$= p(t_{\text{ai}} - t_{\text{ao}})_{\text{des}} + t_{\text{ao}} \tag{9.22}$$

To avoid achieving this excess temperature the heating must be controlled at reduced output from $T_3$. A compensator loop would do this adequately.

It should also be noted that in the integrations above, $t_{\text{ao}}$ has been assumed constant during the unoccupied period, $T_3 - T_1$. $t_{\text{ao}}$ will most likely drop significantly during this period, but the average steady state $t_{\text{ao}}$, $t_{\text{ao ss}}$, to which the cooling curve is tending can be ascertained in a similar fashion to $t_{\text{ai ss}}$, above. $t_{\text{ao ss}}$ will lag behind $t_{\text{ao}}$ and will differ from it as $t_{\text{ao ss}}$ is the outside temperature perceived through the fabric which influences $t_{\text{ai}}$.

## 9.5  Preheat time

The preheat time can be determined from the intersection of the cooling curve and the preheat curve. Equations (9.21) and (9.22) can be used to derive the intersection, but first the equations are made less cumbersome by using the following terms:

$$\delta t = t_{\text{d}} - t_{\text{ao}}$$

$$\delta t_{\text{des}} = (t_{\text{ai}} - t_{\text{ao}})_{\text{des}}$$

$$\delta t_{\text{p}} = t_{\text{p}} - t_{\text{ao}}$$

$$\Phi = \text{load factor}$$

$$= \frac{\delta t}{\delta t_{\text{des}}}$$

$$x = \frac{\text{unoccupied time}}{\tau}$$

$$= \frac{T_3 - T_1}{\tau}$$

These terms make the cooling curve:

$$\frac{T_2 - T_1}{\tau} = \ln\left[\frac{\delta t}{\delta t_{\text{p}}}\right] \tag{9.23}$$

and the preheat curve:

$$\frac{T_3 - T_2}{\tau} = -\ln\left[\frac{p\,\delta t_{des} - \delta t}{p\,\delta t_{des} - \delta t_p}\right] \qquad (9.24)$$

Equation (9.24) added to equation (9.23) gives:

$$x = \ln\left[\frac{\delta t}{\delta t_p}\right] - \ln\left[\frac{p\,\delta t_{des} - \delta t}{p\,\delta t_{des} - \delta t_p}\right] \qquad (9.25)$$

or:

$$e^x = \frac{\delta t\,(p\,\delta t_{des} - \delta t_p)}{\delta t_p\,(p\,\delta t_{des} - \delta t)}$$

from which $\delta t_p$ can be derived:

$$\delta t_p = \frac{p\,\Phi\,\delta t_{des}}{\Phi + e^x(p - \Phi)}$$

or:

$$t_p = t_d - \Phi\,\delta\,t_{des}\left[\frac{(p - \Phi)\,(e^x - 1)}{\Phi + e^x(p - \Phi)}\right] \qquad (9.26)$$

This equation can be used as the basis of a BEMS optimiser algorithm. Alternatively, the preheat time can be used for an algorithm. This is determined by substituting equation (9.26) into equation (9.24), producing:

$$\frac{T_3 - T_2}{\tau} = \ln\left[\frac{p e^x}{\Phi + e^x(p - \Phi)}\right] \qquad (9.27)$$

As the two equations above show, the preheat time varies with the load factor, $\Phi$. This variation is drawn graphically in Fig. 9.12, which is based on equation (9.26). A value of $\tau$ of 40 000 s (11.1 h), was chosen for the graphs in Fig. 9.12 with $T_3 - T_1 = 15h$.

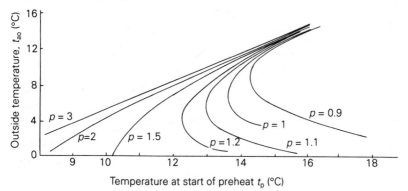

**Fig. 9.12** Relationship between $t_p$ and $t_{ao}$.

## 9.6  Plant size

As the plant size ratio, $p$, reduces, so a distinct bend develops. To understand this characteristic better, it is useful to relate the preheat temperature to the preheat time by examining equation (9.24) and a graph of it (Fig. 9.13).

Equation (9.24) also exhibits the bending, becoming more marked at lower values of plant size ratio, $p$. The turning-points of the curves are the lowest temperatures that the building can drop to for the heating system to be able to achieve the required temperature by occupancy. Any lower than these temperatures and the building will be cold at the start of occupancy.

For a given plant size ratio, $p$, unoccupied time, $\tau x$, the turning-point temperature, or the minimum $t_{ai}$ or $t_p$ for successful preheating, can be determined from differentiating equation (9.26) and equating to zero to find the minimum value. The variable in equation (9.26) is $\Phi$, the load factor, which in turn is a function of $t_{ao}$. So it is necessary to differentiate equation (9.26) with respect to $t_{ao}$:

$$t_p - t_{ao} = \frac{p\,\Phi\,\delta t_{des}}{\Phi + e^x(p - \Phi)} \tag{9.26}$$

noting that:

$$\frac{\mathrm{d}\Phi}{\mathrm{d}t_{ao}} = \frac{-1}{(t_d - t_{ao})_{des}} = \frac{-1}{\delta t_{des}}$$

and for the minimum turning-point:

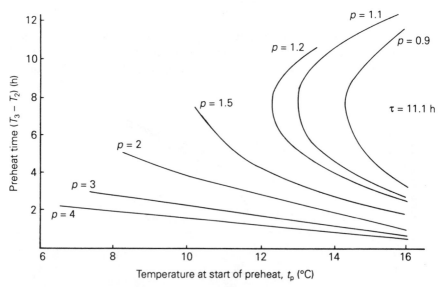

**Fig. 9.13**  Preheat curves for various plant sizes.

$$\frac{dt_p}{dt_{ao}} = 0$$

we get:

$$\Phi = \frac{pe^{x/2}(e^{x/2} - 1)}{e^x - 1} \tag{9.28}$$

Substituting this into equation (9.26) for the preheat temperature at the turning-point is a little complex, but substitution into the preheat period, equation (9.27) is easier:

$$\frac{T_3 - T_2}{\tau} = \ln \left[ \frac{pe^x}{\Phi + e^x(p - \Phi)} \right] \tag{9.27}$$

$$= \ln p + x - \ln [\Phi(1 - e^x) + pe^x]$$

$$= \ln p + x - \ln \left[ \frac{pe^{x/2}(e^{x/2} - 1)}{e^x - 1} (1 - e^x) + pe^x \right]$$

$$= \ln p + x - \ln [- pe^x - pe^{x/2} + pe^x]$$

so:

$$\frac{T_3 - T_2}{\tau} = \frac{x}{2}$$

or:

$$T_3 - T_2 = \frac{T_3 - T_2}{2} \tag{9.29}$$

The turning-point will always be in the middle of the unoccupied period. The preheat temperature at this point is found from equations (9.26) and (9.28):

$$\delta t_p = p \delta t_{des} \frac{e^{x/2} - 1}{e^x - 1}$$

$$t_p = p \delta t_{des} \frac{e^{x/2} - 1}{e^x - 1} + t_{ao} \tag{9.30}$$

Once the inside temperature has fallen below this value of $t_p$, then it is not possible to achieve the required temperature, $t_d$, by the start of occupancy, $T_3$.

There will be no turning-point outside the design temperature range, that is as long as $t_{ao}$ is not lower than $t_{ao \, des}$, provided that the plant size ratio, $p$, is such that:

$$\Phi \geqslant 1.0$$

or:

$$\frac{pe^{x/2}(e^{x/2} - 1)}{e^x - 1} \geqslant 1.0$$

yielding:

$$p \geqslant \frac{e^x - 1}{e^{x/2}(e^{x/2} - 1)}$$

For $\tau = 11.1$ h and $T_3 - T_1 = 15$ h, the plant size would have to be:

$$p \geqslant \frac{2.863}{1.97(1.97 - 1)}$$

$$\geqslant 1.5$$

Equation (9.24), the preheat temperature and time equation, shown in Fig. 9.13, is the locus of the preheat temperature and preheat time. Turning the graphs in Fig. 9.13 anticlockwise through 90° relates the loci to the conventional time and design temperature of Fig. 9.1. Figure 9.14 shows some of the loci, for $\tau = 11.1$ h and $\tau x = 15$ h.

As $t_{ao}$ decreases, so the preheat time increases. But the preheat temperature, $t_p$, initially reduces, then it increases after the turning-point. The locus event-

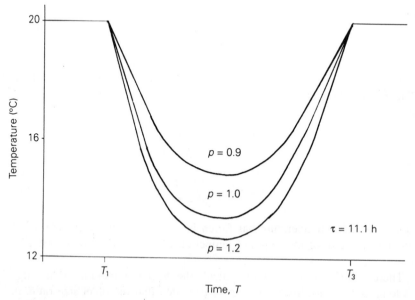

**Fig. 9.14**  Preheat loci.

ually goes back to the time $T_1$, at a preheat temperature of $t_d$ – i.e. the heating should not be switched off. The value of $\Phi$ when the locus reaches $T_1$ is when:

$$T_3 - T_2 = T_3 - T_1 = \tau x$$

Putting this into equation (9.27):

$$x = \ln\left[\frac{pe^x}{\Phi + e^x(p - \Phi)}\right]$$

$$e^x = \frac{pe^x}{\Phi + e^x(p - \Phi)}$$

$$\Phi = p$$

When this load is achieved, then:

$$\Phi = p = \frac{\delta t}{\delta t_{des}}$$

$$= \frac{t_d - t_{ao}}{(t_{ai} - t_{ao})_{des}}$$

$$= \frac{(t_d - t_{ao})\,H_{des}}{F_2\,Q_{des}}$$

Putting this value of $p$ into the first-order heating equation, equation (9.18) yields:

$$\frac{(t_d - t_{ao})\,H_{des}}{F_2\,Q_{des}} = \frac{H_{des}}{F_2}(t_{ai} - t_{ao}) + \Sigma\,(mC_p)\,\frac{dt_{ai}}{dT} \tag{9.18}$$

As $t_d = t_{ai} = t_p$ at $T_1$, then the heating system is only capable of dealing with the steady state heat loss and cannot cope with any stored heat loss, so:

$$\Sigma\,(mC_p)\,\frac{dt_{ai}}{dT} = 0$$

If the locus has no bending point, then the plant size is large and it can cope with all intermittent heating loads within the unoccupied time $T_3 - T_1$.

## 9.7 Weekend shutdown and search period

In the first-order model we have used to derive the preheat curve, the preheat time can be of any duration within the unoccupied period, $T_3 - T_1$. Some commercial BEMS optimiser algorithms use search periods, during which the BEMS is determining when to start the heating. Typical search periods are about 8 h. Unfortunately, during cold weather and/or with a small plant size ratio, $p$, this may not be sufficient to achieve comfort conditions by occupancy.

The unoccupied period, $\tau x$, influences the preheat period and this changes over weekends and holidays. This is best seen in the following example.

*Example*
Calculate the preheat time and preheat temperature for a weekday and a weekend with the following conditions and data:

$$p = 1.2, \quad \tau = 11.1\,\text{h}, \quad \Phi = 1.0, \quad \delta t_{\text{des}} = 20\,\text{K}$$

occupancy ends at 6 p.m. and commences at 9 a.m.

*Solution*
For the weekday:

$$x = \frac{15.0}{11.1} = 1.351, \quad e^{1.351} = 3.861$$

equation (9.27) gives:

$$\frac{T_3 - T_2}{11.1} = \ln\left[\frac{1.2 \times 3.861}{1.0 + 3.861(1.2 - 1.0)}\right]$$

$$= \ln(4.63/1.77)$$

$$T_3 - T_2 = 11.1 \times 0.96$$

$$= \underline{10.67\,\text{h}}$$

From equation (9.26):

$$\delta t_p = 13.6$$

as: $\Phi = 1.0$, then $t_{ao} = 0°C$
giving: $t_p = 13.6°C$
For the weekend:

$$x = \frac{15.0 + 48}{11.1} = 5.676, \quad e^{5.676} = 291.8$$

equation (9.27) gives:

$$\frac{T_3 - T_2}{11.1} = \ln\left[\frac{1.2 \times 291.8}{1.0 + 291.8(1.2 - 1.0)}\right]$$

$$= \ln(350/59.4)$$

$$T_3 - T_2 = 11.1 \times 1.77$$

$$= \underline{19.65\,\text{h}}$$

From equation (9.26):

$$\delta t_p = 0.4$$

as: $\Phi = 1.0$, then $t_{ao} = 0°C$
giving: $t_p = 0.4°C$

For this example the weekend preheat period in cold weather is almost a day long. In practice, the heating would be brought on, at a reduced level, by a frost protection configuration in the BEMS before $t_p$ reached 0.4°C.

The preheat loci for the above example is shown in Fig. 9.15. There is no turning-point in the weekend locus, whereas there is one in the weekday locus. From equation (9.28) the weekday turning-point is:

$$\Phi = \frac{p e^{x/2}(e^{x/2} - 1)}{e^x - 1} \tag{9.28}$$

$$= \frac{1.2 \, e^{0.676}(e^{0.676} - 1)}{e^{1.351} - 1}$$

$$= 0.8$$

So:

$$t_{ao} = 4°C$$

There is a turning-point for the weekend locus but it is outside the design temperature range $\delta t_{des}$:

$$\Phi = 1.13, \quad \text{and} \quad t_p = -2.7°C$$

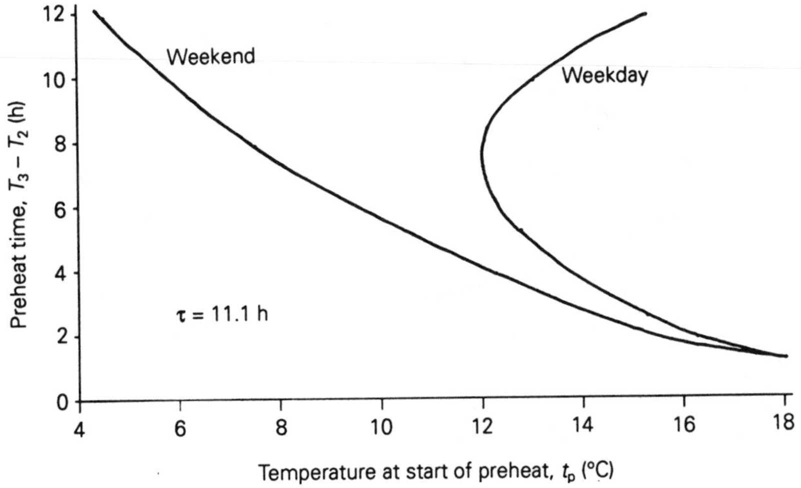

**Fig. 9.15** Weekend and weekday preheat loci.

## 9.8  Influence of thermal mass

A building's thermal mass, or thermal capacity, greatly affect its response. The greater the thermal capacity, then the greater is the time constant, $\tau$. $\tau$ appears in equation (9.26) for $t_p$ in the term, $x$, which equals $(T_3 - T_2)/\tau$:

$$t_p = t_d - \Phi \delta t_{des} \left[ \frac{(p - \Phi)(e^x - 1)}{\Phi + e^x(p - \Phi)} \right] \tag{9.26}$$

and in the preheat time equation, equation (9.27):

$$\frac{T_3 - T_2}{\tau} = \ln \left[ \frac{pe^x}{\Phi + e^x(p - \Phi)} \right] \tag{9.27}$$

As $\tau$ increase, so $x$ decreases. This raises the turning-point temperature and makes the preheat locus shallower. This is demonstrated in Fig. 9.16 and it can also be seen by examining equation (9.30):

$$t_p = p \delta t_{des} \frac{e^{x/2} - 1}{e^x - 1} + t_{ao} \tag{9.30}$$

*Example*
Calculate the turning-point temperature, and the corresponding value of $t_{ao}$ for building A and plant with the details below:

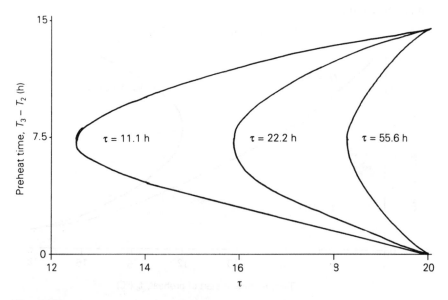

**Fig. 9.16**   Variation in preheat locus with time constant, $\tau$.

$$p = 1.2, \ \tau = 11.1 \, \text{h}, \ t_d = 20°C, \ \delta t_{des} = 20 \, \text{K}$$

occupancy ends at 6 p.m. and commences at 9 a.m.

Compare these with building B with a time constant of 22.2 h.

*Solution*

For building A, $x = 1.351$, $e^x = 3.863$ and $e^{x/2} = 1.97$

For building B, $x = 0.676$, $e^x = 1.97$ and $e^{x/2} = 1.4$

To determine $t_{ao}$ we can use equation (9.28):

$$\Phi_A = \frac{1.2 \times 1.97 \times (1.97 - 1)}{3.863 - 1}$$

$$= 0.8$$

So: $t_{ao} = 20 - 20 \times 0.8$

$$t_{ao} = 4°C$$

$$\Phi_B = \frac{1.2 \times 1.4 \times (1.4 - 1)}{1.97 - 1}$$

$$= 0.69$$

So: $t_{ao} = 20 - 20 \times 0.69$

$$t_{ao} = 6.2°C$$

It is worth remembering that the turning-point is at the same preheat time, $(T_3 - T_1)/2$. The heavier building B reaches this point at a higher temperature, $t_{ao}$, than lighter building A.

To determine $t_p$ we can use equation (9.26):

$$t_{p\,A} = t_d - 0.8 \times 20 \left[ \frac{(1.2 - 0.8)(3.863 - 1)}{0.8 + 3.863(1.2 - 0.8)} \right] \tag{9.26}$$

$$t_{p\,A} = 12.2°C$$

$$t_{p\,B} = 20 - 0.69 \times 20 \left[ \frac{(1.2 - 0.69)(1.97 - 1)}{0.69 + 1.97(1.2 - 0.69)} \right]$$

$$t_{p\,B} = 16.0°C$$

Building B, the building with the greater thermal capacity, has a higher turning-point, at 16°C, and it occurs at a higher outside temperature of 6.2°C. The turning-point time for both buildings is independent of $\tau$, and is the same. So it can be concluded that for a given outside temperature, $t_{ao}$, the heavier building will have to have its heating switched on earlier. As the plant sizes are the same, the energy consumed by the heavier building will be more.

## 9.9  Emitter output

In the original equation used to develop the optimiser model, equation (9.12), the heat input from the boiler and the output from the emitter were:

$$p_1 \dot{m} C_p(t_f - t_r) = p_2 B \, (t_m - t_{ai})^n$$

Then to simplify the solution of the equation it was assumed that the boiler, or boilers, were at maximum output during the preheat period and therefore they would dictate the heating system output. This was held to be a reasonable assumption, except when $p_1$ was much larger than $p_2$ and the emitters would limit the heat output. This case will be considered now, first by way of an example.

*Example*
Determine how the output of a radiator heating system varies with load if $p_1 = 1.5$ and $p_2 = 1.2$. The steady state heat loss is:

$$Q_{des} = \frac{H_{des}}{F_2} (t_{ai} - t_{ao})_{des}$$

$$= 100 \, kW$$

where $(t_{ai} - t_{ao})_{des}$ = design temperature difference (K)
$$= 20 - 0$$

*Solution*
Assuming design conditions of $t_m = 75°C$ and $t_{ai} = 20°C$, then B = 0.546 as:

$$0.546 \times (75 - 20)^{1.3} = 100$$

The greatest design load would be when the inside of the building got as low as the outside temperature of 0°C. When heating commenced, the output from the emitters would be:

$$1.2 \times 0.546 \times (75 - 0)^{1.3}$$

$$= 180 \, kW$$

The maximum output from the boilers is:

$$1.5 \times 100$$

$$= 150 \, kW$$

So the boilers restrict the emitters' output to a constant 150 kW until:

$$1.2 \times 0.546 \times (75 - t_{ai})^{1.3} = 150$$

$$t_{ai} = 9.7°C$$

From $t_{ai} = 9.7°C$ to $20°C$ the emitters' output will reduce from 150 kW to 120 kW, as shown in Fig. 9.17.

When the emitters' output is varying, the preheat differential equation (9.18) is altered to:

$$p_2 B(t_m - t_{ai})^{1.3} = \frac{H_{des}}{F_2}(t_{ai} - t_{ao}) + \Sigma\,(m^*C_p)\frac{dt_{ai}}{dT}$$

The left-hand side of this equation can be simplified by a binomial expansion to give:

$$p_2 B t_m^{1.3}\left[1 - \frac{1.3t_{ai}}{t_m}\right] = \frac{H_{des}}{F_2}(t_{ai} - t_{ao}) + \Sigma\,(m^*C_p)\frac{dt_{ai}}{dT}$$

where from design conditions $B = \dfrac{H_{des}}{F_2}\dfrac{\delta t_{des}}{(t_m - t_d)^{1.3}}$

Putting in the time constant, $\tau$, gives:

$$\frac{p_2 \delta t_{des}\, t_m^{1.3}}{(t_m - t_d)^{1.3}}\left[1 - \frac{1.3t_{ai}}{t_m}\right] = (t_{ai} - t_{ao}) + \tau\frac{dt_{ai}}{dT}$$

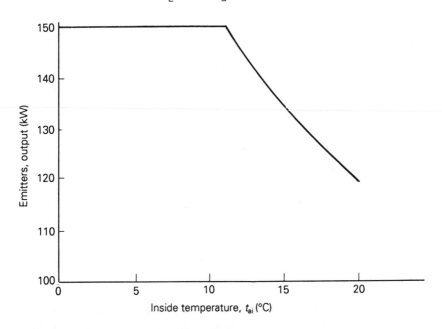

**Fig. 9.17**  Variation in emitters' heat output.

$$p^* \delta t_{des} \left[ 1 - (1.3 t_{ai}/t_m) \right] = t_{ai} - t_{ao} + \tau \frac{dt_{ai}}{dT}$$

$$p^* \delta t_{des} = t_{ai}(1 + 1.3 p^*/t_m) - t_{ao} + \tau \frac{dt_{ai}}{dT} \tag{9.31}$$

where $p^* = \dfrac{p_2 \, t_m^{1.3}}{(t_m - t_d)^{1.3}}$

Integrating equation (9.31) yields:

$$(T_3 - T_2) \, \Gamma = - \ln \left[ \frac{p^* \delta t_{des} - (\Gamma t_d - t_{ao})}{p^* \delta t_{des} - (\Gamma t_p - t_{ao})} \right] \tag{9.32}$$

where $\Gamma = \{ 1 + [1.3 p^*/t_m] \}$

$$\approx 1$$

as $1.3 p^* < < t_m$. This may be seen from the previous example where:

$$p^* = \frac{1.2 \times 75^{1.3}}{(75 - 55)^{1.3}}$$

$$= 1.8$$

So:

$$1.3 \times 1.8 = 2.34 << 75$$

and:

$$\Gamma = 1 + (2.34/75)$$

$$= 1.03$$

So equation (9.32) becomes:

$$\frac{(T_3 - T_2)}{\tau} = - \ln \left[ \frac{p^* \delta t_{des} - (t_d - t_{ao})}{p^* \delta t_{des} - (t_p - t_{ao})} \right]$$

$$= - \ln \left[ \frac{p^* \delta t_{des} - \delta t}{p^* \delta t_{des} - \delta t_p} \right] \tag{9.33}$$

This is the same as equation (9.24), except that $p$ has been replaced by $p^*$. Figure 9.18 shows the preheat loci for various values of $p^*$, and it can be seen that the turning-point has been greatly reduced by the effectively larger plant size.

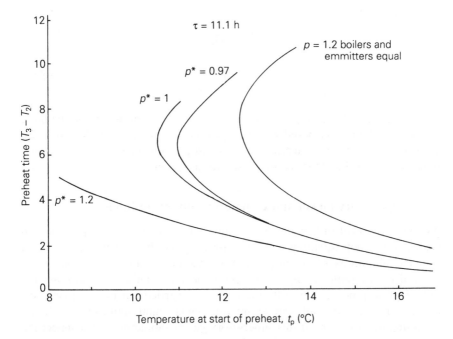

**Fig. 9.18** The effect of varying emitter output.

## 9.10 Comparison with Birtles and John's equation

As mentioned earlier, one of the most successful empirical algorithms for optimum start in BEMSs is based on Birtles and John's equation:

$$\ln (T_3 - T_2) = A_{BJ}(t_p - t_d) + B_{BJ} \qquad (9.8)$$

where $A_{BJ}$ = a constant associated with the thermal weight of the building, and $B_{BJ}$ = a constant associated with the time between switching on the heating and the interior starting to heat up.

This performs well, except at low outside temperatures. So an outside temperature term was later added:

$$\ln (T_3 - T_2) = A_{BJ}(t_p - t_d) + B_{BJ} + C_{BJ}\, t_{ao} \qquad (9.9)$$

where $C_{BJ}$ = a constant.

Although this equation does not look like the first-order equations we have just been considering, the graph of equation (9.8), as shown previously in Fig. 9.8, is not so dissimilar. In fact this graph can be quite closely fitted by a first-order equation where $\tau = 12.2\,\text{h}$ and $p = 1.5$. Indeed, it has been shown [13] that in a comparison with the first-order model, the constant, $A_{BJ}$, is approximately given by:

$$A_{BJ} \approx \frac{\tau H_{des}}{pQ_{des}}$$

$$\approx \frac{\tau}{p(t_{ai} - t_{ao})_{des}} \qquad (9.34)$$

As Birtles and John's equation is empirical, one cannot determine the three constants. Algorithms based on the equation use default values which are adapted as the algorithm 'learns' from its past performance. A recursive least-squares method ([4], [14]) is often used for adaption.

## 9.11  Supervisory jacket and commerical optimiser loops

As was mentioned in Chapter 6 regarding the commercial PID program, so the optimiser loop equations discussed above cannot be written straight into a commercial optimiser loop program. Abnormal data that may be erroneous or atypical (e.g. a boiler going to lock-out or a sensor failure) could upset the self-adaption process. This filtering process is carried out by a **supervisory jacket**, which is extra software around the fundamental optimiser algorithm.

An important feature of this supervisory jacket should be to disconnect the operation of the compensator loop from its connection to the heating system and to open the 3-port valve fully to the boiler system. This will allow full heating during preheating. If the compensator were left connected, the heating system output would vary according to the outside temperature and the self-learning process of the optimiser would be 'confused'. On a mild day the compensator would restrict the heat output and the building would take longer than expected to achieve the required temperature. Likewise, on a cold day the compensator would allow full output of the heating, so that the building would get up to temperature quicker than expected. The self-adaption would be making large and erroneous changes.

Fig. 9.19 shows the characteristics of a commercial optimiser module for heating. In the example shown the optimiser module activates a boiler loop and a 3-port valve loop at the optimum time by a digital output, OSS(OCC) (optimum start/stop (occupancy)). The connections to the loops are via the set point select bits, (SS).

On the left of the module are analogue addresses relating to sensors – e.g. the inside and outside temperature sensors, and the heating set point. The optimiser algorithm is based on a first-order model, and in the configuration of the module the heating-up and cooling-down temperature slopes are required. These can be obtained from observation of graphs from logged data of the building inside temperature. As these are difficult to estimate, default values, pre-set in the supervisory jacket, can be used. The default values will be large, but the self-adaption will gradually set them to more accurate values.

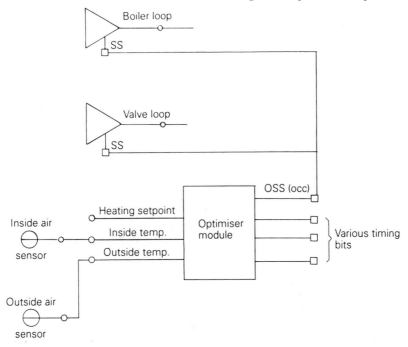

**Fig. 9.19** Characteristics of a commercial optimiser loop module.

Optimum stop is also available in the module, which will switch off the heating at the optimum time, so that the building will cool down to a comfortable target temperature by the end of occupancy.

## 9.12  Savings with optimiser loops

A prime claim in the argument that BEMSs save energy and money is that they have optimiser loops which are good savers. However, there is little analytical evidence as to the savings that can be expected, apart from the findings discussed in the first chapter.

An analysis of the expected savings from an optimiser, compared to continuous heating, has been carried out by Fisk ([9], [15]), using a first-order model of the building, similar to the one discussed in this chapter. The saving, $S$, is given by:

$$S = \frac{T^*}{T + T^*} \left[ 1 + \frac{1}{\beta\alpha} \ln \left\{ \beta \exp\left(-\alpha\right) - \beta + 1 \right\} \right] \qquad (9.35)$$

where $T$ = unoccupied period (h);

$T^*$ = occupancy period (h)

$= 24 - T$

$$\beta = \frac{Q_{occ}}{Q_{max}};$$

$Q_{max}$ = maximum heat output from heating system

$$= pQ_{des} \ (W);$$

$Q_{occ}$ = heat output during occupancy to maintain steady state design inside temperature (W)

$$= \frac{Q_{des} \ (t_{ai \ des} - t_{ao})}{(t_{ai \ des} - t_{ao \ des})}$$

$$= \Phi \ Q_{des}$$

$$\alpha = \frac{T^*}{\tau}$$

$\tau$ = first-order time constant (h).

In the derivation of equation (9.35) the continuous heating used for comparison was with a heat input of $Q_{occ}$. The factor, $\beta$, is related to the plant size ratio, $p$, as can be seen by the following manipulation of the above definitions:

$$\beta = \frac{Q_{occ}}{Q_{max}}$$

$$= \frac{\Phi \ Q_{des}}{p \ Q_{des}}$$

$$= \Phi/p$$

where $\Phi$ = load factor due to the weather, as used earlier.

As $p$ increases, so $\beta$ reduces, which increases $S$, the savings.

*Example*

What are the savings for the single-storey, partitioned office block, with a time constant of 5.9 h, used in a previous example? The occupancy is from 9 a.m. to 6 p.m. and the steady state heat loss is 64 kW, and the plant size ratio, $p$, is 1.25. Take the outside temperature as 7°C, with $\delta t_{des} = 20$ K and $t_{ai \ des} = 20$°C.

*Solution*

From the data:

$$\Phi = \frac{20 - 7}{20} = 0.65$$

$$\beta = \frac{0.65}{1.25} = 0.52$$

$$\alpha = \frac{6 \ p.m. - 9 \ a.m.}{5.9} = 1.53$$

Substituting these into equation (9.35):

$$S = \frac{T^*}{T + T^*}\left[1 + \frac{1}{\beta\alpha}\ln\{\beta\exp(-\alpha) - \beta + 1\}\right] \qquad (9.35)$$

we get:

$$S = \frac{9}{15 + 9}\left[1 + \frac{1}{0.52 \times 1.53}\ln\{0.52\exp(-1.53) - 0.52 + 1\}\right]$$

$$= 0.375\,[1 + 1.26 \times \ln\{0.52\exp(-1.53) - 0.52 + 1\}]$$

$$= 12.7\%$$

The maximum saving that could be made would be by having an extremely large heating plant, so that $\beta$ tends to zero:

$$S = \frac{T^*}{T + T^*}\left[1 + \frac{\exp(-\alpha) - 1}{\alpha}\right]$$

$$= 18.3\%$$

Even this is not very close to the ratio of hours occupancy to the hours run with continuous heating – i.e. 9/24 (0.375). This is due to the storage of heat in the fabric and its loss during unoccupied periods, as well as during occupancy.

## References

[1] Technical Report No. 54, Property Services Agency, 1973. Croydon, UK.
[2] Birtles, A. and John, R. (1985) A new optimum start algorithm. *Building Services Engineering Research and Technology*, **6**, 3.
[3] Sharma, V., Hibbert, P. and Archer, P. (1982) A value for money guide to optimiser selection, *Building Services Environmental Engineering*, 5, 1, September.
[4] Ogata, K. (1987) *Discrete-time Control Systems*, Prentice-Hall, Englewood Cliffs, NJ.
[5] Dufton, A. F. (1934) The warming of walls. *Journal of the Institute of Heating and Ventilating Engineers*, **2**, 21.
[6] McLaughlin, R. K., McLean, R. C. and Bonthron, W. J. (1981) *Heating Services Design*, Butterworths, Sevenoaks.
[7] Bassett, C. R. and Pritchard, M. D. W. (1968) *Heating*, Longman, Harlow.
[8] Clarke, J. A. *Energy Simulation in Building Design*, Adam Hilger, Bristol.
[9] Fisk, D. J. *Thermal Control of Buildings*, Applied Science Publishers, London.

[10] Crabb, J. A., Murdoch, N. and Penman, J. M. (1987) A simplified thermal response model. *Building Services Engineering Research and Technology*, **8**, 1.
[11] O'Callaghan, P. W. (1980) *Building for Energy Conservation*, Pergamon, Oxford.
[12] CIBSE (1986) CIBSE Guide, Volume A, Section A9, Estimation of plant capacity, Chartered Institution of Building Services Engineers, London.
[13] Levermore, G. J. (1988) Simple model for an optimiser. *Building Services Engineering Research and Technology*, **9**, 3.
[14] Iserman, R. (1981) *Digital Control Systems*. Springer-Verlag, Berlin.
[15] Fisk, D. J. and Bloomfield, D. P. (1977) Optimisation of intermittent heating. *Building and Environment*, **12**; also BRE Current Paper CP 14/77.
[16] Letherman, K. M. (1981) *Automatic Controls for Heating and Air Conditioning Principles and Applications*, Pergamon, Oxford.

# 10
# Monitoring and targeting

Two of the great benefits of a BEMS are its ability to communicate and its capability of monitoring plant, as has been pointed out in Chapter 1. The monitoring of plant performance often relates to logging sensor data for later transposing to graphs, the logging only being limited by the memory size of the outstations. Frequency of monitoring is in the hands of the operator and too much stored data can be as much of a handicap as lack of data.

However, this chapter is not primarily concerned with the logging of room temperature sensors, flow water temperature sensors, and so on, but with the overall performance of the plant and the building, for energy efficiency and maintenance.

## 10.1 Monitoring and alarms

The most basic part of monitoring relates to the standard alarms which, for instance, indicate that a sensor is reading high or low or is out of limits. Similar alarms can also apply to loops, drivers and digital inputs. But, in addition, drivers can also have maintenance interval alarms. A **logic hours run module** is required to facilitate this, as shown in Fig. 10.1. This configuration enables an alarm to be raised when an item of plant – here a pump with a binary driver – has gone beyond its period for maintenance. With this facility, **condition-based maintenance** can be implemented.

The logic hours run module counts the hours for which the source bit, S, is on and sends the output, O, to the hours run destination analogue address. In this module is a routine to check whether the hours run has exceeded the interval limit which has been set (input at I), and if so, it will set the interval

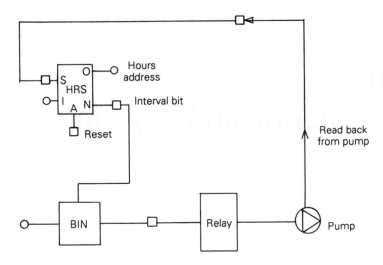

**Fig. 10.1** Maintenance internal alarm for a pump.

bit, from output N, to ON or 1. When the reset input node, connected to A, is set to ON or 1, then the hours run total is set to zero.

With other logic modules, the logic hours run module can monitor the time during occupancy that the room temperature is above a certain limit, say, 22°C, or below a limit, say, 18°C. Both accumulated times are useful for monitoring the efficiency and performance of the heating system.

## 10.2 Energy audit

A BEMS can take monitoring a stage further than simply logging hours run of plant and alarms. Fuel and electricity meters can be interfaced serially to an outstation. Digital signals are sent from the meter counting the dial movements. This energy data can regularly and dynamically update a spreadsheet (see later) in the central station. Various charts and diagrams can be produced from the spreadsheet on the window-based BEMS's software, as shown in Fig. 10.2

Working to the axiom that a diagram is worth a page of writing and many pages of numbers, a Sankey diagram ([1], [2]) can be drawn from all the data collected by the BEMS. As Fig. 10.3 shows, it has scaled arrows to indicate where the energy is going.

## 10.3 Electricity monitoring

Electricity is comparatively easy to monitor. The main intake meter, belonging to the electricity company, will allow total consumption to be monitored if it

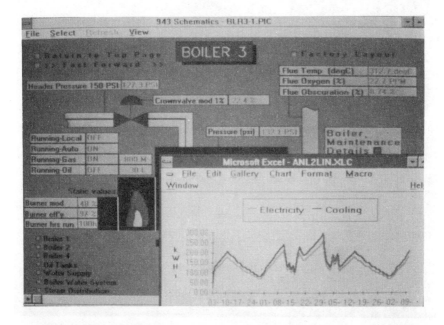

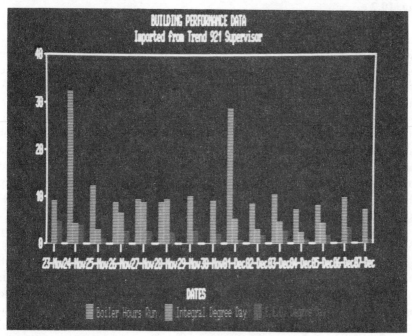

**Fig. 10.2** Spreadsheet data and graphs, and a graph in a window.

Bar  Line  Import  Clear  Save  Quit
Import new data into worksheet

| | A | B | C | D | E | F | G | H |
|---|---|---|---|---|---|---|---|---|
| 21 | | | | | | | | |
| 22 | | | ! | IMPORTED TREND DATA TABLE | | ! | | |
| 23 | | | ! DATES | Boiler | Integral | E.E.O. ! | | |
| 24 | | | ! | Hrs.Run | Degr.Day | Degr.Day ! | | |
| 25 | | | ! 23-Nov | 0 | 9.03 | 4.4 ! | | |
| 26 | | | ! 24-Nov | 32.2 | 4.00 | 3.8 ! | | |
| 27 | | | ! 25-Nov | 12.12 | 2.91 | 0.83 ! | | |
| 28 | | | ! 26-Nov | 8.82 | 6.47 | 2.43 ! | | |
| 29 | | | ! 27-Nov | 9.26 | 8.82 | 2.42 ! | | |
| 30 | | | ! 28-Nov | 8.61 | 9.23 | 2.14 ! | | |
| 31 | | | ! 29-Nov | 0 | 9.00 | 2.64 ! | | |
| 32 | | | ! 30-Nov | 0 | 9.14 | 2.02 ! | | |
| 33 | | | ! 01-Dec | 20.59 | 5.28 | 0.78 ! | | |
| 34 | | | ! 02-Dec | 8.33 | 3 | 1.7 ! | | |
| 35 | | | ! 03-Dec | 10.35 | 4.5 | 2.6 ! | | |
| 36 | | | ! 04-Dec | 7.11 | 2.12 | 0.76 ! | | |
| 37 | | | ! 05-Dec | 0 | 4.11 | 1.72 ! | | |
| 38 | | | ! 06-Dec | 0 | 9.64 | 3.23 ! | | |
| 39 | | | ! 07-Dec | 0 | 7.24 | 0.72 ! | | |
| 40 | | | ! | (sens29) | (sens34) | (sens39)! | | |

08-Dec-86  11:45 AM      CMD

**Fig. 10.2 c.**

has a port on it for a serial connection, e.g. by RS232-C, or other suitable means, for pulse signals to be sent to a BEMS outstation. For the discerning energy manager, sub-meters can be installed around the building to determine where the electricity is used. Many BEMS manufacturers can supply serially interfaceable meters for this purpose.

Instead of fixed meters, portable monitoring equipment, not interfaced to the BEMS, can be put on to various items of equipment. This uses clamps which go around the live electrical cable forming the primary winding of a **current transformer**, the secondary winding being in the clamps connected to an ammeter device in the equipment. With the voltage of the supply being almost constant, simple computation allows the measurement of the electrical consumption, provided that the power factor is known.

If the main meter is a maximum demand MD meter, then careful interfacing to the BEMS is required. This is because the MD meter consists of two parts: a unit measuring consumption (kWh) like an ordinary meter, and one which measures the demand kW (some companies use KVA demand), over half-hour intervals. The BEMS outstation will require a pulse from the kWh meter and another from the demand meter, indicating the start of each half-hour interval of if it is to monitor the MD. If there is only one pulse output from the meter, then the configuration in Fig. 10.4 can be used for monitoring the meter, although synchronization with the meters and MD will not be exact.

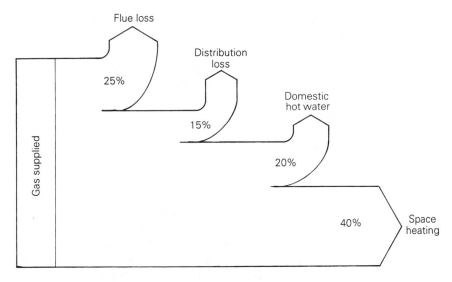

**Fig. 10.3** A Sankey diagram.

At the heart of the configuration is a **logic counter module**, (CNTR), which counts pulses, at S, which are on or off for more than 15.6 ms. This pulse time gives a limiting upper frequency response of 30 Hz. Notice that this module monitors the digital input channel at 15.6 ms intervals, which is much faster than the temperature sensors are monitored as it is independant of the sequence, or program, cycle time which is much longer, typically 5 s. A **fast sequence cycle time** is available if prompt action is required once a pulse has been counted, to avoid the delay of the normal cycle time.

Outputs from the module give the cumulative total, from M, and the consumption rate, from R (the change in the cumulative consumption over a given period which is the average kW demand). In the CNTR is a scaling factor, F, which relates each pulse to kWh, and a reschedule time, T, which defines the

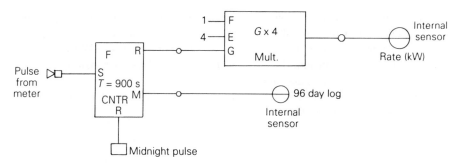

**Fig. 10.4** Meter monitoring configuration.

period, in seconds, over which the rate, or demand, is measured. In the example shown the CNTR is reset by a midnight pulse, at R, to count each day's consumption, which is logged at the internal sensor. For a typical log, this would give 96 days' data. The multiplication function module MULT determines the kW rate from the rate output, R. As here T is set to 900 s (15 min), the MULT module multiplies this by four to give the kW rate.

The MD consumer is charged for the units consumed, as well as for the maximum demand recorded. Such meters are only used for large users, with supplies usually above 40 kVA [3].

The demand meter has a kW (or kVA) circular dial and a hand moves as the consumption in kWh is recorded. This hand pushes another hand. After a half-hour interval, the pushing hand is reset to zero, but the pushed hand stays at the maximum demand reading. The pushing hand then starts measuring the consumption for the next half-hour. The scale of the MD meter is in kW, and the pushed hand is read and reset by the meter reader each month.

The half-hourly resetting signal from the MD meter can be interfaced to the BEMS, in a similar manner to that in Fig. 10.4, using a CNTR module, so that the BEMS can monitor the demand from the meter. In the example, above, there is no separate half-hour pulse from the meter, so the BEMS's demand may not be synchronized with the meter's which could hinder load shedding.

### 10.3.1   Load shedding

If the kW electrical demand goes too high in any half-hour in a month, then the user has to pay for this worst half-hour in the month. It is therefore worthwhile to keep the maximum demand at a low and steady level. A popular use of a BEMS is to monitor the demand and switch off plant on a priority and size basis. Two ways of configuring a BEMS to load shed are the predictive method and the offset method [4], [5].

### 10.3.2   Predictive method

The cumulative electrical consumption is shown in Fig. 10.5, as sampled by a BEMS every 5 min, for the first 15 min at a site. The aim is to keep the kilowatt demand to less than 80 kW, or a consumption of 40 kWh in half an hour. Already the consumption is at 30 kWh and a slope of consumption can be predicted for the demand not to exceed 80 kW.

The kilowatt demand can be determined from the rate of change of the consumption with time, that is:

$$K = \frac{dC}{dT}$$

where $K$ = demand (kW), and $C$ = cumulative consumption (kWh).

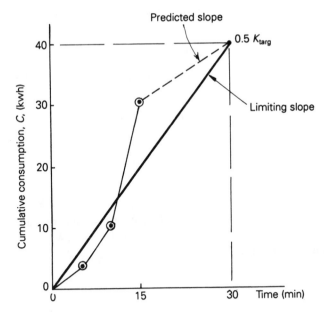

**Fig. 10.5**   Predictive load shedding.

If the BEMS monitors the consumption at regular intervals of $\delta T$ minutes (5 min in Fig. 10.5), in each half-hour period, then at the $i$th interval the kilowatt demand, $K_i$, is:

$$K_i = \frac{60\,(C_i - C_{i-1})}{\delta T} \tag{10.1}$$

where $C_i$ = cumulative consumption at interval $i$ as from the start of the half-hour sampling period (kWh).

The kilowatt demand at the end of the half-hour period is:

$$K_n = \frac{60\,C_n}{n\delta T} = 2\,C_n$$

where $n$ = number of intervals in a half-hour.

Shown in Fig. 10.5 is the limiting slope, determined by the target kilowatt demand, $K_{targ}$, which in this case is 80 kW. If the consumption goes above this line, then the consumption has to be reduced. The minimum electrical load that can be left switched on is that of the predicted slope:

$$\text{predicted slope } = \frac{60\,(0.5\,K_{targ} - C_i)}{(n-i)\delta T}$$

which for the example is:

$$\frac{60\,(0.5 \times 80 - 30)}{(6-3)5}$$

$$= 40\;\text{kW}$$

The consumption slope during the previous 5 min can be calculated from equation (10.1):

$$K_3 = \frac{60\,(C_3 - C_2)}{5} \tag{10.1}$$

$$= 12(30 - 10)$$

$$= 240\;\text{kW}$$

If this rate of consumption continued, 200 kW of equipment would have to be switched off. Conversely, if the rate dropped below 40 kW, equipment could be switched on to the level of 40 kW.

### 10.3.3   Offset method

With this method, the limiting slope is raised at the start of the demand interval by an offset, as shown in Fig. 10.6. Loads are only shed when the offset limiting slope is exceeded. This allows for larger kilowatt demands earlier in

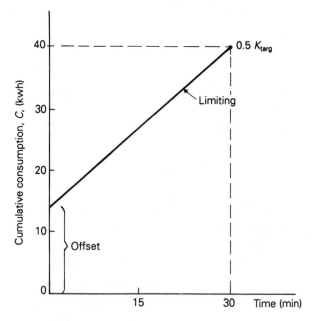

**Fig. 10.6**   Limiting slope with offset.

the interval than the previous method. However, the offset limiting slope is less steep, so it has an overall lower kilowatt demand.

### 10.3.4 Shedding priority

Load shedding primarily saves maximum demand charges, although it may also save some electrical energy. But the decision has to be made as to which items of plant should be switched off, and the priority order in which they are to be switched. (This is discussed in more detail in references [4] and [5].) But it is worth cautioning that careful thought should be given to what loads are shed, and indeed whether load shedding is carried out.

Frequently, the decision is made to switch air conditioning refrigerant compressors. These are not tolerant of too frequent switching and can easily be severely damaged. Induction motors also do not respond well to frequently being turned on and off, due to high inductive currents, although 'soft starters' greatly reduce these currents. The switching off of lights must not cause a safety hazard, so this is a further restriction.

## 10.4 Heat monitoring

Compared to electricity monitoring, heat monitoring is difficult. This is because both flow rate and temperature difference must be measured. Either an interfaceable heat meter, which integrates the two measurements, is used, or the BEMS directly reads the flow rate and temperature difference and uses its own configured software to calculate the heat flow.

For a hot-water heating circuit, the temperature of the flow and return will most probably be measured in the plant room close to the BEMS outstation. Unfortunately, due to the transit time between the outgoing flow and the incoming return, the two will be out of synchronization, as Fig. 10.7 shows.

The instantaneous temperature difference varies between 10 K and 0 K, so the corresponding heat metered would also vary likewise. Also a small error of temperature could correspond to a considerable error of heat output. For instance, for a heat supply of 100 kW with a 10 K temperature difference between flow and return a 0.1 °C error represents 1 kW.

Flow rate must also be measured and integrated with temperature difference to determine the amount of heat. There are a number of flow measuring devices for water systems. Many are based on differential pressure measurement around a constriction in the flow. The pressure differential is related by Bernoulli's equation ([26], [27]) to the fluid velocity. Such devices are the **orifice plate**, **Venturi**, **Dall tube** and **nozzle**. The orifice plate is the most widely used and it is cheap.

Pressure differential has to be changed into an electrical signal for a BEMS to interface to one of the above meters, but an **axial flow turbine meter**

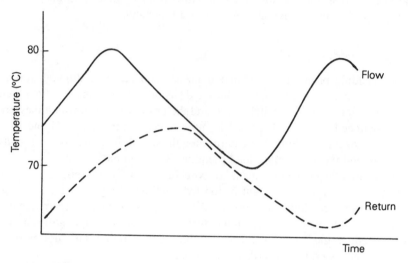

**Fig. 10.7** Flow and return temperatures.

directly produces an electrical signal. The turbine is a multi-bladed rotor suspended in the fluid stream with the axis of rotation parallel to the direction of flow. Each of between four to eight blades of the rotor are made of ferro-magnetic material, which forms a magnetic circuit with a permanent magnet and coil within the meter housing.

Turbine flow meters and differential pressure meters can get clogged up if the water is not maintained in a clean condition. So there is a trend towards using non-intrusive flow meters, which do not get clogged up. Examples of such meters are **electromagnetic, ultrasonic** and **cross-correlation** flowmeters.

The electromagnetic meter utilizes the Faraday Effect, where a moving conductor in a magnetic field generates an electric current. The conductor, in this case, is the water in the pipe. In practice, the water will not be pure and so it should have a small conductivity.

Bentley deals with flow measurement systems in detail, some of which have not been mentioned here [6]. Whatever the method of flow measurement, heat meters are expensive and from past experience need to be well maintained, and in well-maintained systems, to be reliable. Interfacing of heat meter pulses will be very similar to the configuration for electricity meter pulses.

## 10.5  Spreadsheets and graphical techniques

As was seen in an earlier chapter, BEMSs' central stations can have spread-sheet programs and data bases. Spreadsheets are basically tables with rows and columns of numbers. A spreadsheet program is like a word processing package except that numbers are manipulated rather than words [24], and it can perform much 'number crunching' according to formulae entered by the user. From these numbers graphs, histograms and pie charts can be drawn readily; therefore it is a useful tool for a BEMS user to have, especially to manipulate energy data and temperatures. An increasing number of BEMS manufacturers are interfacing their central station software to spreadsheets, so that the spreadsheet can automatically be updated with, for instance, meter readings and temperatures from outstations, when the central station is dialled up by the outstations to give their logged data. From the meter reading the spreadsheet could calculate the latest consumption and readily display the latest consumption graph.

A distinct advantage of spreadsheets is that **what-if questions** can be analysed. For instance, if the cost of fuel rises, then a spreadsheet of monthly consumptions can work through all the data and future monthly costs predicted.

Common spreadsheets are SuperCalc, Microsoft Excell and Lotus 1-2-3. The earliest spreadsheet was VisiCalc (a shortening of visible calculator) to run on Apple II PCs in the late 1970s. Lotus 1-2-3 was then developed to run on IBM-compatible machines.

The basic spreadsheet is a matrix of headed columns, lettered for identification, and rows, numbered for identification, as shown in Fig. 10.8(a). Each location is called a **cell**. The formulae for the spreadsheet calculations are entered on another sheet, and the user can view either the 'results' sheet or the formulae sheet. The two sheets are shown in Fig.10.8(b). The figure also shows a portion of output from a spreadsheet for oil consumption at a large boilerhouse.

Here the first column is headed 'Date' and the first cell under it is '03-May-92'. If this is referred to as cell A8, then the 'stored' oil column is B and the B8 cell has 30 594 litres in it. Using this notation the formula used for calculating some of the other cell values can be derived. The formula for the used fuel, 'Litres used', column F, is:

$$B(n) - B(n + 1) + C(n + 1) = F(n + 1)$$

where $n$ = a row number. We can check this by noting that the fuel used against 31-May-92, F9, is:

$$30\ 594 - 55\ 301 + 54\ 532 = 29\ 825$$

as is F9. Also the price per litre is entered and the total cost calculated. The YRT columns refer to yearly running totals which are explained shortly.

Generally spreadsheet programs are limited to the amount of data that they can hold on their spreadsheet matrices. For instance, it can hold as much fuel data as shown in Fig. 10.8 as there are rows; this may perhaps be as many as

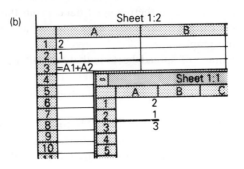

(a)

(b)

(c)

Name;   Atkins House
Address;  Sabiri Way, Milestown.

Account No;  53476   Oil  35 second.   Supplier; Fiddlers.

| Date | Stored | Deliv-ered | Price p/litre | Cost of delivery | Litres used | Oil YRT | Del. cost YRT |
|---|---|---|---|---|---|---|---|
| 03-May-92 | 30594 | 40922 | 15.08 | 6,171.04 | 55651 | 645300 | 97,324.51 |
| 31-May-92 | 55301 | 54532 | 14.63 | 7,978.03 | 29825 | 629120 | 97,358.27 |
| 05-Jul-92 | 44868 | 13640 | 15.63 | 2,131.93 | 24073 | 625304 | 97,104.60 |
| 02-Aug-92 | 26957 | 0 | 15.63 | 0.00 | 17911 | 623281 | 93,043.12 |
| 06-Sep-92 | 32549 | 27280 | 15.63 | 4,263.86 | 21688 | 621450 | 93,237.71 |

**Fig. 10.8**  Spreadsheet of empty cells, above, and of a site's consumption, below.

a thousand. For details of a number of sites and large amounts of data for reference a **data base program** can be used, where the information is held in files, rather like a card index, which can be quickly manipulated. Frequently outside the BEMS area, databases are used to hold mailing lists and account details. A commonly used database is Ashton-Tate's dBASE. However, the art of good monitoring is to avoid 'data diarrhoea' and to transform columns of data into readily understood graphs and charts.

Often consumption data is presented as a histogram, as in Fig. 10.9, which a spreadsheet program can produce very quickly. But to compare one year's

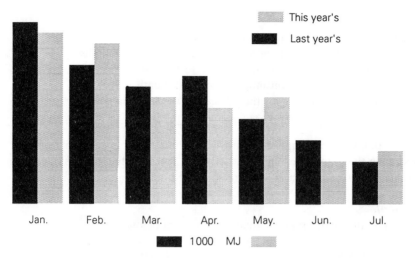

**Fig. 10.9** A histogram of consumption.

consumption with another is difficult. As is shown in Fig. 10.9, some months are higher and some lower than the previous year's.

A useful technique is to develop a trend graph, indicating whether the consumption is tending to increase or decrease. Such a graph is the yearly running total graph (YRT). This technique is also used for analysing firms' sales, especially where seasonal factors influence quantities sold, and a similar method applies to the determination of the retail prices index (RPI). Figure 10.10 shows a YRT from data used in a later example.

In the YRT the consumption for a complete year (all 12 months) is calculated. The YRT for the following 13th month is calculated by the formula:

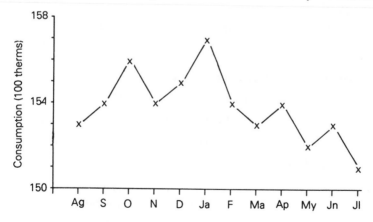

**Fig. 10.10** A yearly running total of consumption.

$$YRT_{13} = YRT_{12} + M_{13} - M_1$$

where $YRT_{13}$ = yearly running total for the 13th month;

$YRT_{12}$ = yearly running total for the previous 12 months;

$M_{13}$ = monthly consumption for 13th month;

$M_1$ = monthly consumption for first month.

In more general terms, for the $n$th month the formula is:

$$YRT_n = YRT_{n-1} + M_n - M_{n-12} \tag{10.2}$$

If one month's consumption is above the same month's consumption a year ago, then the graph goes up slightly. If it is less then the graph slopes down. In this way, seasonal variations are smoothed out.

*Example*

Calculate the yearly running totals for the data below:

| Month | Consumption (100 therms) | | |
|---|---|---|---|
| | 1990/91 | 1991/92 | 1992/93 |
| August | 4 | 3 | 4 |
| September | 5 | 6 | 6 |
| October | 7 | 9 | 5 |
| November | 11 | 9 | |
| December | 20 | 21 | |
| January | 25 | 27 | |
| February | 27 | 24 | |
| March | 18 | 19 | |
| April | 14 | 13 | |
| May | 8 | 6 | |
| June | 8 | 9 | |
| July | 7 | 5 | |
| Total | 154 | | |

*Solution*

From equation (10.2) the YRT for August 1990 is:

$$YRT_{Aug\,91} = YRT_{July\,91} + M_{Aug\,91} - M_{Aug\,90}$$

$$= 15\,400 + 300 - 400$$

$$= 15\,300$$

Similarly, for the following months one gets:

| Month | YRT (100 therms) | |
|---|---|---|
| | 1991/92 | 1992/93 |
| August | 153 | 152 |
| September | 154 | 152 |

| Month | YRT (100 therms) | |
|---|---|---|
| | 1991/92 | 1992/93 |
| October | 156 | 148 |
| November | 154 | |
| December | 155 | |
| January | 157 | |
| February | 154 | |
| March | 153 | |
| April | 154 | |
| May | 152 | |
| June | 153 | |
| July | 151 | |

Overall the trend is down, as is shown by the graph of the YRT in Fig. 10.10.

It is interesting to note that YRTs can be determined very easily from monthly meter readings. One simply takes last year's reading away from this year's to obtain the YRT.

The variations in consumption may be due to the weather, in which case the YRT of the monthly average temperature, $\bar{t}_{ao}$ will also show a similar variation.

## 10.6 Degree-days

The variation in the heating consumption is primarily due to the coldness of the weather. A common measure of weather coldness is the **degree-day**. Degree-days derive from the energy consumed in heating. From the integrated balance equation the energy consumed is:

$$\int \dot{m}C_p(t_f - t_r)\, dT = \int B(t_m - t_{ai})^{1.3}\, dT = \int A(t_{ai} - t_{ao})\, dT$$

Here the storage effects in the fabric have initially been ignored and the time period assumed to be reasonably long – i.e. greater than a week. The above equation may be turned into a discrete equation:

$$\sum_{i=1}^{n} \dot{m}C_p(t_{fi} - t_{ri})\delta T = \sum_{i=1}^{n} (t_{mi} - t_{aii})^{1.3}\, \delta T = \sum_{i=1}^{n} A(t_{aii} - t_{aoi})\delta T \qquad (10.3)$$

where the time period is $n\delta T$. This yields an equation with the average values over the same period:

$$\dot{m}C_p n\delta T(\bar{t}_{fn} - \bar{t}_{rn}) = Bn\delta T(\bar{t}_{mn} - \bar{t}_{ain}) = An\delta T(\bar{t}_{ain} - \bar{t}_{aon}) \qquad (10.4)$$

where $\bar{t}_{fn}$ = average flow water temperature over the period $n\delta T$, $\bar{t}_{rn}$, $\bar{t}_{mn}$, $\bar{t}_{ain}$ and $\bar{t}_{aon}$ are average values over the period $n\delta T$. This is in fact the balance equation, although the average and the period $n$ symbols are normally omitted, and $n\delta T$ is cancelled out.

To determine the energy consumption over this period, $n\delta T$, then either the boiler output, the heat emitter output or the fabric heat loss parts of the equation can be used. But the first two need the average values $\bar{t}_{fn}$, $\bar{t}_{rn}$, $\bar{t}_{mn}$, which need to be determined from extensive monitoring. It is therefore easier to use the fabric heat loss part as this only relies on $\bar{t}_{aon}$ and $\bar{t}_{ain}$. $\bar{t}_{aon}$ need not even be monitored as it can be readily obtained from meteorological records, and $\bar{t}_{ain}$ should be maintained at a fairly constant level, at least during occupancy. It should be noted that this average inside temperature is the inside temperature produced due to the heating alone. However, there will also be heating due to internal gains, such as lighting, equipment, people and sunshine. Although these gains are not considered in the heating system design calculation, if they are utilized, even unintentionally they have to be considered in the energy consumption determination. This is done by redefining the components of the inside temperature as $t_{ai\ cont}$, the inside temperature at which the building is maintained by the controls, and $t_g$, a temperature due to the gains. So:

$$\bar{t}_{ain} = t_{ai\ cont} - t_g$$

$\bar{t}_{ain}$ is often referred to as the **balance point temperature** of the building, $t_{bal}$. The balance point temperature, $t_{bal}$, is so named as when the outside temperature, $t_{ao}$, is above $t_{bal}$, then no heating is required, and conversely when $t_{ao}$ is below it, then heating is required.

For a continuously heated building, the energy consumed maintaining a controlled inside temperature of $t_{ai\ cont}$, over $N$ days is from equation (10.3):

$$24\,A \sum_{i=1}^{N} (t_{bal} - t_{aoi})$$

where $\delta T$ is 24h and:

$$t_{ai\ cont} = t_{bal} + t_g$$

The term:

$$\sum_{i=1}^{N} (t_{bal} - t_{aoi}) \tag{10.5}$$

is the degree-days for N days referred to the base temperature, $t_{base}$, of $t_{bal}$. Sometimes the 24 hours in the day is implied in the degree-day units but here, as equation (10.5) shows, degree-days are simply the sum of temperature differences and so the units are temperature difference (K).

Traditionally $t_{base}$ has been taken as 15.5°C (60°F). This derived from work done many years ago, primarily in the 1930s and 1940s [7], which showed that there was a good correlation between monthly energy consumption and monthly degree-days with a base temperature of 15.5°C. For hospitals, with higher inside temperatures, a base temperature of 18.5°C is taken [8]. Monthly degree-day figures are published and available from the Department of the Environment Energy Efficiency Office and various journals and magazines.

Correction factors are available [9] to adjust a yearly degree-day total to a total to a different base temperature, $t_{base}$. This may be necessary as the base temperature should be equal to a building's balance temperature $t_{bal}$. For modern, well-insulated buildings $t_{bal}$ can be around 10°C, well below the standard base temperature of 15.5°C. The gains (solar, people and equipment) can supply sufficient heat to maintain the building at a comfortable temperature. However, these correction factors only apply to yearly degree-day totals and are for the determination of annual fuel consumption:

$$\sum_{i=1}^{N} (t_{base} - \delta t_{base} - t_{aoi}) = \varphi \sum_{i=1}^{N} (t_{base} - t_{aoi}) \qquad (10.6)$$

where $\varphi$ = base temperature correction factor, and $\delta t_{base}$ = a reduction in $t_{base}$, so that:

$$t_{base} - \delta t_{base} = t_{bal}$$

Values of $\varphi$ can be calculated, but equation (10.6) is correct for only one value of N, the annual number of 365 days. Figure 10.11 shows a graph of $\varphi$ for various base temperatures, derived from reference [8]. Alternatively, a formula derived by Hitchin [10] can be used for calculating the monthly degree-days to a different base temperature:

$$\text{degree days per month} = N_{month} \frac{(t_{base} - \bar{t}_{ao\ month})}{1 - \exp(-k)(t_{base} - \bar{t}_{ao\ month})} \qquad (10.7)$$

where $N_{month}$ = number of days in the month considered;
$\bar{t}_{ao\ month}$ = average monthly outside air temperature (°C);
$k$ = a constant, which varies with site

| Site | k |
|------|------|
| Heathrow | 0.66 |
| Manchester | 0.7 |
| Glasgow | 0.74 |
| Cardiff | 0.78 |
| Birmingham | 0.66 |
| Mean | 0.71 |

Equation (10.6) is incorrect for general values of N different from 365, as can be seen in the following example.

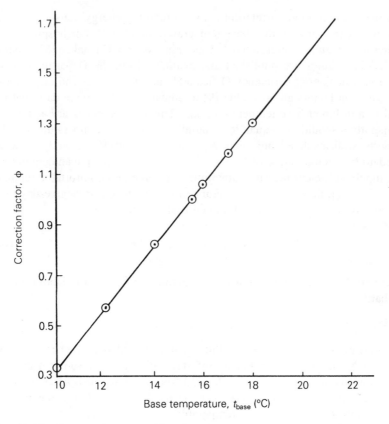

**Fig. 10.11**   Degree-day correction factors.

*Example*

The average outside temperatures for three days are:

$$\bar{t}_{ao1} = 10.5°C, \ \bar{t}_{ao2} = 12.5°C, \ \bar{t}_{ao3} = 6.5°C$$

and $t_{bal} = 13°C$. Calculate the degree-days to a base temperature of 13°C and $t_{base} = 15.5°C$ and determine the values of $\varphi$ from equation (10.6).

*Solution*

For the first day, the degree-days are 5 K and from equation (10.6):

$$(15.5 - 2.5 - 10.5) = \varphi(15.5 - 10.5)$$

$$\varphi = 0.5$$

For the second day, the degree-days are 3 K, and for the first two days equation (10.6) gives:

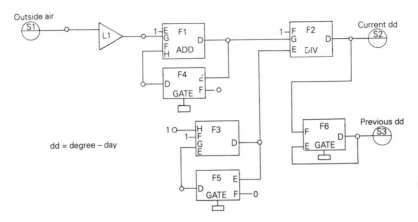

**Fig. 10.12**   Degree-day configuration.

$$(2.5 + 0.5) = \phi(5 + 3)$$
$$\phi = 0.375$$

On the third day the degree-days are 9 K, and for all three days equation (10.6) gives:

$$(2.5 + 0.5 + 6.5) = \phi(5 + 3 + 9)$$
$$\phi = 0.56$$

Clearly, as this example shows, the application of a correction factor is mathematically wrong for all but defined periods such as a year.

Degree-days can be measured with a BEMS, and the configuration for this is shown in Fig. 10.12.

Loop L1 has its set point at the required base temperature and its error signal output will be the temperature difference. ADD module, F1, then adds this to the cumulative temperature difference (which is derived via the gate, F4), and the DIV module, F2, divides by the number of readings outputted from the loop. ADD module, F3, counts the readings outputted from the loop. With input H set at 1 and G connected to the output, D, the address node from D is incremented by 1 each time the module is serviced, at the same service step as the other modules and loop. Each gate will be pulsed at midnight to set the calculation to zero, except for GATE module, F6, which will send the current degree-day reading on internal sensor S2 to internal sensor, S3.

A simpler configuration, based on minimum and maximum function modules, would provide adequate though less accurate results. But this is the traditional way of measuring degree-days with an ordinary minimum–maximum thermometer, and the definition of the average daily temperature is [25]:

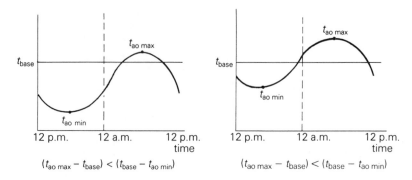

**Fig. 10.13**   Degree-day calculations.

$$\overline{t}_{ao} = \frac{t_{ao\ max} + t_{ao\ min}}{2}$$

where $t_{ao\ max}$ = maximum daily temperature (°C), and

  $t_{ao\ min}$ = minimum daily outside temperature (°C).

This is satisfactory if $t_{ao\ max}$ is below $t_{base}$ but when $t_{ao\ max}$ is just above $t_{base}$, as shown in Fig. 10.13, then the degree-days for the day, DD, are:

$$DD = \frac{(t_{base} - t_{ao\ min})}{2} - \frac{(t_{ao\ max} - t_{ao\ min})}{4}$$

If $t_{ao\ min}$ is just below $t_{base}$, then:

$$DD = \frac{(t_{base} - t_{ao\ min})}{4}$$

These empirical equations can be appreciated if it is assumed that the daily temperature variation is sinusoidal, and numerical integration, such as Simpson's Rule, is used to determine the average temperature under the $t_{base}$ line.

The daily variation in temperature has been shown as sinusoidal in Fig. 10.13, as it is often regarded, although this is rather an approximation for the winter months [19].

## 10.6.1   Variable-base degree-days

Although degree-days can be useful, from earlier chapters we can see that the building internal temperature, $t_{ai}$, will vary with the heat load and the type of control. Fortuitous heat gains will also affect $t_{ai}$. It has been reported that in a reasonably well-insulated house $t_{base}$ might be 16°C in December and 9°C in April. The difference is attributed to solar gains [9]. So to be accurate, the degree-day base for a building should be varied.

ASHRAE provide a **variable-base degree-day method** (VBDD) to reflect more accurately these gains [11]. Various factors are quoted to account for internal gains and solar gains. The monthly degree-days are calculated to variable base temperatures from the monthly average temperature by formulae similar to equation (10.6).

It is interesting that the CIBSE Energy Code Part 2(a) [12] does not use either standard degree-days or VBDD, but simply the average outside temperature. There is the justified comment that the degree-day method 'requires some measure of interpretive skill'.

## 10.7 Annual fuel consumption

From the annual degree-day total the annual fuel consumption can be calculated. The method is based primarily on work by Billington [13], who estimated the accuracy to be ± 25%. These errors are bourne out by work in the USA [11]. The method is outlined in the CIBSE Guide, Section B Part 18 [9]. The example below demonstrates this method.

*Example*
Calculate the annual fuel consumption for the building with the following details:

Calculated heat loss from the building 1500 kW
Indoor design temperature 20°C
Outdoor design temperature − 1°C
London location with annual degree-days 2034 K
Heating system efficiency 0.6
Building occupied 5 days per week, 8 hours a day
The building is classified in the terminology of the Guide as: traditional, with normal glazing, equipment and occupancy, and is regarded as heavyweight.

*Solution*
The CIBSE Guide (Table B18.7) [9] suggests that the average temperature rise maintained by miscellaneous gains alone is 4°C. In terms used earlier, $t_{ai\,cont}$, the inside temperature at which the building is maintained by the controls, $t_g$, a temperature due to the gains, and $t_{bal}$ balance point temperature:

$$t_{bal} = t_{ai\,cont} - t_g$$

$$t_{bal} = 19 - 4$$

$$= 15°C$$

From Fig. 10.11 the correction factor for the degree-days to the base temperature of 15°C is 0.94. If the heating system was operated continuously throughout the day, and it exactly matched the design heat loss, then it would be on at full load for the **equivalent full load operating time**, $E_q$, of:

$$E_q = \frac{24 \times 2034 \times 0.94}{20 - (-1)}$$

$$= 2185\,h$$

But the heating system is operated intermittently and the occupation is not continuous. The CIBSE Guide gives the following correction factors to account for this:

| | |
|---|---|
| 5-day week | 0.85 |
| Intermittent heating with system with a long time lag and a heavy building | 0.95 |
| 8-hour day | 1.00 |

So $E_q$ becomes:

$$2185 \times 0.85 \times 0.95 \times 1.00$$

$$= 1764\,h$$

It is interesting to note that because of the building's thermal storage, the 5-day week only reduces the heat demand by 0.85, not by the direct ratio of:

$$\frac{5}{7} = 0.71$$

From the equivalent hours the annual heat requirement is:

$$1764 \times 1500$$

$$= 2.64 \times 10^6\,kWh$$

or more correctly in GJ:

$$9504\,GJ$$

The annual fuel requirement will therefore be:

$$\frac{9504}{0.6}$$

$$= 15,840\,GJ$$

## 10.8 The performance line

Besides using degree-days for determining the annual fuel consumption of a building, they can also be used for monthly targets.

From our earlier explanation of the theory of degree-days it will be seen that the fuel consumption for heating a building should be related to the coldness of the weather, or degree-days. This has been demonstrated in a paper by McNair and Hitchin [14] which showed that the gas consumption in 96 dwellings in the UK was indeed related to degree-days. The following relationship was obtained:

$$C = 61 + 70 \times DHL \times \frac{DD}{2222} + 59\,N_{\text{person}}$$

where $C$ = annual gas consumption (therms yr$^{-1}$);

$DHL$ = design heat loss (kW);

$N_{\text{person}}$ = number of persons in household;

$DD$ = degree-days. The multiple correlation was $r = 0.74$.

Hence a graph of monthly consumption against monthly degree-days should show a relationship similar to that in Fig. 10.14.

The line through the points is the performance line, and it can be determined statistically by regression analysis. The slope, $s$, is given by:

$$s = \frac{N \Sigma x_i y_i - (\Sigma x_i)(\Sigma y_i)}{N \Sigma x_i^2 - (\Sigma x_i)^2} \qquad (10.8)$$

where the summation, $\Sigma$, is over $N$ pairs of data, $x_i$ and $y_i$;

$N$ = number of months considered;

$x_i$ = degree-days, along $x$-axis, for $i$th month;

$y_i$ = fuel consumption, along $y$-axis, for $i$th month.

The intercept, *int*, is calculated from:

$$\text{int} = \frac{(\Sigma y_i)(\Sigma x_i^2) - (\Sigma x_i)(\Sigma x_i y_i)}{N \Sigma x_i^2 - (\Sigma x_i)^2} \qquad (10.9)$$

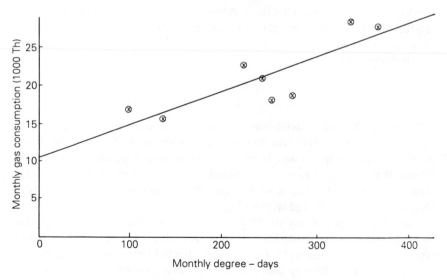

**Fig. 10.14** A performance line.

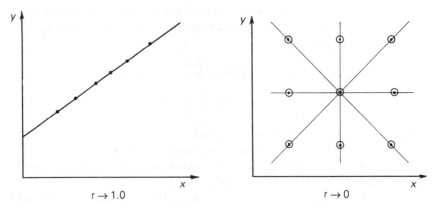

**Fig. 10.15**   Good and poor relationships.

The intercept represents the weather independent consumption; the domestic hot water and the distribution and flue losses. It is sometimes referred to as the **base load**. Any fuel for process heat or other weather-independent processes would also be included. The line can be determined from the monthly data in a heating season. Strictly, non-heating season data (i.e. summer consumptions) should not be included in the determination of the line as the summer consumption does not vary with weather and so gives a false impression of the line. However, problems can arise with the heating season having fractions of months.

An interesting statistical relationship which can be derived is the correlation coefficient, $r$. This quantifies the goodness of fit of the line to the data. For a perfect fit of the line to the data, $r$ tends to one. If there is no fit, or relationship, as shown in Fig. 10.15, then $r$ tends to zero.

$r$ is derived by:

$$r = \frac{N \Sigma x_i y_i - (\Sigma x_i)(\Sigma y_i)}{\sqrt{\{N \Sigma x_i^2 - (\Sigma x_i)^2\}\{N \Sigma y_i^2 - (\Sigma y_i)^2\}}}$$

$r^2$ is the **coefficient of determination** and is a measure of how much data is explained by the straight-line relationship. For instance, if $r^2 = 0.6$, then 60% of the fuel consumption data is related to the weather (degree-days), but 40% is not. If the value of $r$, and consequently $r^2$, is low (and there are statistical confidence levels that can be worked out), then there is no reliable relationship between consumption and degree-days.

Surprisingly, in a study of 20 large heating installations, (blocks of flats heated from a central boilerhouse), 16 of them did not have reliable relationships with the weather, [15]. The $r^2$ values for the sites and the intercepts as a fraction of total heating season consumption are shown in Fig. 10.16. The significant value of $r^2$ for a statistically valid relationship is 0.57.

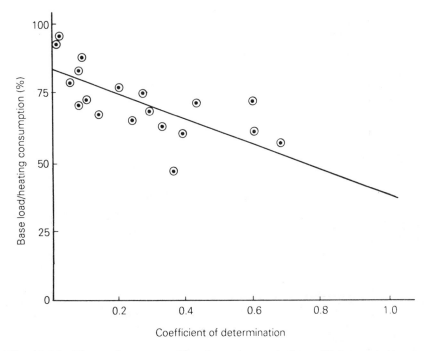

**Fig. 10.16** The performance of heating schemes before efficiency measures.

This poor relationship with weather suggests that the heating systems were poorly controlled. Also the high base loads implied large losses, again due in part to poor control. So a hypothesis can be inferred from this, that poorly controlled sites have high base loads and low $r$-values compared to similar, well-controlled sites.

There is some evidence for this hypothesis, because after the controls at the sites were improved and correctly set, as well as some minor energy conservation work, the base loads reduced and $r$-values improved, as Fig. 10.17 shows. Similar results have been found at a north-eastern England group heating scheme and at a London school [15].

*Example*

One of the large heating installations mentioned above was examined in detail. It consisted of five tower blocks of 214 dwellings supplied from a central boilerhouse with two 880 kW boilers and a 600 kW boiler. The calculated heat loss for the dwellings for an average inside air temperature of 19°C and a design outside air temperature of − 1°C assuming one air change per hour was 979 kW. Assuming two air changes, the heat loss rose to 1117 kW. During the heating season, the heating was on continuously, although there were compen-

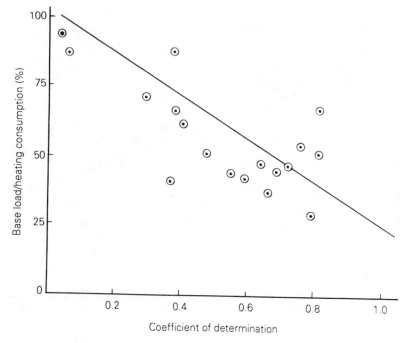

**Fig. 10.17**   The performance of heating schemes after efficiency measures.

sator and thermostat controls in the blocks. The system had the following consumptions:

| Month | Consumption (therms) | Degree-days |
|---|---|---|
| June | 5 737 | 81 |
| July | 4 754 | 25 |
| August | 5 901 | 24 |
| September | 5 737 | 61 |
| October | 16 720 | 97 |
| November | 21 966 | 241 |
| December | 18 688 | 273 |
| January | 27 868 | 367 |
| February | 28 360 | 337 |
| March | 18 196 | 252 |
| April | 22 786 | 221 |
| May | 15 737 | 134 |
| Total | 192 450 | 2113 |

Determine the performance line and analyse it in the light of the above data.

Take the heating season to be from October to May inclusive.

*Solution*
The performance line, to be determined by the method of least squares, is:

$$y = sx + int$$

where $y$ = monthly consumption (therms);
$\quad x$ = monthly degree-days (K);
$\quad s$ = slope (therms degree-day $^{-1}$);
$\quad int$ = intercept (therms).
For the least-squares analysis;

$$\Sigma x_i = 1922 \quad \Sigma y_i = 170\,321 \quad \Sigma x_i^2 = 5.2 \times 10^5$$

$$\Sigma y_i^2 = 3.79 \times 10^9 \quad \Sigma x_i\, y_i = 4.35 \times 10^7$$

In equation (10.8) these values give:

$$s = 44.4 \text{ therms } K^{-1}$$

and in equation (10.9):

$$int = 10\,620 \text{ therms}$$

The performance line is that shown in Fig. 10.14. The correlation coefficient, $r$, is 0.86, a reasonable fit, indicating that 74% of the data is explained by the line.

The slope, $s$, should be related to the design heat loss of the dwellings, which was 979 kW for $-1°C$ outside and 19°C inside. Under these design conditions for one day's continuous heating, with no heat gains considered, the balance point temperature of the building would be 19°C, and the degree-days would be 20 K. Hence the heat loss per degree-day would be:

$$\frac{979 \text{ kW} \times 24 \text{ h}}{20 \text{ K} \times 29.3 \text{ kWh/Th}}$$

$$= 40.1 \text{ Th K}^{-1}$$

With an air change rate of 2, this would give:

$$44.7 \text{ Th K}^{-1}$$

This is very close to the performance line slope of 44.4, but it must be remembered that the air change rate is not known, and other factors such as boiler and system efficiency and controls will affect the slope and intercept (this is discussed further in reference [14]).

The base load or intercept, $int$, should be close to the summer monthly consumption, but:

$$\text{average base load } = \frac{\text{June} + \text{July} + \text{August} + \text{September}}{4}$$

$$= \frac{5737 + 4754 + 5901 + 5737}{4}$$

$$= 5532 \, \text{Th}$$

which is well below the intercept at 10 620 Th. One reason for this may be that the dwellings were being overheated, as the boilers are capable of a combined output of 2360 kW, and the balance point temperature is above 15.5°C, the base temperature for the degree-days. The balance point temperature, and the degree-day base temperature to make the intercept equal the summer average base load, is found from the intercept of the performance line and the summer average base load:

$$5532 = 10\,620 + 44.4x$$

$$x = -\,114.6\,\text{K}$$

To make the intercept coincide with the summer average base load at zero degree-days, 114.6 degree-days has to be added to each of the 8 points on the performance line. Hence the new degree-day total is:

$$1922 + (8 \times 114.5)$$

$$= 2838\,\text{K}$$

This produces a correction factor, $\varphi$, of:

$$\frac{2838}{1922}$$

$$= 1.48$$

From Fig. 10.11 this value of $\varphi$ corresponds to a base temperature of 19.5°C. Considering that most of the dwellings will have heat gains to produce at least a 2–3 K room temperature rise, then it would seen that there is some overheating.

It is interesting to find what happens if the least-squares analysis is wrongly conducted on the whole 12 months' data. The performance line becomes:

$$y = 70x + 3526$$

giving a higher slope nearer to an air change rate of 6 $h^{-1}$, and an intercept below the summer average base load. The latter would indicate the need for a lower degree-day base temperature and a balance point temperature below 15.5°C. These facts show the errors due to the inclusion of the summer months' consumption. But as a lesson in interpreting statistics, the correlation coefficient is now 0.93, higher than the previous line, so giving a better fit to the data, even though some of the data should not have been included!

Assuming that a building does have a good relationship with degree-days, then the performance line can be the basis for a future target. For instance, if the heating controls are set to maintain a lower inside temperature, then a target line below the current performance line can be set.

If the distribution losses are reduced by increased thermal insulation of pipework, then the intercept will be reduced, having a similar effect to setting down the temperature.

Further insulation of the building, however, will reduce the slope of the performance line as the building's heat loss is reduced.

If the heat loss of a building is known, for instance, from the design calculations for a new building, then a performance line can be derived from data collected by the BEMS and the slope compared with the heat loss.

Unfortunately, the ventilation and infiltration air change rate, N, will not be known and will probably vary with door and window opening. A pressurization test will indicate the air change rate [21], but this is difficult on large buildings and rarely done. Other factors affecting the performance line are the controls, solar radiation and wind (these are dealt with later in this chapter).

An alternative to the performance line that can easily be set up on a BEMS is the **energy signature**. As shown in Fig. 10.18, this consists of the daily consumption against the average outside daily temperature, $t_{ao}$. It yields the balance temperature of the building, which is the discontinuity in the curve. Summer consumptions can be included on this signature giving further points above the balance temperature.

Unfortunately, the best-fit line for the signature by regression analysis is

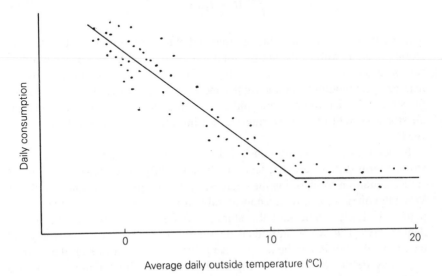

**Fig. 10.18** An energy signature.

complicated by the discontinuity. The balance temperature needs to be known before the two parts of the line can be treated separately.

A method used in PRISM (PRIncetown Scorekeeping Method), determines the most appropriate base temperature for degree-days to give the best-fit straight line [17]. Summer consumptions are included in the data to determine the straight line, although the example above indicates that this might increase the correlation but give more error.

## 10.9 Fabric storage effects

All the methods that produce linear relationships between consumption and weather data are essentially steady state. This is satisfactory as long as dynamic effects, such as thermal storage in the building fabric (and variations in inside temperature due to controls), do not significantly affect the overall energy consumption. Over a short period of time, such as a day or so, then the heat going into and out of the fabric will be a significant part of the energy consumption. Building fabric often has a time constant in terms of days, as we have discussed in Chapter 9 on optimisation; and the heat stored and its take-up is affected by the outside temperature in the past, as well as the present. This has implications for the accuracy of degree-days over a few days and for degree-hours. The dynamic balance equation explains the effect mathematically. As in Chapter 9 on optimisers, the dynamic balance equation during the heating period is:

$$pQ_{\text{des}} = \frac{H_{\text{des}}}{F_2} \, (t_{\text{ai}} - t_{\text{ao}}) + \Sigma \, (m^*C_{\text{p}}) \frac{dt_{\text{ai}}}{dT} \qquad (9.18)$$

where with the inclusion of the internal and external fabric of the building for storing heat, as well as the air, the total effective thermal mass of the building can be grouped into one summed term, $\Sigma(m^*C_{\text{p}})$. The left-hand term is the heating system output, and the right-hand term is the steady state heat loss and the storage of heat in the fabric and the air. In comparison with the fabric, the air stores very little heat. During the heating off period, the left-hand side is zero.

To determine the energy consumed this equation must be integrated. The storage term (the differential term) is the only difference between the steady state calculation for deriving the degree-day consumption and equation (9.18). When the integration is over a considerable time (e.g. a week), then the weekly pattern is fairly stable and the storage effects do not impede the use of degree-days. But when individual days are considered, then the storage of energy in the fabric can be a significant difference, even though the degree-days may be the same. This is especially true of a Monday morning after a cold weekend. The extra heat to warm up the fabric can be very significant,

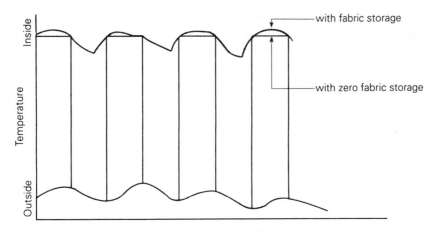

**Fig. 10.19** Effect of fabric storage on temperature.

whereas for an equally cold day later in the week the energy consumption can be much less. An example will show this more clearly.

The influence of the thermal storage in a building's fabric is shown in Fig. 10.19, where the inside temperature graph of a building is compared to a theoretical building with no thermal storage (and perfect thermal control) that drops to the outside temperature when the heating is switched off.

*Example*
Compare the heat input to the office building in Fig. 9.12 in Chapter 9, at the start of the week to the input later in the week. Assume that the heating comes on after a weekend off, and that the heating is brought on by an optimiser before the start of occupancy at 9 a.m. Occupancy ends at 5 p.m.

Compare this to an identical office with a larger effective thermal capacity and the time constant is 16 h. The heating plant is 25% oversized for both buildings.

*Solution*
From the example calculations on this building, above, the heat stored in the fabric and air at design conditions was 1355 MJ, the fabric heat loss 48 kW and the air heat loss 16 kW. Hence the plant size is:

$$(48 + 16) \times 1.25 = 80\,\text{kW}$$

By inspection the steady state heat consumption over the occupancy time of one day, 8 h, operating at the design temperature difference of 20 K, is:

$$80 \times 8 = 640\,\text{kWh}$$

$$= 2304\,\text{MJ}$$

So the heat stored is comparable to a severe day's consumption. Also as an indicator, the time for the heating system to get the heat into the fabric, if the steady state heat loss were ignored, would be:

$$\frac{1355 \text{ MJ}}{80 \text{ kJ s}^{-1}}$$

$$= 16\,938 \text{ s, or } 4.7 \text{ h}$$

For more exact calculations, equation (9.27) gives the preheat time as:

$$\frac{T_3 - T_2}{\tau} = \ln \left[ \frac{pe^x}{\Phi + e^x(p - \Phi)} \right] \tag{9.27}$$

from this the preheat consumption is:

$$pQ_{des}(T_3 - T_2)$$

$$= pQ_{des}\,\tau \ln \left[ \frac{pe^x}{\Phi + e^x(p - \Phi)} \right]$$

The consumption during the occupancy period should be the same for all days if the outside conditions are the same, provided that initially the heating has warmed the fabric sufficiently. With the short preheat times of some BEMSs, this will not be the case.

As the preheat consumption is the point of interest, the difference for a weekday preheat and the preheat at the end of a weekend is due to the different values of $x$ in equation (9.27).

For the example office block with $\tau = 5.9$ h:

$$x_{w \text{ end}} = 64/5.9$$

$$= 10.85$$

and:

$$e^{x_{w \text{ end}}} = 51\,534$$

$$x_{week} = 16/5.9$$

$$= 2.71$$

and:   $$e^{x_{week}} = 15$$

So the ratio of weekend preheat to weekday preheat, with $t_{ao}$ set to 0°C (i.e. $\Phi = 1.0$), is:

$$\dfrac{\ln\left[\dfrac{1.25\times 51\,534}{1+51\,534(1.25-1)}\right]}{\ln\left[\dfrac{1.25\times 15}{1+15(1.25-1)}\right]}$$

$$= 1.18$$

The weekend preheat uses 18% more energy than a weekday preheat. When the weather is milder, say, $t_{ao} = 10°C$, ($\Phi = 0.5$), the ratio is:

$$\dfrac{\ln\left[\dfrac{1.25\times 51\,534}{0.5+51\,534(1.25-0.5)}\right]}{\ln\left[\dfrac{1.25\times 15}{0.5+15(1.25-0.5)}\right]}$$

$$= 1.09$$

For the similar building with a time constant of 16 h, then:

$$x_{w\ end} = 64/16$$

$$= 4$$

and:

$$e^{x_{w\,end}} = 54.6$$

$$x_{week} = 16/16$$

$$= 1.0$$

and:

$$e^{x_{week}} = 2.72$$

making the ratio, with $\Phi = 1$:

$$\dfrac{\ln\left[\dfrac{1.25\times 54.6}{1+54.6(1.25-1)}\right]}{\ln\left[\dfrac{1.25\times 2.72}{1+2.72(1.25-1)}\right]} \tag{10.10}$$

$$= \dfrac{1.54}{0.703}$$

$$= 2.19$$

a considerable increase.

The numerator in equation (10.10) is 1.54, so the heating on Monday, including the preheating, is on for:

$$(1.54 \times 16) + 8 = 32.6 \, \text{h}$$

For Tuesday, and other weekdays under similar conditions, the heating is on for:

$$(0.703 \times 16) + 8 = 19.25 \, \text{h}$$

For the whole week, the ratio of Monday heating to that of the week is:

$$\frac{32.6}{(32.6 + 4 \times 19.25)}$$

$$= 30\%$$

With 30% of the heating of the week being used on the Monday, and Sunday evening, a comparison of Monday's heating with that of Tuesday, for identical outside conditions, is not equal as a degree-day or degree-hour comparison would make it. For a number of outside conditions, the ratio is given in Table 10.1.

**Table 10.1**   Weekend to weekday preheat ratios

| Outside temperature, $t_{ao}$ (°C) | Weekend to weekday preheat ratio ($\tau = 5.9$ h) | ($\tau = 16$h) |
|---|---|---|
| 0 | 1.18 | 2.19 |
| 10 | 1.09 | 1.71 |
| 15 | 1.08 | 1.65 |

Monitoring with a BEMS should reveal the ratio of heating for the start of the week and other weekdays, and although outside conditions are unlikely to remain constant, it will give some insight to the fabric capacity and also the optimiser performance.

It is often noticeable that the inside temperature of a building may creep up during the week as the fabric store of heat becomes 'full', as shown in Fig. 10.19. So degree-day and degree-hour calculations over days and hours may well give erroneous results due to this storage effect. For these short time periods, a more sophisicated model, such as the first-order model of equation (9.18), or a detailed dynamic computer simulation should be used.

## 10.10  Other influences on consumption

Degree-days are simply a measure of the outside air temperature, and although most of the above discussion of energy consumption has been related to degree-days other weather influences, such as solar radiation and the wind, also affect consumption. These can partly be accounted for in the use of

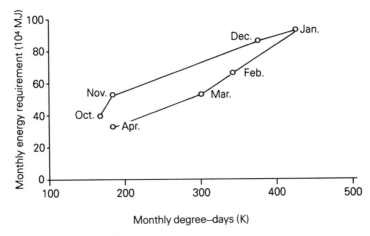

**Fig. 10.20**  Effect of large solar gain on the performance line.

variable base degree-days, where the balance point temperature varies during the year. Controls and system efficiency also play a crucial role in a building's energy consumption for heating. All these influences are discussed in more detail in reference [18], but some of the salient details are considered here.

It has been shown [18], and confirmed [19], that there is a strong correlation between the monthly global solar radiation and the air temperature of the following month. The air temperature lags behind the solar radiation. This gives rise to a strong correlation between the degree-days for a heating season and the solar radiation. For nine months of the CIBSE Example Weather Year (1 October 1964 to 30 September 1965 [20]), for Kew, $r^2$ is 0.97 [17]. In general, the relationship between solar radiation and degree-days may be expressed as a straight-line equation:

$$S_m = S_o - a\, DD_{m+1}$$

where $S_m$ = monthly global solar radiation, for month $m$ (W m$^{-2}$);
$\quad S_o$ = intercept of straight line (W m$^{-2}$);
$\quad a$ = slope of line (W m$^{-2}$ K$^{-1}$);
$DD_{m+1}$ = degree-days for following month, $m + 1$ (W m$^{-2}$).

A **solar aperture** term can relate the useful contribution of the sun to the building's heating. Although the determination of a solar aperture for a building is complex [14], its dimensions are m$^2$ and it can be related to the building's glazed area.

Despite the fact that a number of papers report that the solar influence is difficult to detect from energy data [14], if a building were to utilize a lot of solar radiation, then its performance line would exhibit the type of hysteresis shown in Fig. 10.20.

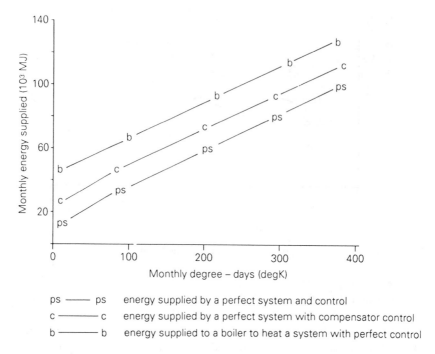

**Fig. 10.21**   Boiler and control efficiency effect.

In April and November the degree-days were similar but the solar contributions were not, hence the difference in energy consumption. For Fig. 10.20, the building had an assumed solar aperture of 243 m² with 608 m² of glazing of which 190 m² was facing south-east.

The effect of wind is more difficult to analyse. It affects the external surface heat transfer, as well as the infiltration through cracks and openings. Infiltration is influenced directly by the wind speed and also by the temperature of the outside air, due to the **stack effect**, the hot air rising in the building and generating a pressure gradient to pull cold air in at the lower openings and expel the warm air through higher openings [21]. Although the temperature difference can be related to degree-days, the wind velocity is not so well related [16], and the use of dynamic thermal models with comprehensive weather data would be more useful if the analysis were to be to a greater depth than a simple degree-day assessment.

## 10.11  The effect of efficiency and controls

The heating system, and its controls to provide a constant required inside temperature, has a higher efficiency at the higher heat loads. These heat loads can be related to the outside air temperature and hence the degree-days. So the efficiency effect of the heating system and controls will reduce the slope of the performance line while raising its intercept, as shown in Fig. 10.21, compared to the useful heat required, determined from the heat loss calculation.

Derived from reference [16], Fig. 10.21 relates to a heating system with a compensator control and a single boiler. The inefficiency of the compensator relates to the rise in room temperature with rising outside air temperature (and lowering load), discussed in Chapter 8 on compensator control.

## 10.12 Boiler signature

The boiler inefficiency can be determined from a steady state boiler model of which the parameters can be determined from a boiler energy signature, as shown in Fig. 10.22.

The parameters in the signature are:

(i) $\overline{Q}_{fuel}$ = average fuel supplied to the boiler in a certain time (including any boiler off time in the period) (kJ);
(ii) $\overline{Q}_u$ = average useful heat supplied by the boiler to the heating system in a certain time (including any boiler off time in the period) (kJ).

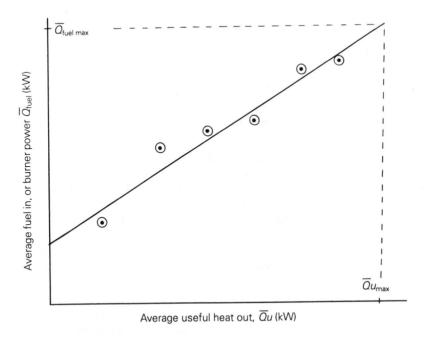

**Fig. 10.22** Boiler energy signature.

Such a boiler energy signature can be determined from a BEMS which monitors both the fuel input and the heat output. These determined over a period of time, to give $\overline{Q}_{\text{fuel}}$ and $\overline{Q}_{\text{u}}$, provide the boiler efficiency, which in itself is valuable. If there are a number of measurements with an amount of experimental error, it will be necessary to determine the best straight line using the least-squares method.

But the boiler efficiency curve can also be determined from the energy signature and the load factor, $\varphi$. $\varphi$ is more difficult to determine, but with a knowledge of the system design, including the flow rates, pipework and valves, monitoring the principal flow and return temperatures will give the load factor.

If these factors are unknown, then the two extreme points of the signature may be determined. The full load, top point of the line (when $\varphi = 1.0$) being:

$$\eta_{\text{max}} = \frac{\overline{Q}_{\text{u max}}}{\overline{Q}_{\text{fuel max}}}$$

where $\eta_{\text{max}} = $ maximum efficiency.

The intercept of the signature (when $\varphi = 0$) is given by:

$$\overline{Q}_{\text{fuel max}} \frac{\beta}{1 + \beta}$$

where $\beta = $ ratio of heat loss through the boiler case and up the flue when the boiler is not fired, to $Q_{\text{u max}}$.

The boiler efficiency curve, in terms of the above parameters, is given by:

$$\eta = \eta_{\text{max}} \left[ 1 - \frac{(1 - \varphi)\beta}{\varphi + \beta} \right]$$

A graph of this equation is shown in Fig. 10.23.

## 10.13   Normalized performance indicators

Once the BEMS has acquired a year's consumption, then the performance of the building and plant can be assessed against performance yardsticks set by the Energy Efficiency Office and published in a series of twelve booklets entitled *Energy Efficiency in Buildings* [22].

To determine the building's performance against these yardsticks, its **normalized performance indicator** is calculated. For this, the heating consumption is adjusted for a standard degree-day year, with allowance for exposure. This is then added to the rest of the consumption and the resulting total is normalized for the area of the building, hours of occupancy and type of use of the building (e.g. whether a primary or secondary school, etc.).

This assessment may well feedback as adjustments to settings and controls

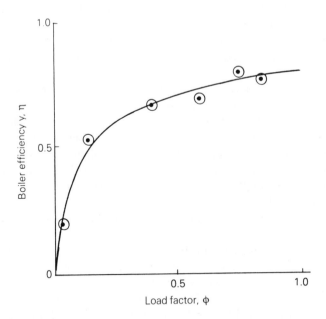

**Fig. 10.23**  Boiler efficiency curve.

on the BEMS and other efficiency measures with the production of energy targets. However, although the BEMS and the other measures may well be capable of achieving these savings, the human factor must be considered [23], as we discussed at the beginning of this book.

## References

[1]  CIBSE (1991) CIBSE Applications Manual, Energy audits and surveys, AM5, Chartered Institution of Building Services Engineers, London.

[2]  Department of Energy (1989) *Energy Audits*, Fuel Efficiency Booklet 1, Department of Energy, London; amended reprint, 1989.

[3]  Hughes, G. J. (1988) *Electricity and Buildings*, Peter Peregrinus, London.

[4]  Fielden, C. J. and Ede, T. J. (1982) *Computer-based Energy Management in Buildings*, Pitman, London.

[5]  Eyke, M. (1988) *Building Automation Systems*, BSP Professional Books, Oxford.

[6]  Bentley, J. P. (1988) *Principles of Measurement Systems*, Longman Scientific and Technical, London.

[7]  Hitchin, E. R. and Hyde, A. J. (1979) The estimation of heating energy use in buildings, Symposium on the Environment Inside Buildings, Institute of Mathematics and its Applications, Southend-on-Sea, May.

[8]   Hyde, A. J. (1980) Degree-days for heating calculations *Building Services and Environmental Engineering*, **2**, 6.

[9]   CIBSE (1986) CIBSE Guide, Volume B, Section B18, Owning and operating costs, Chartered Institution of Building Services Engineers, London.

[10]  Hitchin, E. R. (1983) Estimating monthly degree-days. *Building Services Engineering Research and Technology*, **4**, 4.

[11]  ASHRAE Handbook Fundamentals, American Society of Heating, Refrigeration and Air Conditioning Engineers, Atlanta, 1989.

[12]  CIBSE Building Energy Code, Part 2, Calculation of energy demands and targets for the design of new buildings and services, Section A, Heated and naturally ventilated buildings, Chartered Institution of Building Services Engineers, London.

[13]  Billington, N. S. (1966) Estimation of annual fuel consumption. JIHVE, **34**.

[14]  McNair, H. P. and Hitchin, E. R. (1980) The principal factors that influence gas consumptions in centrally heated houses. *Journal of the Institution of Gas Engineers*, December.

[15]  Levermore, G. J. (1987) The performance of group heating schemes, Combined Heat and Power Association Conference, Torquay, July.

[16]  Levermore, G. J. and Chong, W. B. (1989) Performance lines and energy signatures. *Building Services Engineering Research and Technology*, **10**, 3.

[17]  Fels, M. F. (1986) An introduction. *Energy and Buildings*, **9**, 1–2.

[18]  Owens, P. G. T. (1980) Figuring out energy needs. *Building Services* (CIBSE), **2**, 7.

[19]  Hay, N. and Levermore, G. J. (1988) Reduced weather data for heating calculations, Weather Data Symposium, Chartered Institution of Building Services Engineers, London, May.

[20]  Holmes, M. J. and Hitchin, E. R. (1978) An example year for the calculation of energy demand in buildings. *Building Services Engineer*, **45**.

[21]  Liddament, M. W. (1986) *Air Infiltration Calculation Techniques–an Applications Guide*, Air Infiltration and Ventilation Centre, Warwick.

[22]  Department of Energy (1990) *Energy Efficiency in Buildings*; there are 12 booklets, entitled How to bring down energy costs in schools; Catering establishments; Shops; Further and higher buildings; Offices; Sports centres; Libraries, museums, art galleries and churches; Hotels; High street banks and agencies; Entertainment; Factories and warehouses; Courts, depots and emergency services buildings.

[23]  Levermore, G. J. (1985) Motivation and Training for Energy Targeting, Energy Management Experience Conference Proceedings, London.

[24]  Colantonio, E. S. (1989) *Microcomputers and Applications*, D. C. Heath, Lexington, Mass.

[25] Department of Energy (1989) *Degree Days*, Fuel Efficiency Booklet 7, Department of Energy, London; amended reprint, 1989.

[26] Hansen, E. G. (1985) *Hydronic System Design and Operation: Guide to Heating and Cooling with Water*, McGraw-Hill, New York.

[27] McLaughlin, R. K., McLean, R. C. and Bonthron, W.J. (1981) *Heating Services Design*, Butterworths, London.

# Index